CW01660963

RON MUECK

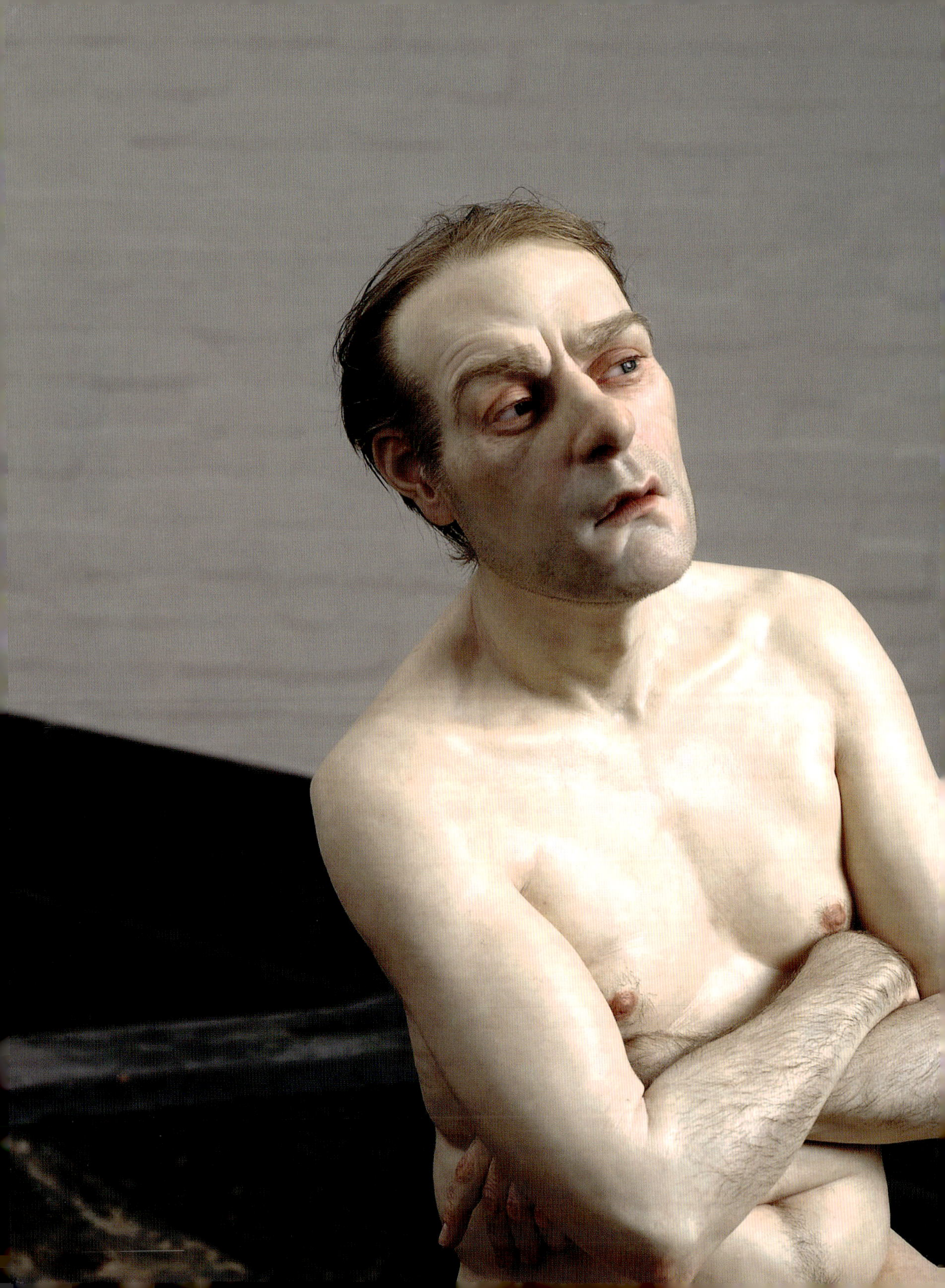

RON MUECK

DAVID HURLSTON

WITH ESSAYS BY LISA BALDISSERA, NICHOLAS CHAMBERS, JAMES FOX, KELLY GELLATLY, TED GOTT, SUSANNA GREEVES, PHILIP LONG, ANGELA NDALIANIS, JUSTIN PATON, CRAIG RAINE, AND ANGUS TRUMBLE

NATIONAL GALLERY OF VICTORIA

YALE UNIVERSITY PRESS, NEW HAVEN AND LONDON

ngv National Gallery of Victoria

Yale

CONTENTS

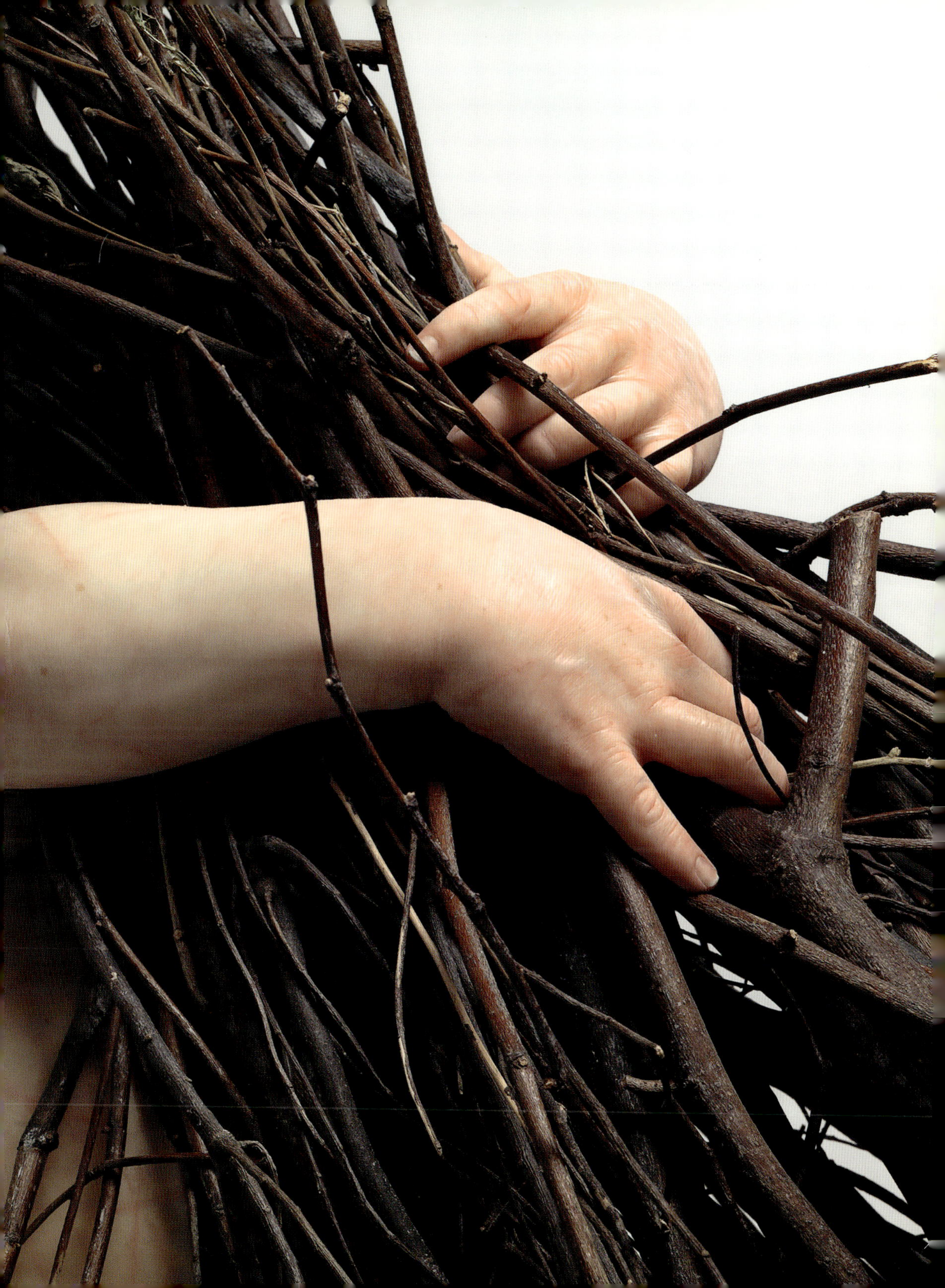

FOREWORD

p. 2
Man in a boat
2002 (detail)
Private collection

p. 7
Woman with sticks
2008 (detail)
Anthony d'Offay, London

Ron Mueck's work first came to the attention of a wide audience when his moving and poignant work *Dead Dad*, 1996–97, was included in the history-making exhibition *Sensation: Young British Artists from the Saatchi Collection*, which opened in London at the Royal Academy in September 1997. Since then he has established a strong international reputation for his moving and poignant sculptures, sometimes colossal, sometimes miniature, which resonate with deep emotion. Special milestones, among many, have been his two-year residency as Associate Artist at the National Gallery, London (starting in 2000), and his highly publicised representation at the Venice Biennale in 2001 with *Boy*, 1999, first exhibited in London in 2000 in the Millennium Dome.

This publication accompanies the National Gallery of Victoria's first major exhibition of Ron Mueck's sculptures. It is fitting that, in his original home town, it is one of the largest and most comprehensive exhibitions of his work ever to be mounted – with four new sculptures, in addition to a number of his most important works, including the now-iconic *Dead Dad*.

We are delighted to be able to present this publication with its insightful perspectives on the works included in the exhibition. The contributions by prominent writers, many of whom have followed Mueck's practice closely for many years, form a fascinating compilation. Indeed, with its detailed catalogue raisonné, this is perhaps the most comprehensive record of Mueck's oeuvre to date. I take this opportunity to thank the authors most sincerely. I also acknowledge the role David Hurlston, NGV Curator of Australian Art, has played in organising and coordinating both the publication and the exhibition, and our Deputy Director Frances Lindsay.

I thank our colleagues from the Art Gallery of New South Wales, the McClelland Gallery + Sculpture Park, the National Galleries of Scotland, the National Gallery of Australia and the Queensland Art Gallery for lending works to the exhibition. I would also like to express our gratitude to Stefan Edlis and Gael Neeson from Chicago and to Anthony d'Offay for their generosity in making key works available. Anthony d'Offay has played a special role in supporting Mueck's career and, in addition to lending works to the exhibition, I acknowledge the instrumental role he has played in facilitating the realisation of this project and thank him most sincerely.

Exhibitions such as this are only possible when they are supported by public-spirited organisations. I wish to acknowledge and thank most warmly the principal sponsor, Mercer. I also thank our support sponsors, Maddocks, Sanpellegrino, Sofitel Melbourne on Collins, *The Age* and JCDecaux.

Finally, and most importantly, I congratulate Ron Mueck on a remarkable body of work and thank him for providing us with a stunning exhibition and the opportunity to produce this publication. As the creator of some of the most widely acclaimed, prominent and identifiable figurative sculptures, Ron Mueck occupies a singular place in the field of international contemporary art. It is particularly pleasing that we have the opportunity to open this exhibition in his home town of Melbourne.

GERARD VAUGHAN
DIRECTOR, NATIONAL GALLERY OF VICTORIA

ACKNOWLEDGEMENTS

The preparation of this publication and associated exhibition has been a collaboration involving many people. First and foremost I would like to acknowledge Ron Mueck, who has been incredibly open in discussion and also very generous with his time. Having got to know him during the course of the project, I have the utmost respect for his sensitivity and artistic sensibility, and also his desire for privacy! He is truly an exceptional artist and I believe that history will judge him to have been a key figure of our time.

The organisation of the exhibition and the many details associated with the preparation of this publication could not have occurred without the assistance of Anthony d'Offay and his staff. Their support and commitment, from the beginning, has been critical. In particular I wish to thank Anthony's assistant Hannah Barry, who has been a mainstay, and also Ted McDonald-Toone.

Support for the project has come from many departments within the NGV, most notably from Communications, Conservation, Curatorial, Education and Programs, Events, Exhibition and Graphic Design, Marketing and Sponsorship, Multimedia, Photographic Services, Publications, Registration, and Risks and Facilities. Individuals who have worked on the project and whom I would particularly like to acknowledge include: Janelle Borig, Exhibitions Conservator; Deirdre Canon, Intern; Julia Cassar, Travel and Projects Coordinator; Trish Cave, Motion Graphic Designer; Jean-Pierre Chabrol, Head of Multimedia; Jasmin Chua, Publications Manager; Luke Doyle, Liaison Librarian; Diana Dzelalija, Exhibition Designer; Jessica Gommers, Senior Graphic Designer; Kirsty Grant, Senior Curator, Australian Art; Philip Jago, former Publications Manager (retired December 2008);

Trish Little, Assistant Cataloguer; Cherie McNair, Senior Exhibitions Coordinator; Adam Meredith, Senior Lighting Technician; Jennie Moloney, Scheduling and Copyright Coordinator; Nicole Monteiro, Exhibitions Manager; Paula Nason, Associate Registrar, Touring Exhibitions and Storage; Megan Patty, Publications and Copyright Assistant; Toby Pola, Senior Art Handler; Erin Reeve, Media and Public Affairs Coordinator; Garry Sommerfeld, Manager Photographic Services; and Daryl West-Moore, Design Manager. Gerard Vaughan, Director, and Frances Lindsay, Deputy Director, have been supportive of the project at all times and I thank them most sincerely. I am also grateful to Paige Amor, Margaret Trudgeon and Catherine Cradwick for their editing of the texts.

On behalf of the NGV I wish to express sincere gratitude to the institutional lenders to the exhibition: Art Gallery of New South Wales, Sydney, Australia; McClelland Gallery + Sculpture Park, Langwarrin, Australia; National Galleries of Scotland, Scottish National Gallery of Modern Art, Edinburgh, Scotland; National Gallery of Australia, Canberra, Australia; Queensland Art Gallery, Brisbane, Australia. I would also like to thank collectors Stefan Edlis and Gael Neeson, as well as Anthony d'Offay for lending works from their collections. We are aware that works by Ron Mueck are greatly cherished by their owners and thank all of the lenders to the exhibition for their understanding and generosity.

Finally I would like to acknowledge and express sincere appreciation to the authors who have contributed to this publication: Lisa Baldissera, Nicholas Chambers, James Fox, Kelly Gellatly, Ted Gott, Susanna Greeves, Philip Long, Angela Ndalianis, Justin Paton, Craig Raine and Angus Trumble. Their insightful and perceptive essays offer new perspectives on Mueck's work.

DAVID HURLSTON,
CURATOR, AUSTRALIAN ART, NATIONAL GALLERY OF VICTORIA

AUTHOR BIOGRAPHIES

LISA BALDISSERA is an independent curator and writer currently residing in Florence, Italy. From 1999 to 2009 she was Curator, Contemporary Art, at the Art Gallery of Greater Victoria, Canada.

NICHOLAS CHAMBERS is Curator, Contemporary International Art, at the Queensland Art Gallery, Gallery of Modern Art, Brisbane.

JAMES FOX teaches Art History at the University of Cambridge. In 2008 he was curator of the *Statuephilia* exhibition of contemporary sculpture at the British Museum.

KELLY GELLATLY is Curator, Contemporary Art, at the National Gallery of Victoria.

TED GOTT is Senior Curator, International Art, at the National Gallery of Victoria. He has been curator of many major exhibitions including, most recently, *Salvador Dali: Liquid Desire*.

SUSANNA GREEVES is a freelance writer and curator based in London, has known Ron Mueck from the beginning of his career as an artist, and has written and lectured on his work.

DAVID HURLSTON has worked in a range of positions at the National Gallery of Victoria, since 1993. Currently he is Curator, Australian Art.

PHILIP LONG is Senior Curator at the Scottish National Gallery of Modern Art, Edinburgh, where he is responsible for the ARTIST ROOMS collection, which includes works by Mueck as well as by Warhol, Koons, Hirst, Kiefer, Nauman and others.

Two women, 2005, with Emily Floyd's *A strategy to infiltrate the homes of the bourgeoisie*, 2005, installation view

ANGELA NDALIANIS is Associate Professor in Cinema Studies at Melbourne University and a Trustee of the National Gallery of Victoria. Her publications include *Neo-Baroque Aesthetics and Contemporary Entertainment* and *The Contemporary Comic Book Superhero*.

JUSTIN PATON is Senior Curator at Christchurch Art Gallery Te Puna o Waiwhetu and has written widely on New Zealand and Australian art.

CRAIG RAINE is a poet, librettist, dramatist, novelist and the editor of the arts tri-quarterly *Areté*. He is also a Fellow in English at New College, Oxford.

ANGUS TRUMBLE is Senior Curator of Paintings and Sculpture at the Yale Center for British Art in New Haven, Connecticut. He was previously Curator, European Art, at the Art Gallery of South Australia in Adelaide.

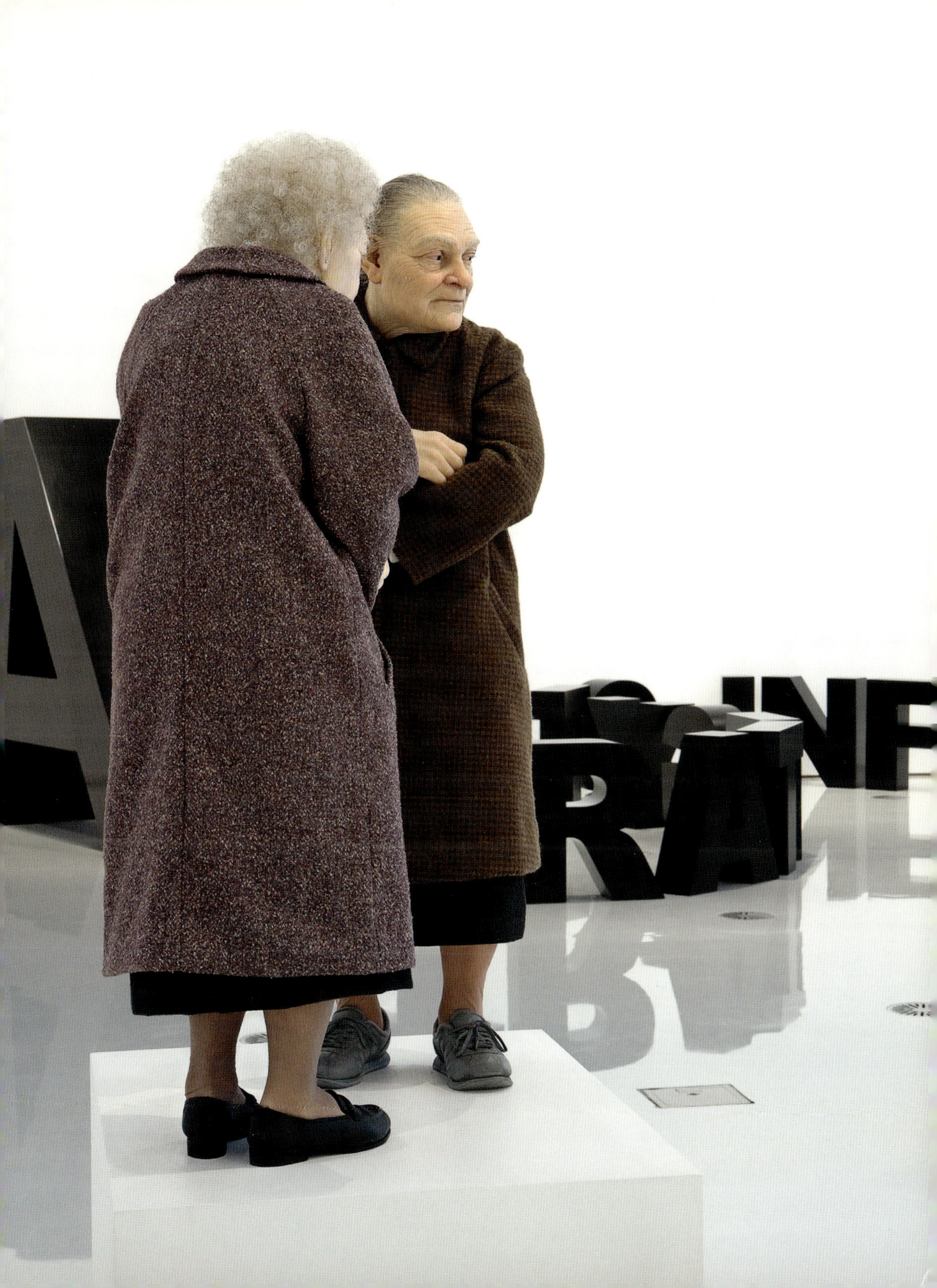

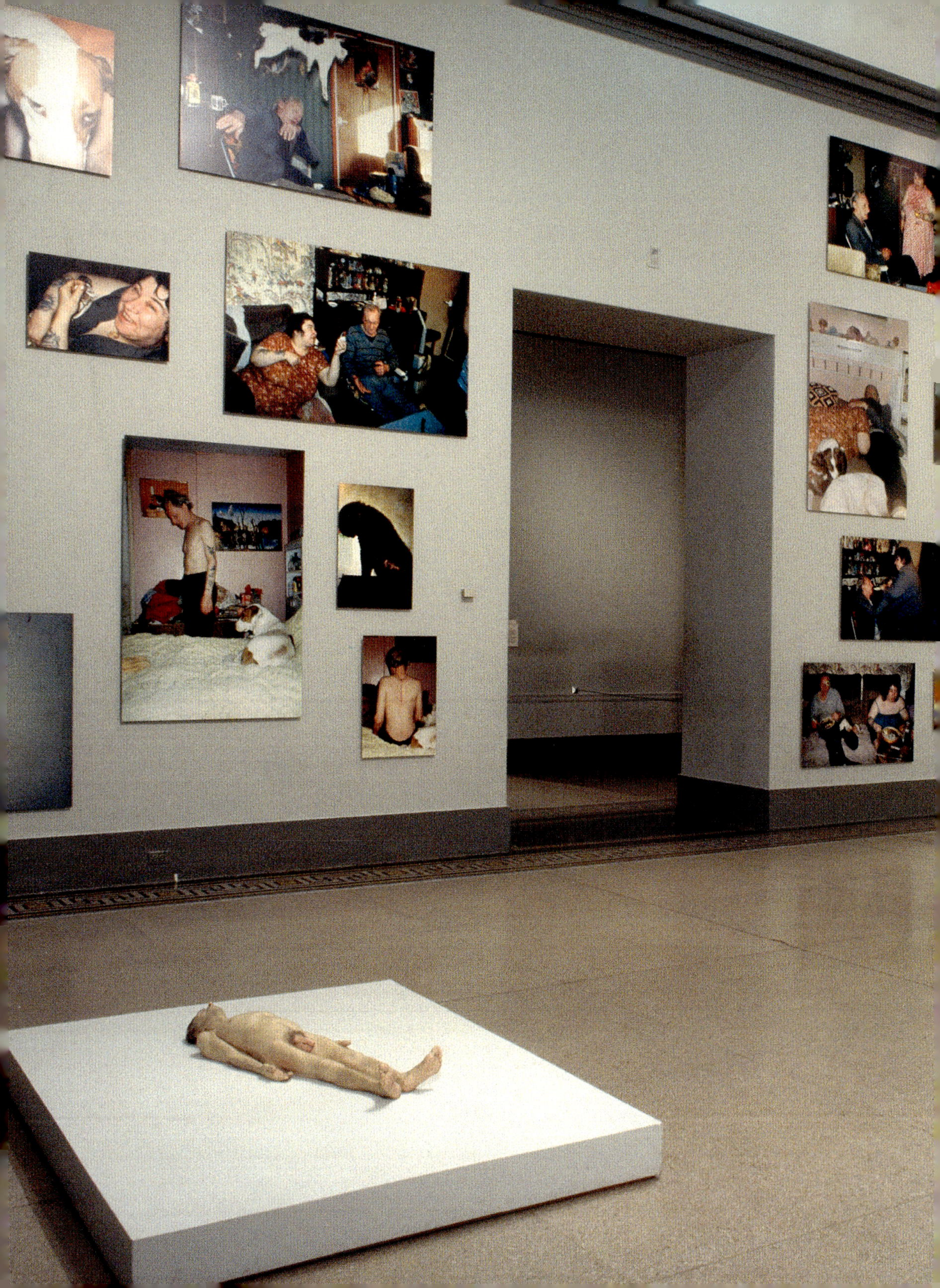

DAVID HURLSTON

INTRODUCTION

Sensation: Young British Artists from the Saatchi Collection, installation view. Brooklyn Museum, New York, 1999–2000

In 1997, a smaller-than-life-size sculpture of a male corpse by then unknown Australian-born artist Ron Mueck appeared in the exhibition *Sensation: Young British Artists from the Saatchi Collection*, which opened at London's Royal Academy of Arts. Of the 110 exhibits by some of Britain's best-known contemporary artists, it was this work, *Dead Dad*, 1996–97, that drew excited attention and enthusiastic responses from the public. What made the piece so compelling was that it was at once astounding in its apparent realism and truly poignant in its humility and vulnerability. It was a work of contemporary art that both amazed and moved people.

Since his dramatic entry onto the international art stage, Mueck has continued to astound audiences with his realistic, figurative sculptures and now occupies a unique and important place in the field of international contemporary art. There is no doubt that it was the exposure he received through *Sensation* that brought Mueck's practice to the attention of a wide audience, however, what led to his inclusion in that exhibition, and indeed to his debut as an artist, had occurred more than a year earlier.

✦✦✦

> Ron made a dragon out of sand to amuse the children. People on the beach gathered and stared at it. What was surprising was that it had life. And that is his gift. It isn't even that it's so cleverly done and is realistic. Sand isn't the stuff to make a lifelike crocodile, is it? I thought, 'This is wonderful', and I asked him to do a sculpture for me.[1]

Pinocchio 1996

Mueck's mother-in-law, the prominent and internationally recognised painter Paula Rego, asked him to make her a small figure of Pinocchio. She included this figure as part of her tableau for the exhibition *Spellbound: Art and Film*, held at the Hayward Gallery in London (22 February – 6 May 1996).

The impish figure, less than a metre in height, came to the attention of influential contemporary art collector Charles Saatchi. Saatchi was so impressed by Mueck's mastery at modelling the human form that he commissioned him to make a group of works for his collection. The resulting sculptures included *Mask*, 1997; *Angel*, 1997; and *Dead Dad*.

✦✦✦

Sensation included works by forty-two of Britain's emerging and established contemporary artists; artists who were gathered together under the rubric Young British Artists (YBA).[2] It was a contentious exhibition that opened in London at the Royal Academy of Arts in September 1997. It then travelled to Berlin's Hamburger Bahnhof Museum für Gegenwart and to the Brooklyn Museum in New York.[3]

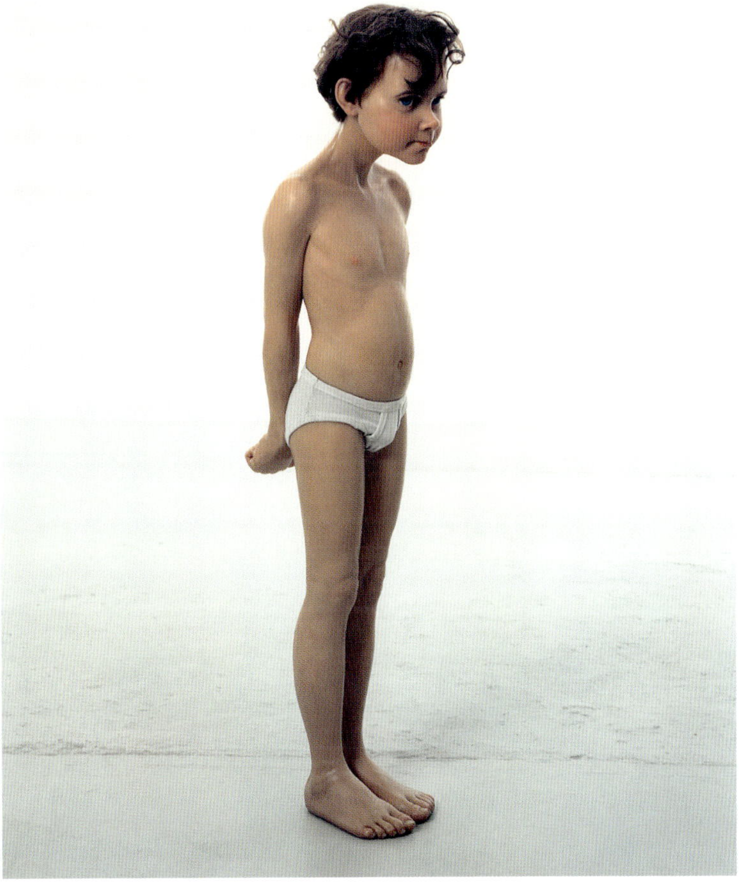

It was scheduled to be shown at the National Gallery of Australia in June 2000, however this leg of the tour was cancelled due to the controversy the exhibition had generated overseas.[4]

Mask, 1997, at *Sensation: Young British Artists from the Saatchi Collection*, installation view. Brooklyn Museum, New York, 1999–2000

The exhibition was praised by many for its boldness and for engaging the broader public with issues in contemporary art. However, it was also met with outrage and protests from some parts of the community, with media attention centring principally on the strong subject matter of some of the works.[5] In something of a *succès de scandale*, the attention served to raise the profile of the exhibition. In London the show drew an audience of almost 300,000. In Berlin it was so popular that it was extended by almost a month and in New York, where Mayor Rudolph Giuliani described it as 'sick stuff', it broke Brooklyn Museum's daily attendance record.

In London, Mueck was represented in the exhibition with *Dead Dad*. In New York and Berlin two additional works were included: *Mask* and *Angel*. Amid the controversy, protests and media attention that surrounded aspects of the exhibition, it was Ron Mueck and his *Dead Dad* that visitors came away talking about. The response was summed-up by journalist Sean O'Hagan from the London *Observer*:

> 'Have you seen *Dead Dad* yet?' became one of those mantras that more often accompany the crossover success of a sleeper hit film. Ron Mueck had gate-crashed the *Sensation* party and stolen the show.[6]

✦ ✦ ✦

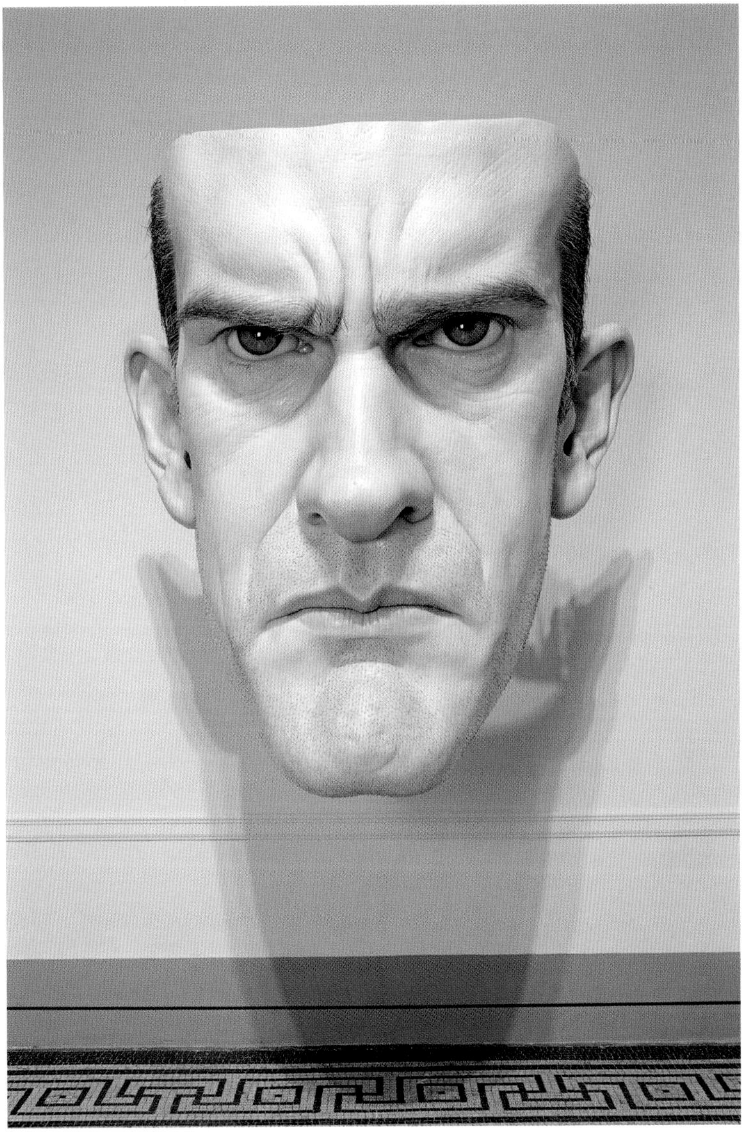

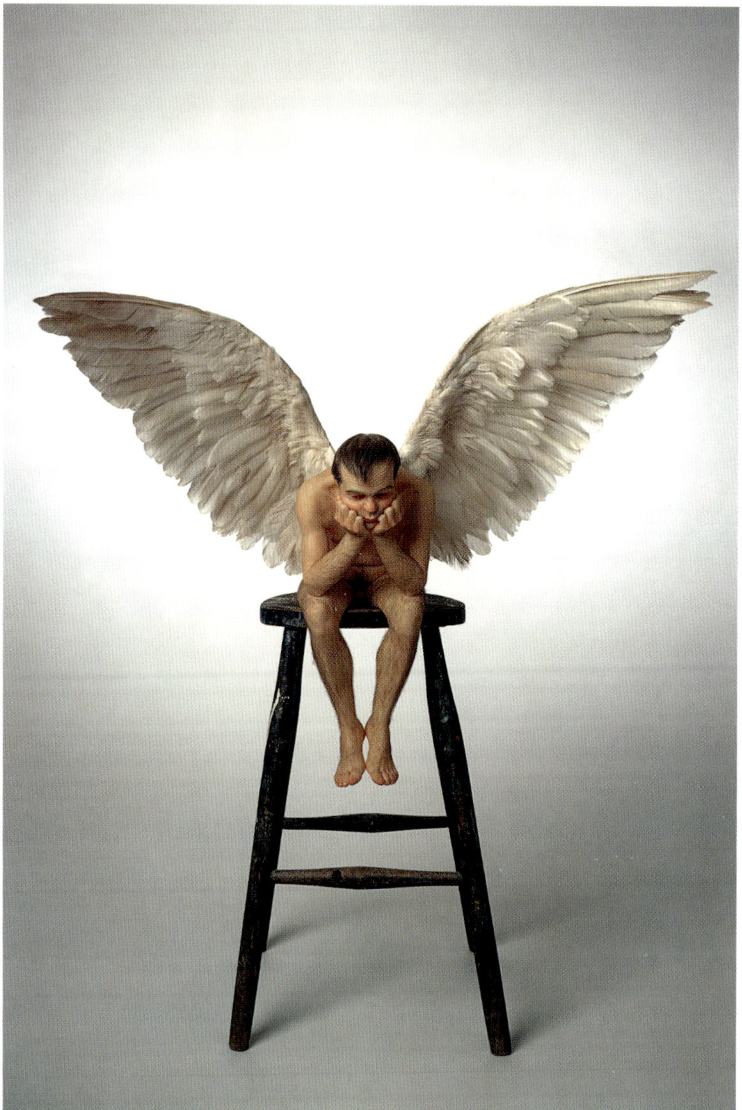

Angel 1997

While Mueck's recognition as an artist owes much to the public exposure received through the *Sensation* exhibition, his practice had been many years in preparation.

Born in Melbourne, Australia, in 1958, Mueck was exposed to creativity and artisanship from an early age. His parents, who had arrived in Australia from Germany in the 1950s, established a successful toy-making business in Melbourne. Aside from the production of soft toys, Mueck recalls his father having made marionette-type puppets that operated through mechanical means rather than with strings.[7] From an early age, Ron Mueck was interested in puppetry and the ability to animate an otherwise lifeless object.

After leaving school in the 1970s, Mueck began working as a puppet maker and puppeteer. Between 1978 and 1983 he was Creative Director of the Australian television series *Shirl's Neighbourhood*, a popular thirty-minute afternoon children's program. The series included a cast of puppet characters that were made and operated by Mueck.[8]

In 1983 Mueck worked as an assistant puppeteer on the Australian episodes of Jim Henson's *Fraggle Rock*. Following this he was invited to spend two months in the United States, working with Henson's team, before travelling to London to work on the feature film *Labyrinth*.[9] Mueck remained in London following the filming, and in 1987 established his own company creating models for the motion picture and advertising industries.

By the 1990s, Mueck had begun using polyester resin and fibreglass in his work. While he had always made things for his own pleasure, it was an increasing frustration with the creative limitations imposed by his work

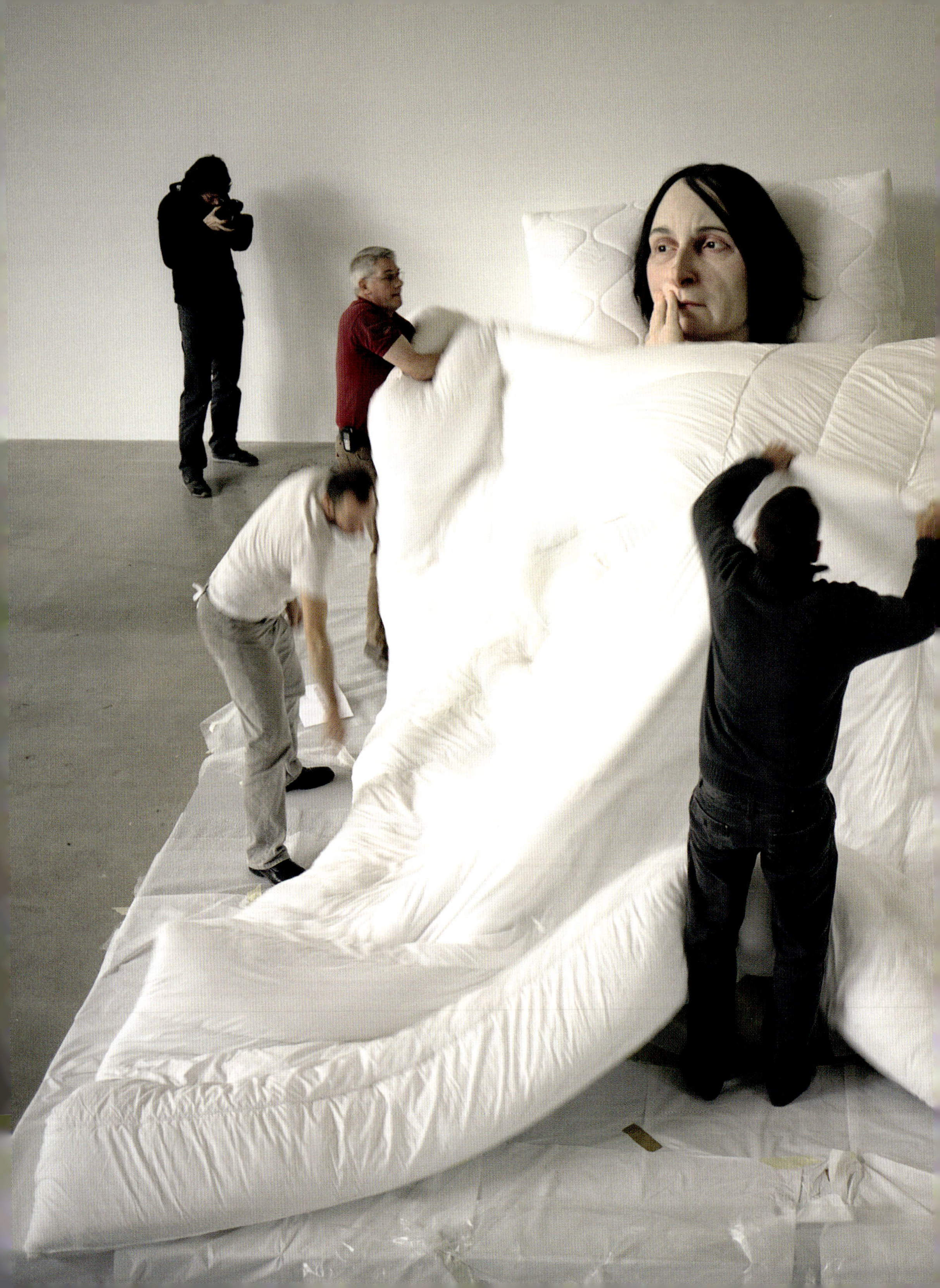

Installing *In Bed*, 2005

in film, television and advertising that prompted him to consider making objects essentially 'for their own sake'.[10] In 1996, Mueck created the first of his lifelike human sculptures. A new direction had begun.

> I had always made things for my own amusement but mostly I was creating things to make a living. The models I had made [for film, television and advertising] always seemed like pleasing objects in their own right, it was just that they had been created for another purpose ... these [new] pieces had no other reason for being and it seemed that was ok.[11]

✦ ✦ ✦

Following his inclusion in *Sensation*, Mueck was taken on by prominent London art dealer Anthony d'Offay.[12] D'Offay was instrumental in building on Mueck's early recognition and has continued to support his career which, since his first publicly exhibited work in 1996, has seen a rapid succession of major achievements. These have included, among many, his two-year residency as Associate Artist at the National Gallery, London, starting in 2000, and his representation at la Biennale di Venezia 49 (the 49th Venice Biennale) in 2001 with *Boy*, 1999.

Since 1996, Mueck has created in excess of forty sculptures, including editions, and is represented in numerous private collections throughout Europe, the United Kingdom and the United States.

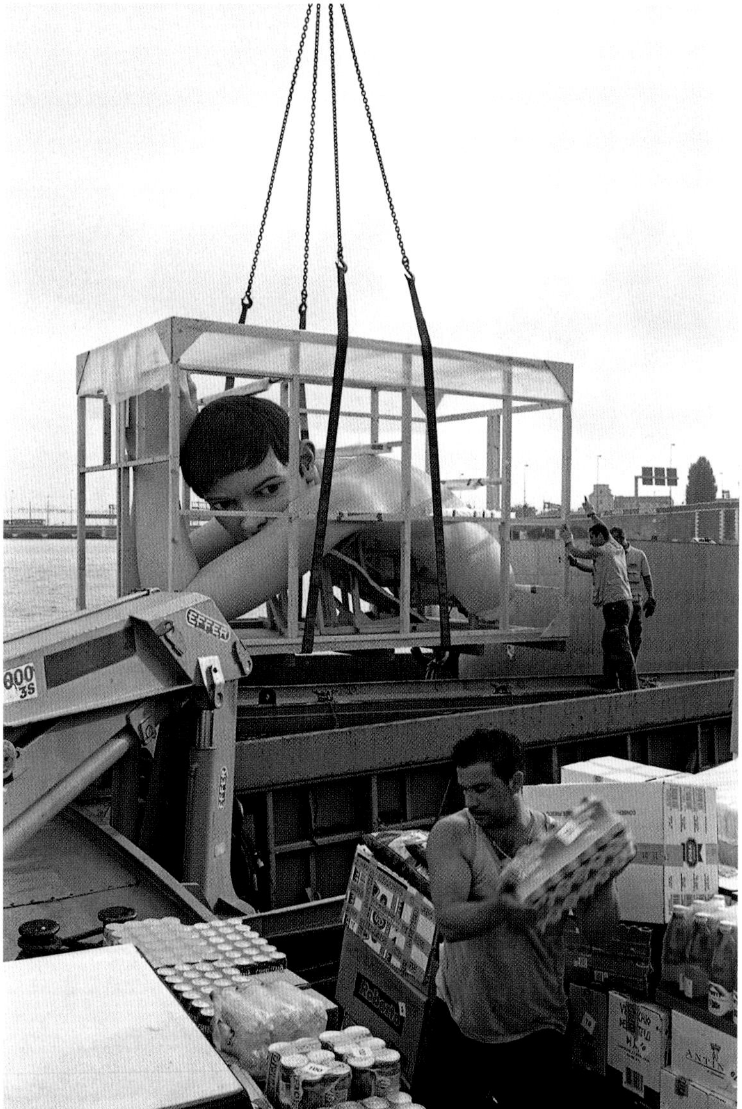
EFFER

Boy, 1999, in transit for the 49th Venice Biennale

Mueck is also represented in many international public collections, including those of the Århus Kunstmuseum, Århus, Denmark; Art Gallery of New South Wales, Sydney, Australia; Hirshhorn Museum and Sculpture Garden, Smithsonian Insititute, Washington DC, United States; Kunstsammlung Nordrhein-Westfalen, Düsseldorf, Germany; McClelland Gallery + Sculpture Park, Langwarrin, Australia; Modern Art Museum of Fort Worth, Texas, United States; Museum Brandhorst, Munich, Germany; National Gallery of Australia, Canberra, Australia; National Gallery of Canada, Ottawa, Canada; National Galleries of Scotland, Scottish Gallery of Modern Art, Edinburgh, Scotland; National Gallery of Victoria, Melbourne, Australia; Queensland Art Gallery, Brisbane, Australia; San Francisco MoMA, California, United States; Tate, London, United Kingdom; and Towada Art Center, Towada, Japan.

✦ ✦ ✦

Working from a small studio in north London, cluttered with tools, equipment and – to an outsider – a disconcerting array of disconnected body parts, Mueck continues to create his sculptures using ingredients such as polyester resin, silicone, polyurethane and acrylic monofilament. Despite the use of these modern materials, his working methods are surprisingly traditional.

Beginning with sketches and maquettes, he models the form in clay using only his hands and a few modelling tools before casting it in either polyester resin or silicone, or sometimes both. Drawing on his many years of experience and an understanding of techniques and materials, he works with great technical fluency. Mueck is also a keen observer, and while much is made of his ability to render details of skin, hair, eyes and physical features, it is the way he does this that instils in his sculptures the essence of life that gives them such indescribable presence. Susanna Greeves, who has closely followed Mueck's career as an artist, identifies this aspect of his practice:

Ron Mueck in his studio, 2009

> There is a Chinese tradition that the painter does not complete the eyes of his subjects, in order to prevent them escaping his control. Mueck lavishes extraordinary care on hand-making his model's eyes in many stages, building up a transparent lens over a colored iris and deep black pupil. When finally he inserts them the effect is startling, as the figure appears to come to life.[13]

✦ ✦ ✦

Some of Mueck's sculptures are puckish portrayals of childhood innocence. Others are acute and poignant observations of stages of life, from birth to adolescence, to middle and old age, and even death. Many are solitary figures, psychological portraits of emotional intensity and of isolation.

> People in all their variations and similarities are pretty fascinating. Occasionally some of these aspects come into focus ...' and I think maybe I could capture that. You just start with your subject (and your own baggage) and see where you end up ... you try to imagine what it's like to be in their place.[14]

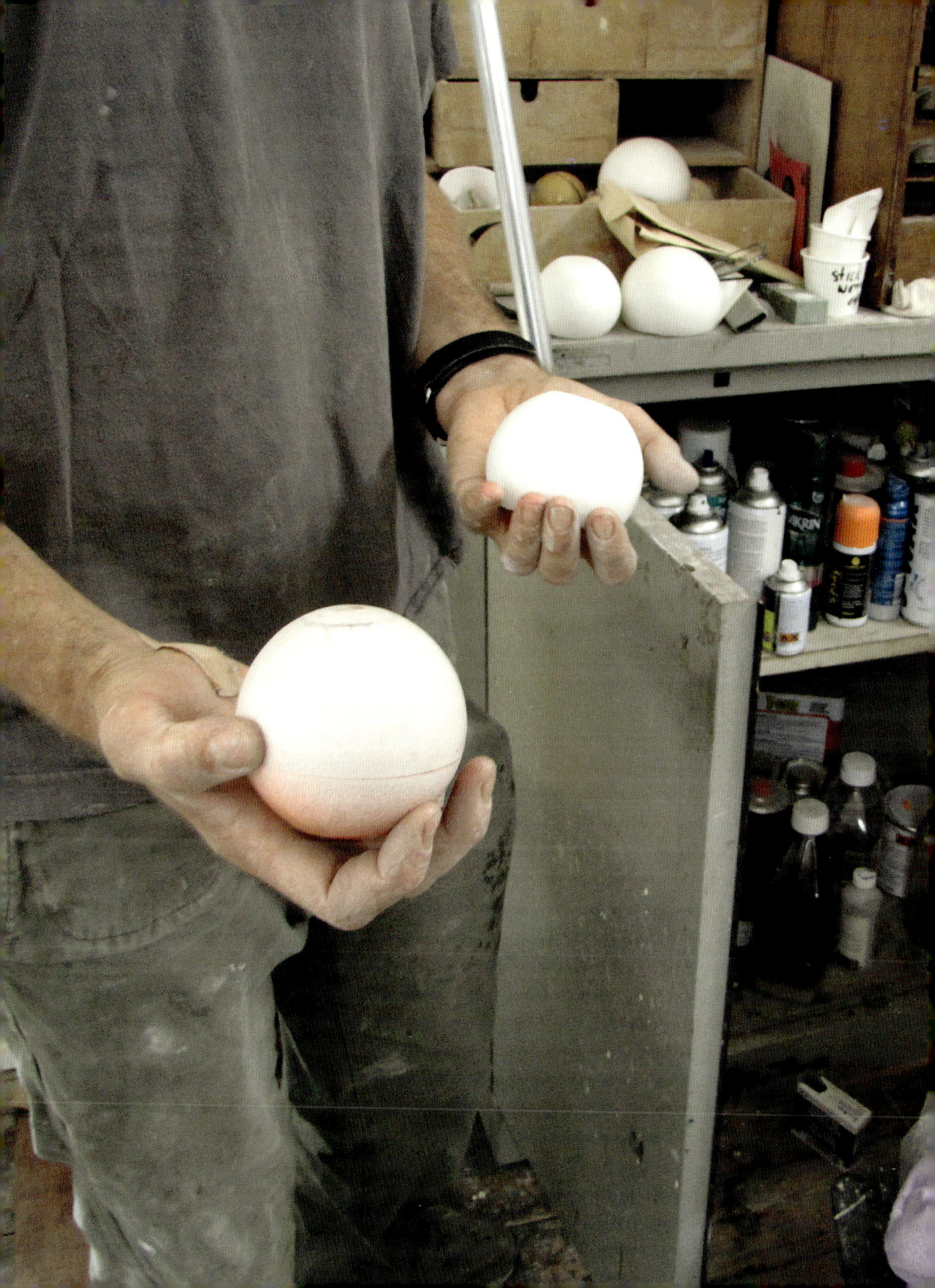

Ron Mueck is a very private person. By his own admission, he is something of an eremite and an outsider in the world of contemporary art. He shuns public interviews and is generally reluctant to talk about his work, preferring instead that people respond to his sculptures in their own personal ways. Because they appear so real, his works naturally invite our interaction; their power lies in their ability to cause us to create our own narrative.

Pregnant woman, 2002, installation view

Often naked and suspended in states of self-consciousness, introspection or deep contemplation, his figures present both emotional and physical states of exposure. As viewers we experience a level of unease that is borne of a voyeuristic awkwardness, as though we have invaded some kind of personal space. However, we also identify with the human condition that these poignant moments express. Mueck is the master of reflection.

More than a decade on from his dramatic entrée onto the contemporary art scene, Ron Mueck continues to move and amaze people with his extraordinary sculptures. He has earned a singular place as the creator of some of the most evocative sculptures of our time.

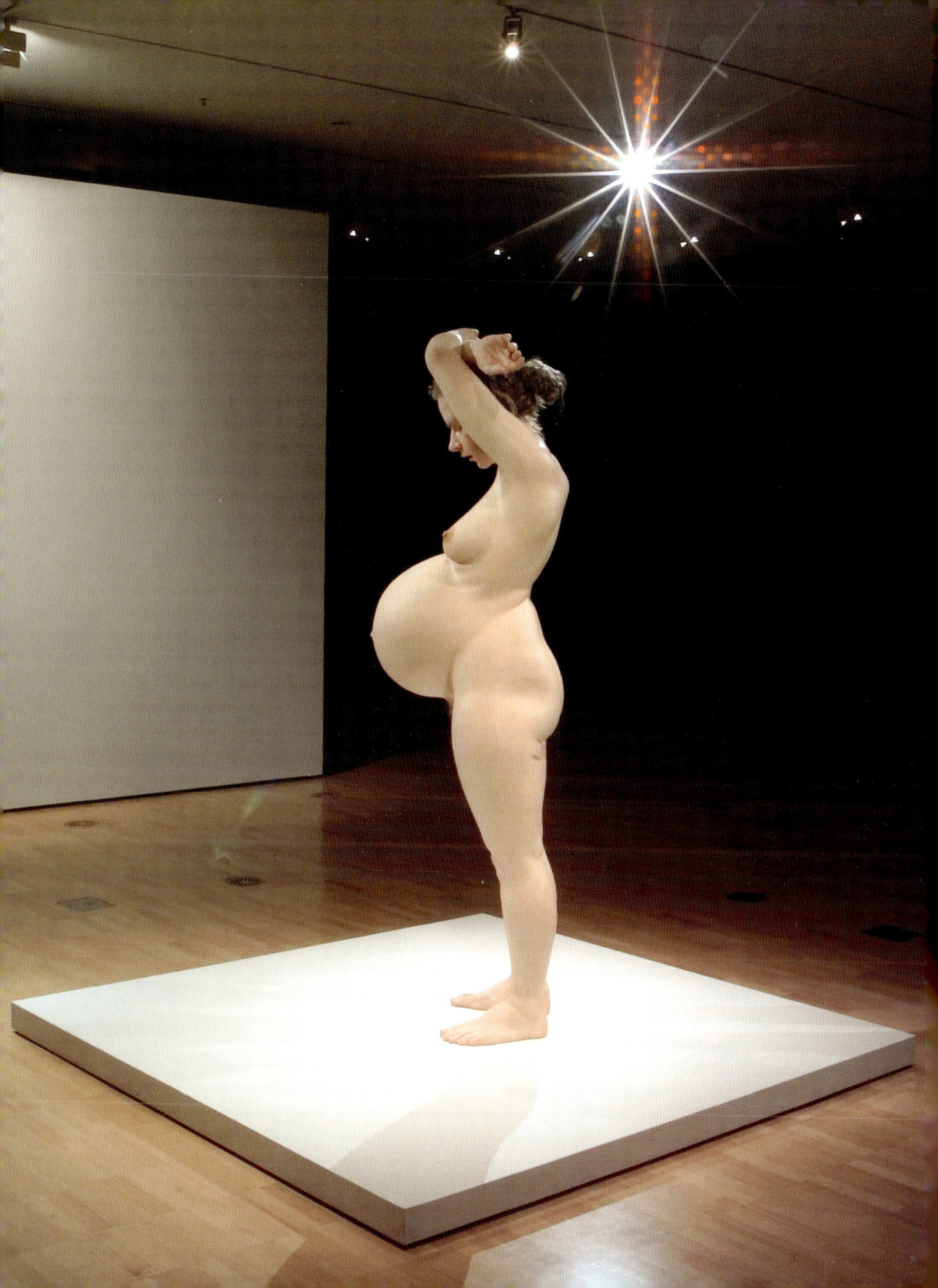

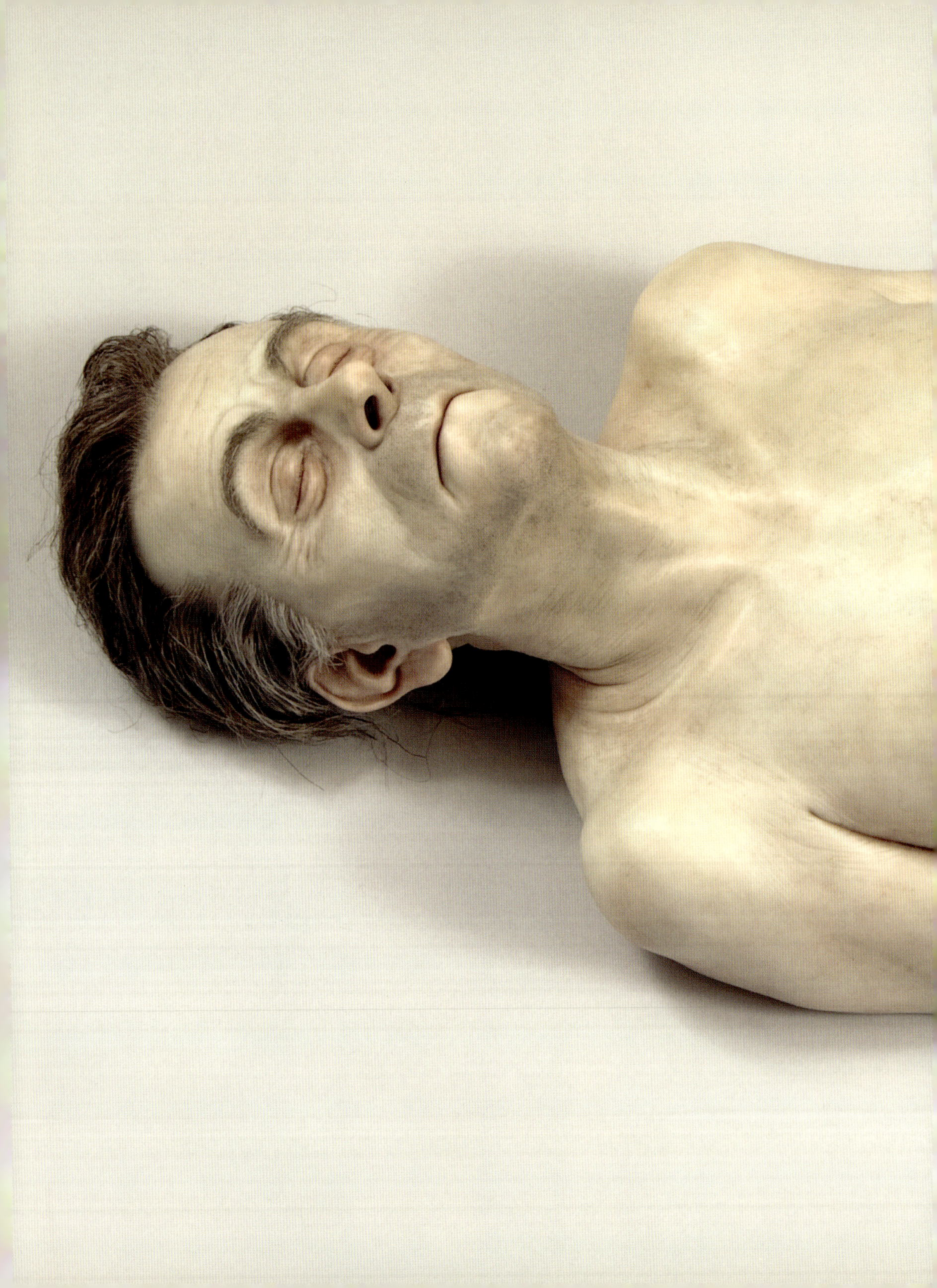

ANGUS TRUMBLE

DEAD DAD

Dead Dad,
1996–97 (detail)
Stefan T. Edlis
Collection, Chicago

Albrecht Dürer the Elder handles his rosary. The miller Harmen Gerritsz van Rijn wears some items borrowed from his son's collection of oriental costume and bric-a-brac, evidently with some unease. Citoyen Denon *père* does his best to stay awake, but nevertheless smiles affectionately. The toothless innkeeper John West of Springfield, Pennsylvania, determinedly wears his hat indoors – Quakers only ever removed them to pray. Régis Courbet gradually ages with much dignity, doubling as an astute manager of the family's substantial interest in cattle at Ornans. The Scarborough physician Frederic Septimus Leighton is erect, proud and cultivated. The retired banker Augustin Degas listens patiently to a Spanish tenor noisily strumming his guitar in the middle of the drawing room. Louis-Auguste Cézanne is shown reading a copy of *L'Evènement*, something he almost certainly never did without provocation. The art teacher and part-time museum curator Don José Ruiz Blasco stares into space, the *ne plus ultra* of gaunt Catalan melancholy in Picasso's youthful study, while old Mr Kossoff, the retired baker of East London, is simply 'Father'. Ron Mueck's, by contrast, is 'Dad' – naked and lately dead.

In each case we encounter not only an image of the artist's father but inevitably also a kind of portrait of the artist as his father's son. *Dead Dad*, 1996–97, is one of only very few sculptures that Mueck has yet created from whose subject all life has drained away.

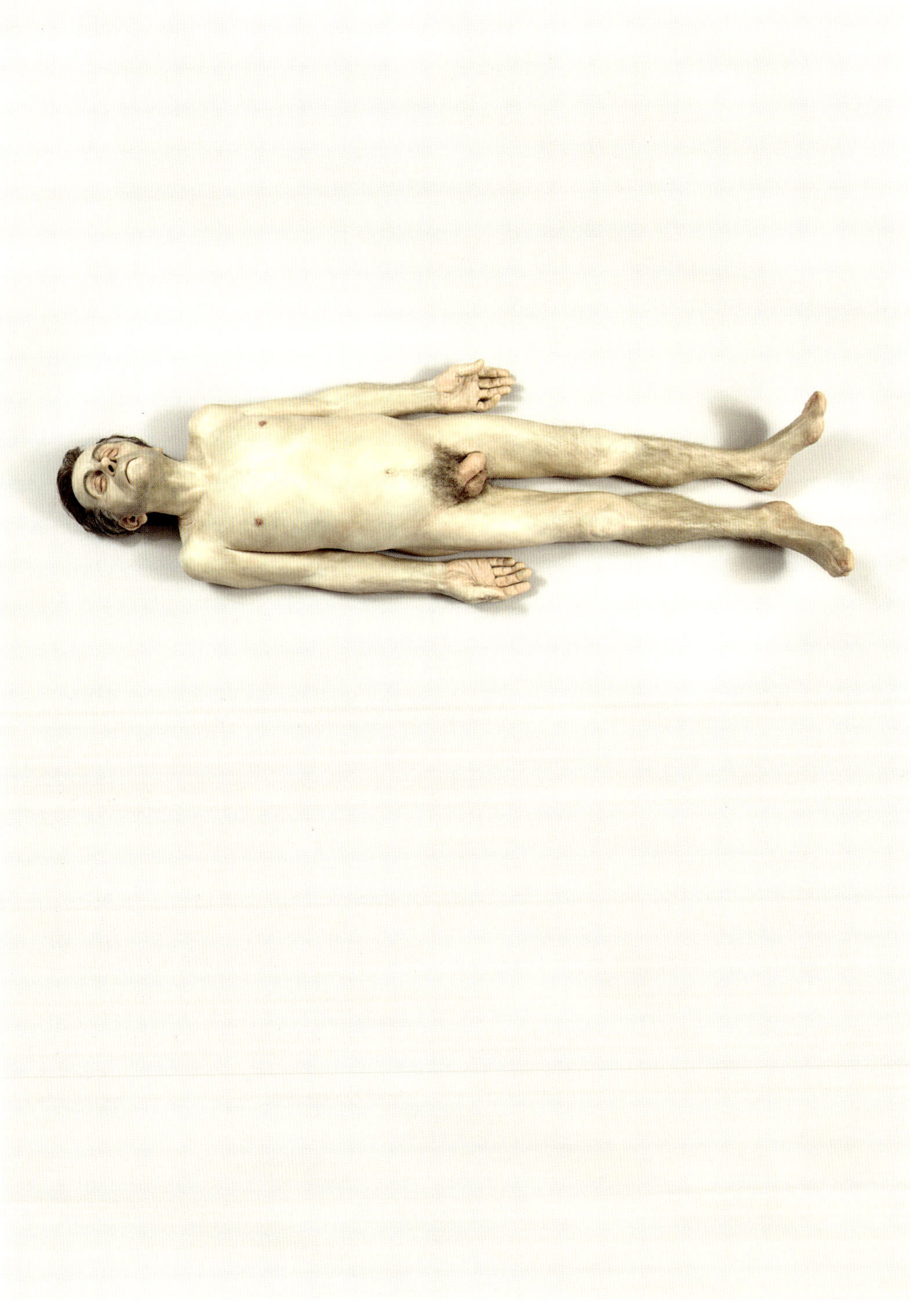

I first saw *Dead Dad* at the Royal Academy of Arts in London, when my own father was seriously ill; nobody who sees this work and has navigated the death of a parent can possibly prevent those experiences from merging powerfully. It was *Dead Dad*'s full head of hair that I recall noticing then, and still notice today. Somewhat incongruously kempt, it reminds me of what well-meaning nurses did to my own father's towards the end – insistently sweeping it straight back over his head, ignoring the meticulous left-hand parting of better days, thereby attaining by accident a slightly raffish and therefore wholly wrongheaded appearance. It was nobody's fault, but irritating nevertheless. Mum spent a good deal of time carefully brushing Dad's hair back the right way – just *comme ça*. Anything more than imperfect shaving can also pose a problem for those responsible for looking after dying men. And whiskers continue to grow for some considerable time after the heart stops beating.

In sculpture, the manipulation of scale can be an exceedingly blunt instrument, and at only 102.0 cm long, *Dead Dad* is, of course, as tiny, psychically limp and vulnerable as *Wild man*, 2005, and *A girl*, 2006, are enormous. However, when incongruous exaggerations of scale, both downward and upward, are as dominant a concern as they are for Ron Mueck – and combined with the microscopically calibrated verisimilitude of subtly tinted resin, fibreglass and silicone planted with synthetic hair, the defining framework of his sculpture – the resulting effects go far beyond some form of visual hyperbole. The emphasis in *Dead Dad* is upon dying as an irreversible process of diminution – the confiscation of every kind of bodily armature – and upon death as shrinkage to nothing. Here the corpse is a metonym for complete exposure, and in that sense it is as if Mueck turns inside out Hans Holbein's sequestered *Body of the dead Christ in the tomb*,

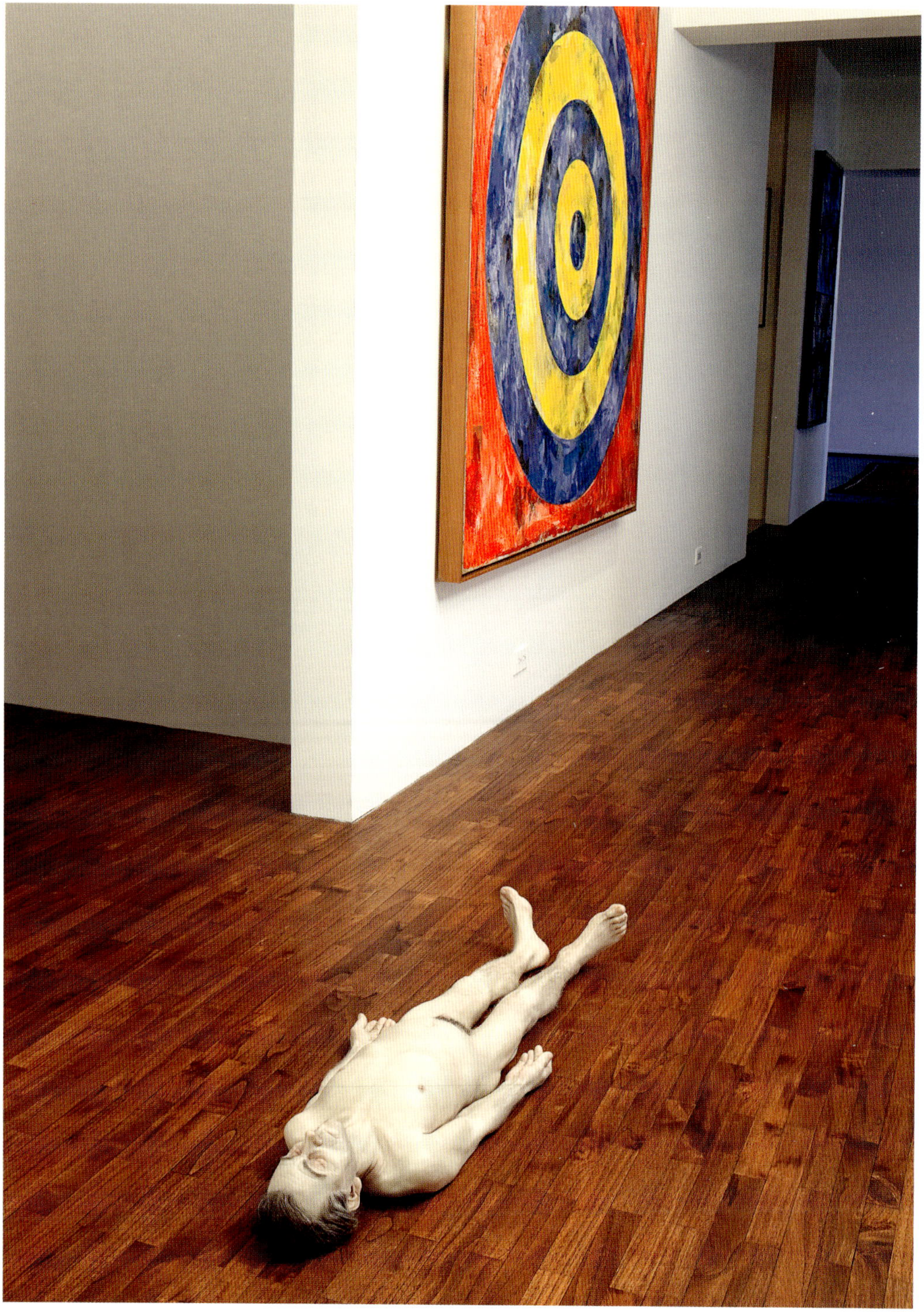

Dead Dad, 1996–97, with Jasper Johns's *Target*, installation view

1521–22, or Andrea Mantegna's *Dead Christ*, *c*.1500, supplanting the marks of the Passion with the carbolic cleanliness of the hospital or clinic; substituting some unspecified, maybe even banal pathology for horrifying wounds; emphatic nakedness for the winding sheet; the cold electric light of day for the darkness of the tomb. Indeed, *Dead Dad* now dwells in spaces so public and anodyne as to be almost embarrassing.

Unlike Dürer the Elder, M. Courbet, Dr Leighton and the rest, I know nothing about Ron Mueck's dad except that he lived and died in Melbourne after the artist settled permanently in London, and that – perhaps in more ways than the critic who first said so ever intended – this is the work that made his name.

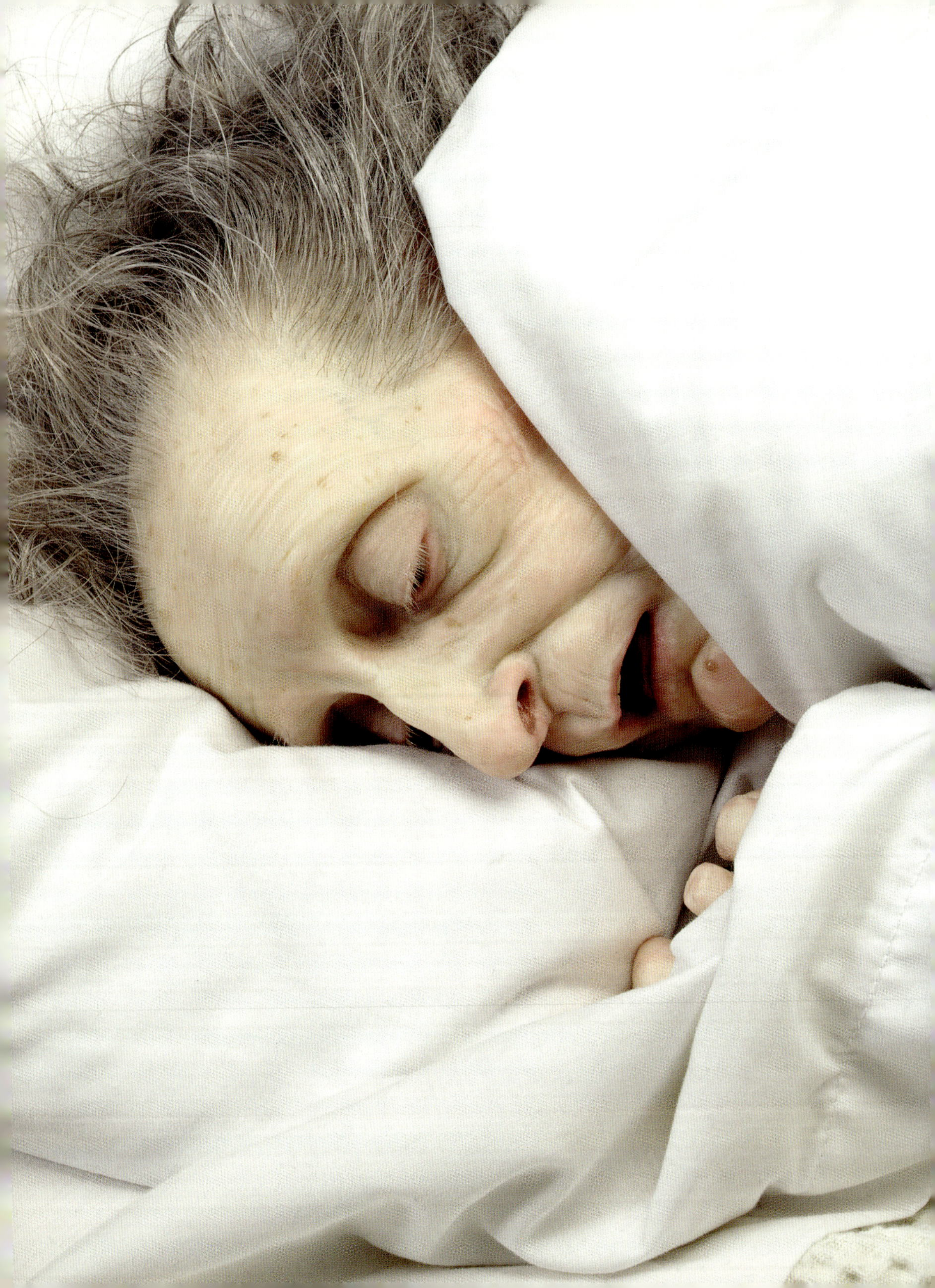

LISA BALDISSERA

THE ART OF EXCESS: FIVE MOVEMENTS

Old woman in bed 2002
Art Gallery of New South Wales, Sydney

1 A young woman in a red dress with fine high heels, a white-haired man in light khakis and a muscular boy in shorts – all surround the marble figures in the centre of the room. The light, which at first seems to be pouring through an open window, after several moments appears to emanate from the perfection of the white stone. The elegant struggle between Pluto and Persephone in Gian Lorenzo Bernini's *Rape of Persephone*, 1621–22, is as controlled as its gathered audience. The sinuous gesture of the two figures wends its way towards the extravagant ceiling of the hall of the Villa Borghese. Still, there is one event that seems to have drawn particular attention: Pluto's grip on the flesh of Persephone's thigh. At precisely the juncture where one muscle overlays another, Pluto's hand dimples the surface with hyperreal exactitude. The thick hand presses into what has somehow reached a point of mimetic arrest, a transfixing note of punctum[1], where stone and flesh mingle in one serpentine movement. Those gathered here might be unfamiliar with the Classical story depicted in the Mannerist sculpture but synaesthesia may also have a role to play: the force of the gesture distilled in the press of Persephone's marble flesh.

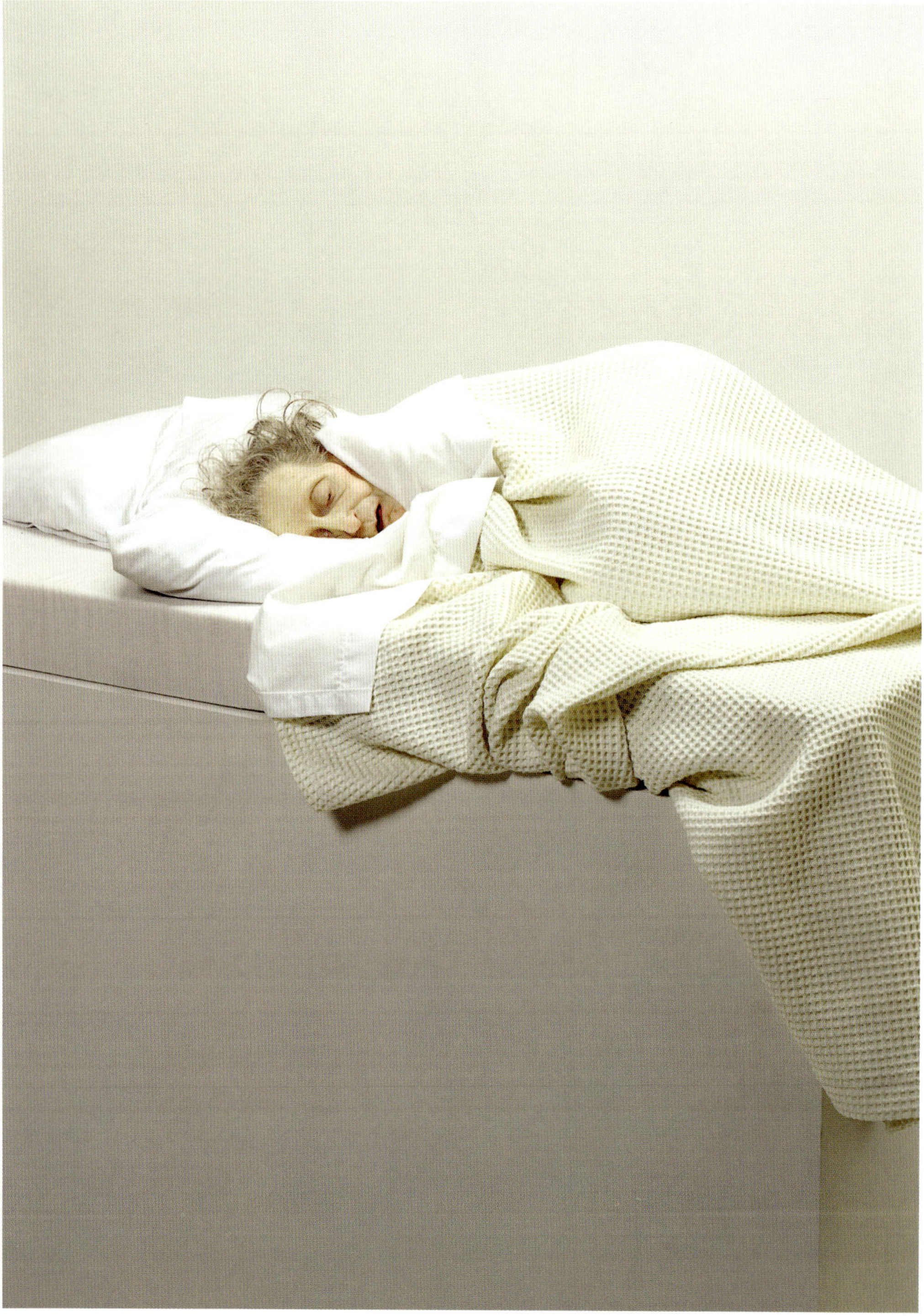

2 Patti Smith, languorous in a torn white slip, kneels on the floor in a white-curtained room and lays a small pitch-toned sculpture of a robed male figure down beside her. Slowly, she topples it, declaring: 'I can't get away from language. This thing is like language to me'.[2] She swaddles it in white cloth, effectively erasing it from the screen.

3 In the anterooms beside Michelangelo's *David*, 1501–04, Thomas Struth's *Audience 2, Galleria dell'Accademia, Firenze*, 2004, one of nine photographs, depicts transfixed audiences encircling the iconic statue. Struth's work was commissioned to commemorate the 500 years since the sculpture's 'birth'.

In an alcove designed in the nineteenth century, for Michelangelo's masterpiece, a young man in a *Viva Italia* T-shirt exclaims, 'It's big!' as he enters the salon where *David* now stands, after more than 350 years in Piazza Signoria. Security guards huddle in front, shouting 'No photo!' to those timorous enough to attempt to suture this witnessing into a structure that will contain it after their visit. Throughout, a woman sits on a crowded bench in the Accademia Gallery with a notebook on her lap, a small vial of sepia and a sable paintbrush poised above an empty page. The sculpture reveals Michelangelo's instinctive understanding of the divine agreement between light and object. *David*'s fawn-coloured stone surface, dulled by weather and restoration, achieves its amaranthine presence through the force of the artist's exaggeration: one hand slung too low and too large reveals Michelangelo's constructed realism and this, more than the convincing gestural weight of *contrapunto*, opens the psychic space of the work to a contemporary witness.

4 Against a backdrop of slate grey, fragments of a second-century frieze have been reconstructed: veined hands, jutting hips and flowing robes are all that remain of the figures that occupied the frieze of the Pergamon Altar, housed in the Pergamon Museum in Berlin since 1929. No sculptural reconstruction has been attempted to replace the gaps in retrieval of this ambitious frieze to the losses of time, war and thieving. Notes tell us the figures were once painted to heighten their spectacular vividness. The spaces between the known, the found and the unknown allow for myriad reconstructions; slate grey becomes a space of projection and possibility between a collapsed bow pulled by a gracefully articulated hand and an exquisitely rendered torso. This Hellenic ruin is ever falling away and coming into being. In fact, absence is its mimetic presence: into the gaps the projections of a diasporic viewer find refuge.

5 A group of children inadvertently mimic Baroque gestures and Mannerist tropes. Ron Mueck's *Old woman in bed*, 2002, prompts them to enact their Classical poses as they lean in, swaying, to understand the piece. The sculpture seems to be the only body that breathes, as synaptic pressures extort each viewer to resolve the frank and shocking effect of the hyperreal. The mimetic confluence of the translucent, papery skin, the intrusion of cheekbone and poverty of the collapsed mouth are heightened by the sculpture's diminutive size. Mueck's refusal of life-size figuration establishes a tender puncture of the suspension of disbelief, incorporating the excessive gesture of Hellenic sculpture that influenced both Michelangelo and Bernini and their apprehension of the figure, which in turn set aesthetic conventions that persist in contemporary treatments of the body. Mueck contributes further to this history, utilising imaginative precedents set in this century by cinematic language and form, which

establish new sites of imagination in contemporary viewers. Special effects technologies and cinematic conventions of the late twentieth century take their cue from earlier film events: Marlene Dietrich's face, lit lovingly by Josef von Sternberg reveals every sensuous curve, eyelash and fold of a lip, becoming a 'sculpture' that materially diminishes the audience gathered in the theatre. As in Mueck's work, light, space and flesh are effectively harnessed by the erotic force of obsession.

✦ ✦ ✦

In the National Gallery of Victoria, Mueck's sculpture, a slight figure of an old woman curled under a modest blanket, a drop of saliva in the corner of her gaping mouth, reveals the artist's elegant aesthetic summary of realism and the hyperreal: Persephone's thigh, David's hand, the cool blank absences of a reconstructed Pergamon and, finally, Smith's lament: the persistence of language.

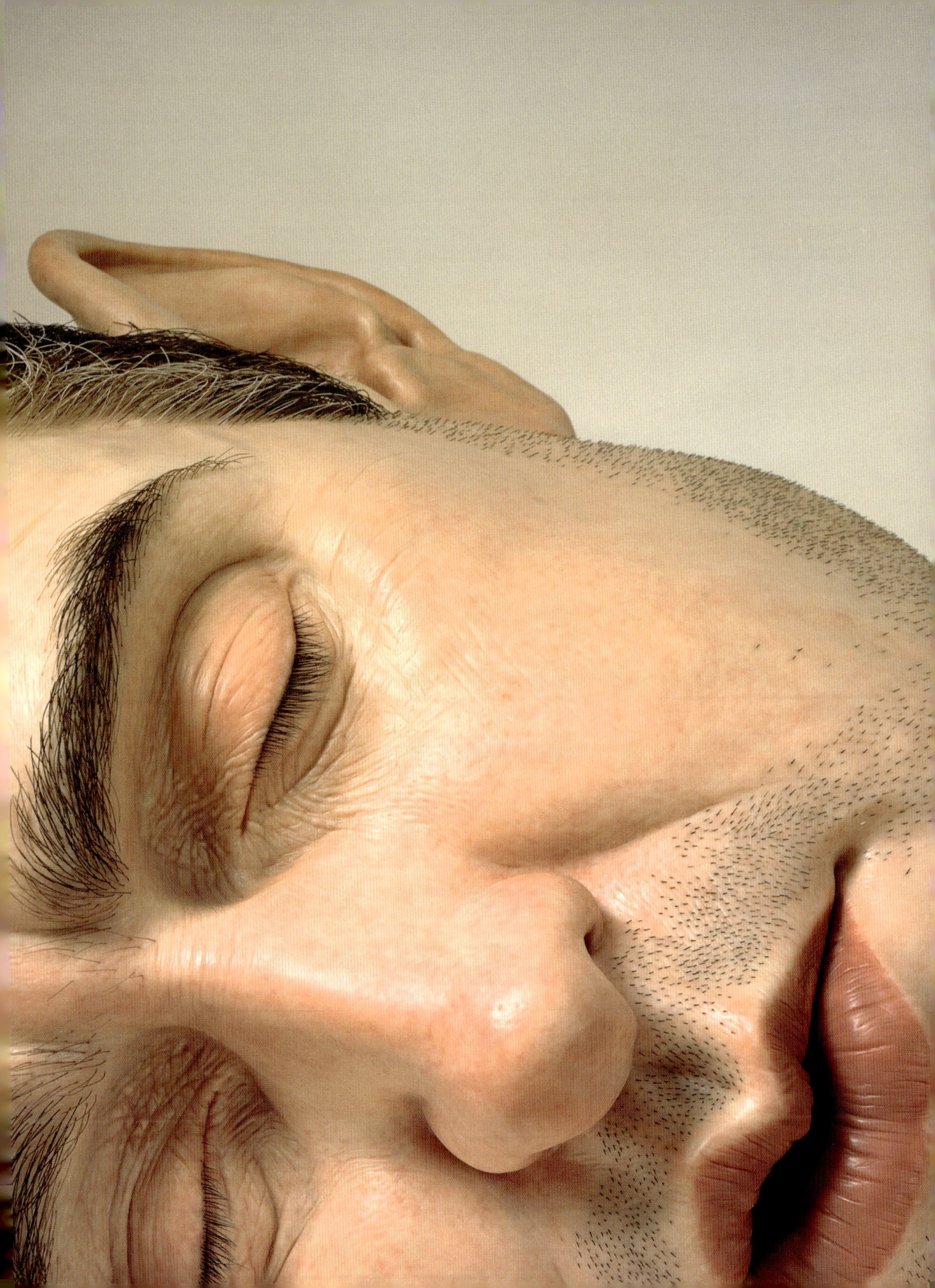

JAMES FOX

MASK II AND THE CURSE OF NARCISSUS

Mask II 2002
Private collection

Within moments of its unveiling at the British Museum, it was clear that *Mask II*, 2002, was going to be a hit.[1] Over the next four months, it was besieged by a constant gaggle of onlookers and accompanied by rhapsodic exclamations, warbling digital cameras and the all-too-frequent 'No touching please!' from the beleaguered staff whose job it was to protect the work. For the countless visitors who had dragged themselves and their families to the museum in search of the Parthenon sculptures, the Rosetta Stone and the Egyptian mummies, Mueck's spot-lit self-portrait looked like an alien entity that had travelled from a distant world, fallen through a Bloomsbury skylight and crash-landed in a building that didn't quite know what to do with it.

Mask II may have been a surprising addition to the British Museum's collection, but it is very much at home in the art historical canon. Its cutting-edge materials, coruscating vividness and the belligerence with which it goes after its audience's visual appetites disguise the fact that, if anything, it belongs to a grand and global lineage of monumental statuary. To my mind, its cultural kinfolk are not Damien Hirst and Tracey Emin but the Egyptian busts of Amenhotep and Ramesses, the boulder-sized Olmec heads from Mexico, the great marble colossi from ancient Rome, and the hundreds of square-jawed giants that have imperiously guarded the coastline of Easter Island for what seems like eternity.

These monumental sculptures were produced for a myriad of reasons. Some celebrated death and others were designed to defy it; some

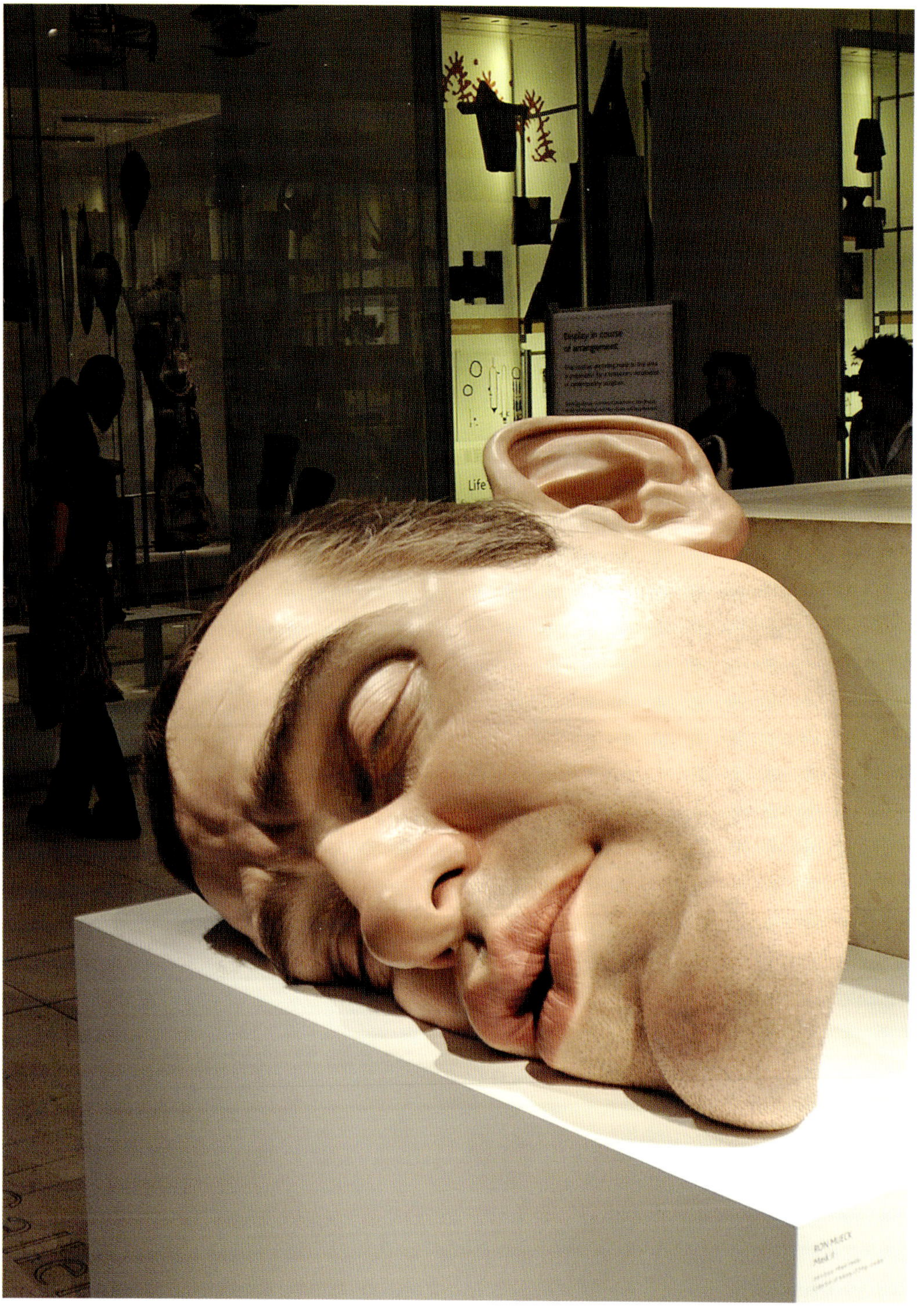
Life
RON MUECK

commemorated the past and others safeguarded the future; some communicated with the gods and others were believed to be the gods. All, however, were underpinned with humanity's perennial fascination with its own image, and by a desire to permanently inscribe that image onto an otherwise indifferent universe. But anyone who knows the tale of Narcissus (the Greek adolescent who fatally covets his reflection) knows that these desires are highly dangerous, and history confirms that the 'hubris' of constructing monumental likenesses is all too often followed by the 'nemesis' of their downfall. We need only recall the scenes of Iraqi men attacking the large bronze statue of Saddam Hussein in 2003 to find evidence that sculpture has lost none of this rebarbative resonance.

One could here be forgiven for asking what bearing any of this has on *Mask II*. I discuss it not simply because Hussein's infamous bronze head happened to boast almost identical proportions to Mueck's mixed-media head, nor because in its appropriation of fragment-form *Mask II* alludes to the iconoclastic fury that had mutilated countless such likenesses in the past. I cite it because in this monumentalised and somehow abstracted self-portrait, Mueck seems to answer the perennial questions concerning the power of sculpture. What is it that encourages societies to devotedly produce sculpture, but also encourages them to angrily destroy it? And why are sculpted likenesses so potent that, according to the Bible, even God himself was jealous of them? *Mask II* suggests that this power is located in their unique ability to manipulate scale, material, form and site in order to transform likenesses into idols, and humans into deities.

This may be mere speculation but only speculation seems possible for an object that, like the faces of the dead, meets every impassioned overture with the same inscrutable indifference. *Mask II* actually thrives on such ambiguity: it willfully oscillates between self-consciousness and

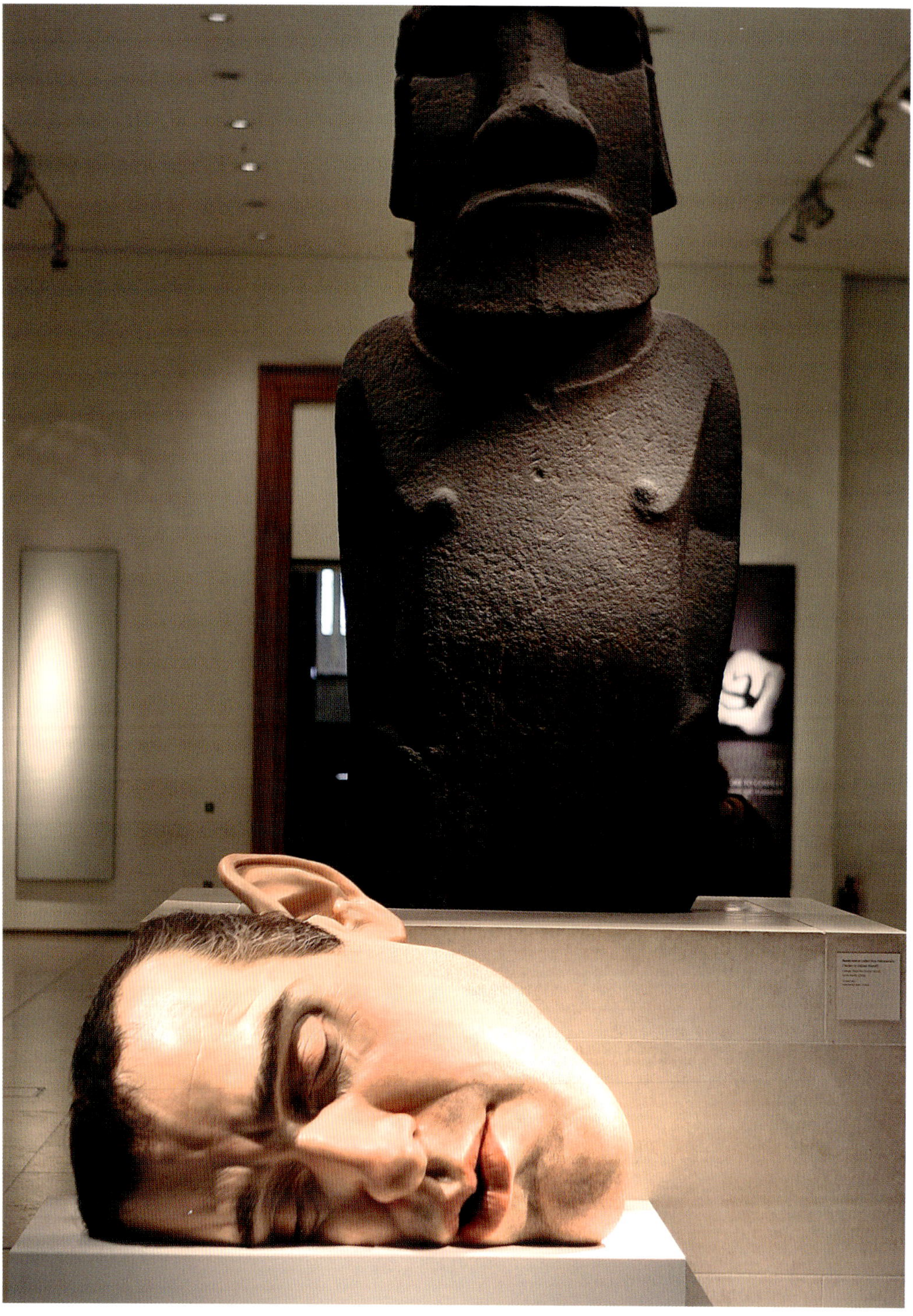

unconsciousness, intimacy and monumentality, beauty and grotesquerie. But most effective of all is its unstable location between hyperrealism and anti-realism. Following its unveiling in the British Museum, I observed how viewers' excitement invariably became disappointment as they turned their attention from its breathtakingly naturalistic front to its hollow, blank back. It was at this point that I swear I saw an almost imperceptible smirk flicker across the features of that giant face. Here was Mueck deliberately collapsing the very illusion he had strived so hard to create, and proving to us – as the pool proved to Narcissus – that however real some images may appear, they are in the end just images.

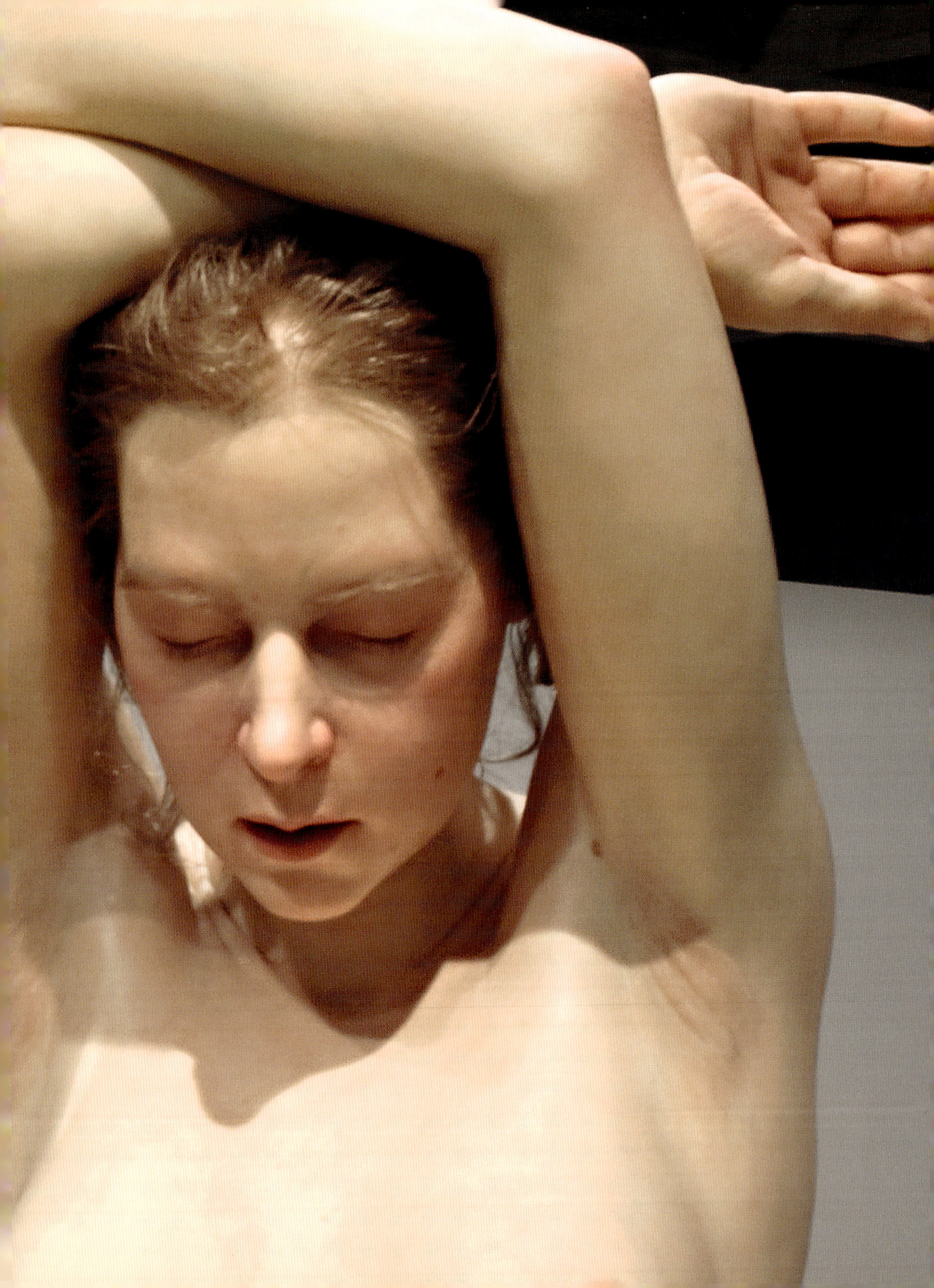

JUSTIN PATON

TAKING THE WEIGHT

Pregnant woman 2002 (detail)
National Gallery of Australia, Canberra

When my partner was pregnant with our first son six years ago, she took a photograph of herself in the same mirror every few weeks. Looking at the photographs recently, I laughed at how much I had forgotten. You forget what an event a pregnancy is, how fast and how extreme, how much space it takes up. And our culture doesn't exactly help you remember. Despite the furious marketing of parenthood and the use of bodies everywhere to advertise everything imaginable, the astonishing spectacle of one body generating another is still a rare sight.

Rising more than eight feet high in a pristine gallery environment, Ron Mueck's *Pregnant woman*, 2002, is impossible not to see. If your first view of the sculpture is from behind, the pregnancy is initially concealed. But what cannot be missed, even at a distance, is the sense of enormous weight descending, of this body as a load-bearing structure. You feel it in the deep curve of the spine, pulled forward by the belly. You feel it in the legs and braced back, and in the feet, planted profoundly flat. And you not only feel but see it when rounding the sculpture to confront, at eye-height, the booming fullness of the belly, with its popped navel and shining *linea nigra*. At life-size, this sight would be extraordinary enough. At this size, it is hallucinatory – the human form stretched larger than seems humanly possible.

With this oversized sculpture of an enormous human event, Mueck presses in on a vast human question: how much space is there for each of us in the world? And how should we occupy that space? Throughout

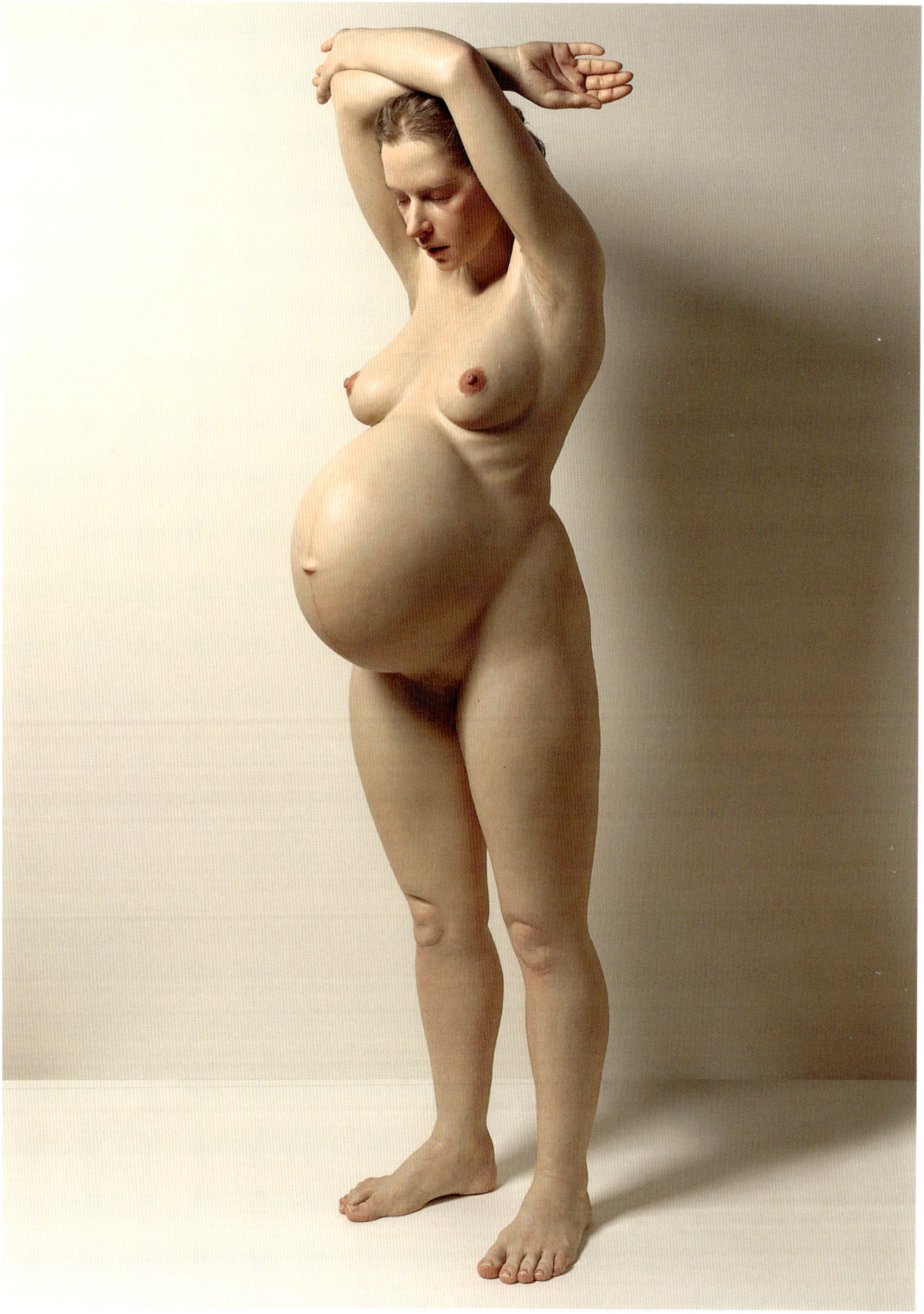

the Western sculptural tradition, the answer is often *actively*. From the writhing figures of the Laocoön group and the rippling Belvedere torso on down to Auguste Rodin's aggressively striding man, this tradition is full of male bodies eager to claim their share of surrounding space. Whether they are athletes, warriors or biblical figures, the argument is the same: that humans are never more vivid and real than when they are reaching, striding, moving.

Then comes *Pregnant woman* and redefines this idea of action. Her arms do not reach. Her heels are not lifted. Her gaze is not fixed on some horizon of victory. By the standards of Western sculpture and its space-invading figures, she is scandalously still. But Mueck's achievement is to generate, within this stillness, a colossal sense of change and increase. From the faint sheen of sweat on her brow, to the way her mouth seems to measure its breaths and the colossal jut of her stomach, every outward detail makes us imagine a vast internal event – hormones rushing in, ligaments yielding, the whole body making ready. The result is monumental figure sculpture of a wonderfully self-questioning kind. Traditional sculptural heroes stand proud and singular. But this figure is heroic because she has let go of her singularity and taken the weight of another human. She has agreed to be two.

Pregnant woman has been called a modern Mary, a contemporary earth mother and a 'hymn to the beauty of the life-giving'.[1] The problem with this praise is that it glides too smoothly over Mueck's audacity – the risks he takes, as a male sculptor, in confronting the matter of pregnancy. What does it mean for a man to make such a sculpture? Is it a case of male rivalry with the female power of procreativity? Aren't there dangers that the resulting object will simply join the contemporary parade of bodies to be stared at? And as a male viewer, am I even qualified to answer these

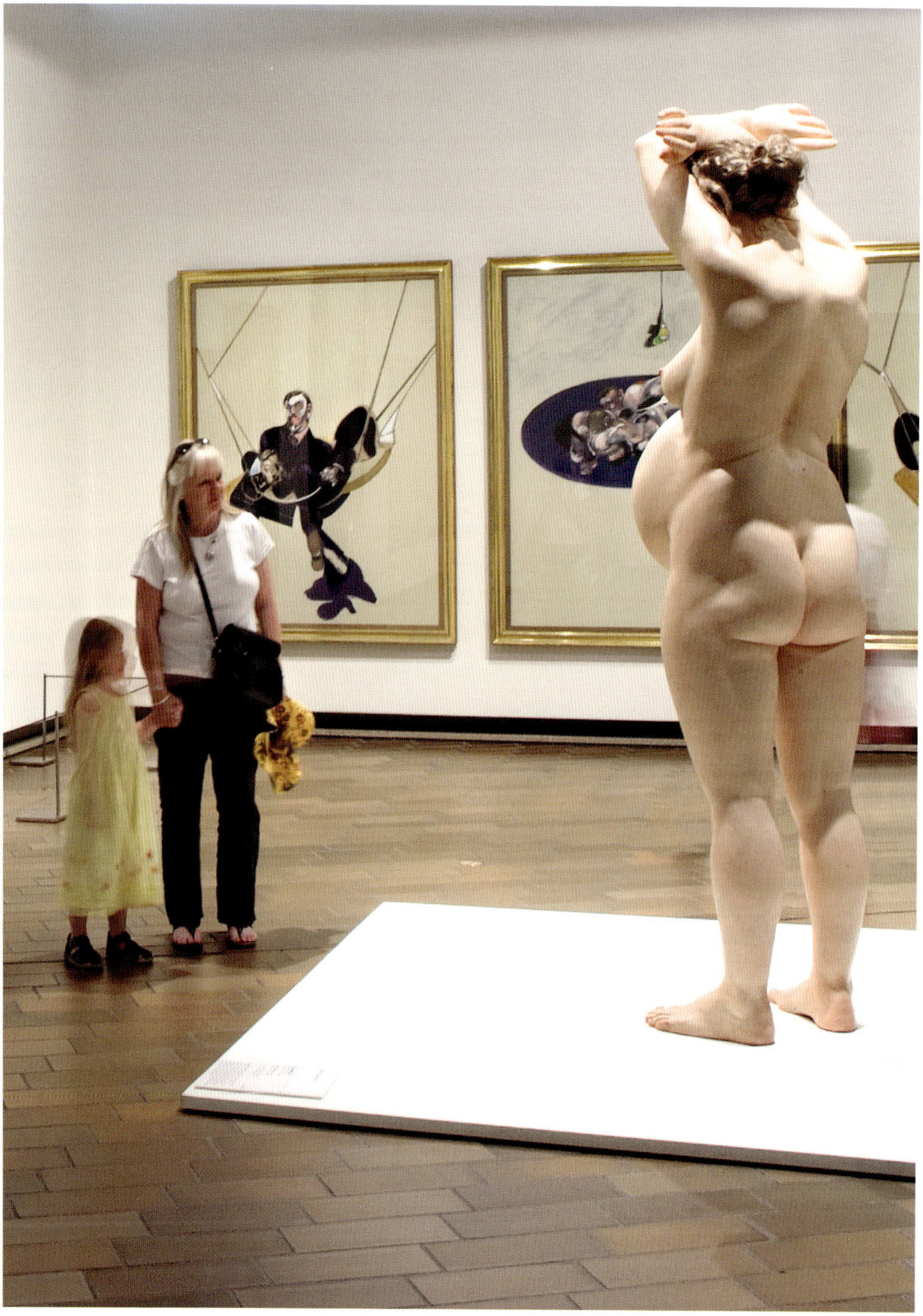

Pregnant woman, 2002, with Francis Bacon's *Triptych*, 1970, installation view

questions? But these doubts and uncertainties do not stand in the way of a proper encounter with *Pregnant woman*. In fact, they are the very source of its power. Rather than celebrating motherhood as a known and universal condition, *Pregnant woman* testifies to the awesome otherness of pregnancy for bystanders at the event. In other words, this is not just a sculpture of how someone else looks. Much more importantly, it is a sculpture about how it feels to look at someone else.

'I can't imagine' we sometimes say, upon hearing of the emotional trials of other people. Can't imagine being born, giving birth, losing someone, dying. And pregnancy, too, defies imagination if you have not experienced it yourself. As a sculptor drawn to extreme life events, Mueck seems to answer simultaneously two powerful impulses. On one hand there is his burning desire to capture such moments, right down to the last follicle. On the other, there is his humble recognition of the limits of what even the most detailed sculpture can capture. And for me this quality of humility and tact is what makes an encounter with *Pregnant woman* unforgettable. The miracle is that a figure so emphatically *there* is at the same time somewhere else. Her eyes are closed, her gaze focused on some inner horizon. She has forgotten us.

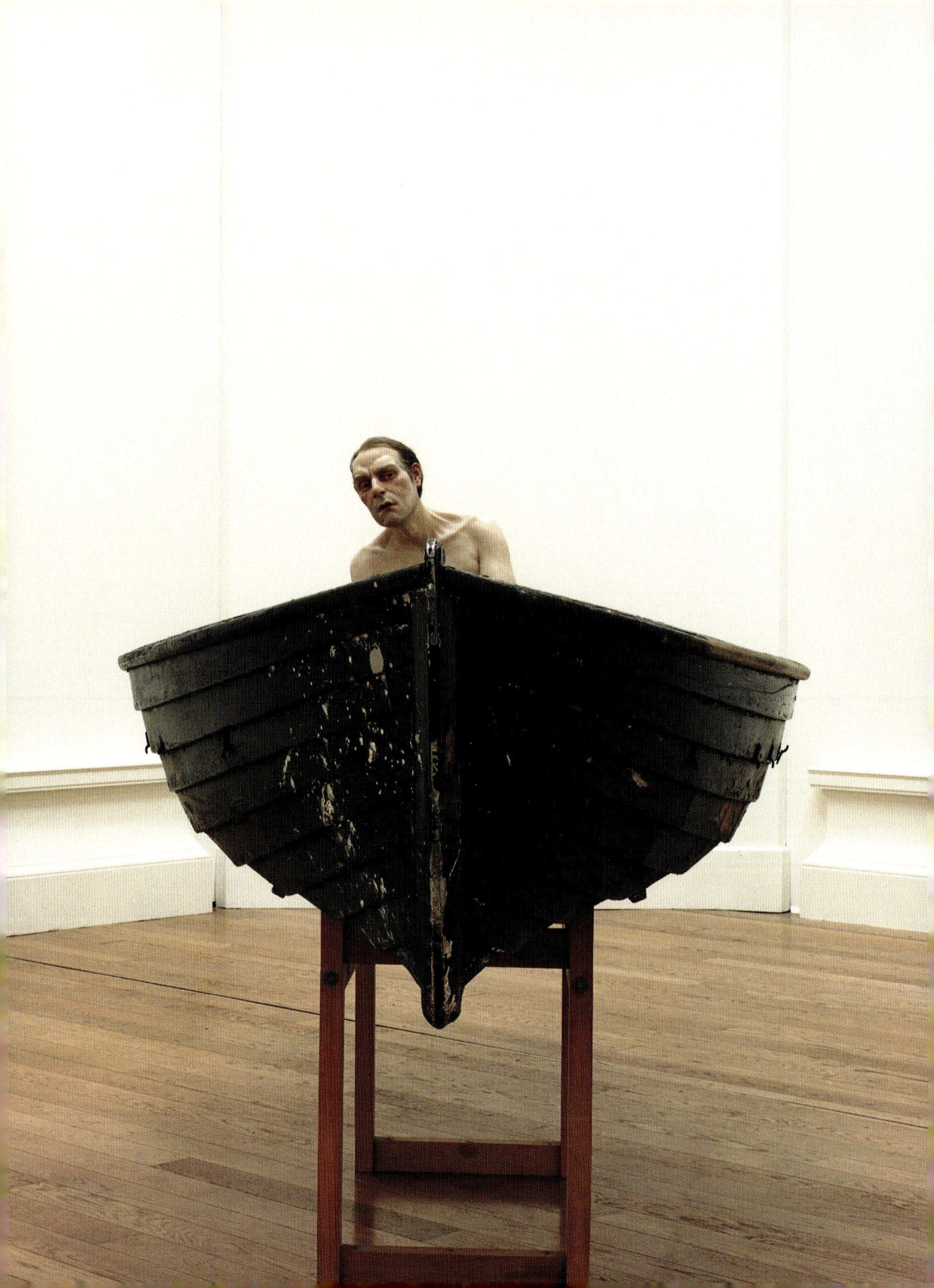

CRAIG RAINE

INVITATION AU VOYAGE

Man in a boat 2002
Private collection

There are splashes of white paint, like tiny stars of lichen, on the bow of the boat. Man in a boat, then, or a mollusc in an open, midnight-blue mussel shell? A visual pun: a portrait of vulnerability, of edibility unprotected by a carapace. The 'man in the boat' is also slang for the clitoris. Why? Because the pudenda look like a narrow boat. Ron Mueck's man is as naked as a newborn baby in the vagina's open boat. An implication of helplessness.

Perhaps.

An *invitation au voyage*, certainly. But rather different from Baudelaire's imagined, ideal destination of *luxe, calme et le volupté* in the company of his beloved. Instead, an unanswered question: 'Where to?'

Walter Pater's famous rhapsody around Leonardo da Vinci's *Mona Lisa*, c.1503–06, was included in the *Oxford Book of Twentieth-Century Verse* by W. B. Yeats, who laid it out typographically as *vers libre*. In *The Critic as Artist*, Oscar Wilde had already acclaimed its self-standing aesthetic status – quoting it practically verbatim – and disclaimed any requirement for accurate description of the original painting. 'Who ... cares whether Mr Pater has put into the portrait of Monna Lisa something that Lionardo never dreamed of?'[1] Wilde thought the Pater a rival work of art, executed by the critic. 'It treats the work of art simply as the starting point for a new creation.'[2]

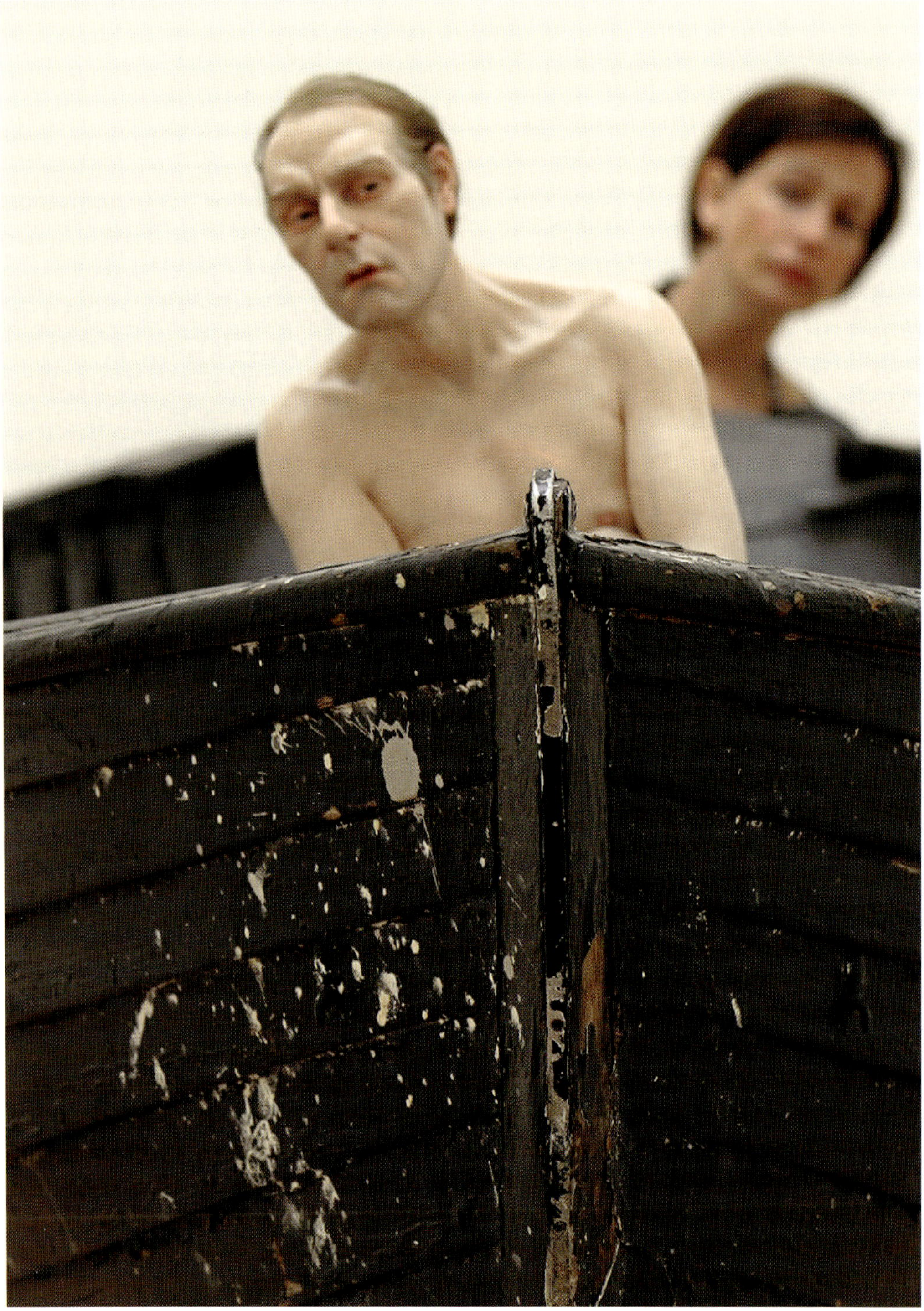

In brusque, denuded summary, Pater's point is that la Gioconda's physicality, her troubled beauty, expresses every malady of the human soul.

Is that *all*?

Pater exists as a warning and T. S. Eliot was right to stigmatise this kind of 'aesthetic' criticism as illegitimate, as thwarted, ersatz creativity. I will try to avoid it.

In *Ulysses*, Leopold Bloom, on his way to Paddy Dignam's funeral in Glasnevin cemetery, glimpses a tramp from the cortege: 'on the curbstone before Jimmy Geary the sexton's an old tramp sat, grumbling, emptying the dirt and stones out of his huge dustbrown yawning boot. After life's journey.'[3] Life's journey: the (appropriately fatigued) cliché is redeemed by the description of the boot.

In a *Paris Review* interview, Jorge Luis Borges asserted that all of the great metaphors were unoriginal:

> When I was a young man I was always hunting for metaphors. Then I found that really good metaphors are always the same. I mean you compare time to a road, death to sleeping, life to dreaming, and those are the great metaphors in literature because they correspond to something essential. If you invent metaphors, they are apt to be surprising during the fraction of a second, but they strike no deep emotion whatever.[4]

Indeed, it is true that with *Man in a boat*, 2002, an allegory irresistibly suggests itself: life as a voyage, life as a journey without a definite destination. There are no oars. The man's arms are folded. He is a naked, middle-aged Moses, afloat in our limitless imaginations and the abstract limbo of the art gallery's 'invisible' walls. He is a man in space.

Blaise Pascal famously said, '*Le silence des vestes éspaces m'éffrayent*' ['The silence of interstellar space terrifies me'], and we are comfortably uncomfortable with that bleak immeasurable dread, that blanket *angst*. But Mueck is offering us something significantly different – a discomfort blanket. Anthony d'Offay, Mueck's dealer, once told me that he thought 'Ron dreams these things'. I would put it rather differently. *Man in a boat* is a classic dream image – inexplicable nakedness in a public place and a rowing boat that clearly belongs to someone else. The enigma of total exposure. Nothing hidden. Nothing disclosed.

I first saw *Man in a boat* at Mueck's National Gallery exhibition in London in 2003 and again at the Scottish National Gallery of Modern Art in Edinburgh in 2006. My notes record the slight paunch, the hairs above the nipples, the hair on the pale forearms, the pinker hands, the strained tendons on the left side of the neck, the slightly angled head, the faint bristle on the chin, the cock all glans and below it, a crumpled scald of skin. The feet are turned in and tucked away. The upper lip is loose and the hair is going grey. Unmistakably, this is not a naked man so much as a man without his clothes.

There are two crucial features: his carefully combed hair, and the expression in his eyes and face. The expression is guarded, wary. Were he sculpted by Pascal, he would be terrified. Instead, he is sculpted by Mueck and is watchful, wary of being watched. His right eyebrow is cocked and curious. He is the opposite of a representative figure, a symbolic figure. This isn't Everyman. He's a particular bloke.

In my collected etchings of Rembrandt, there are many self-portraits: *Self portrait in a cap, laughing*, 1630; *Self portrait open-mouthed, as if shouting*, 1630; *Self portrait, frowning*, 1630; *Self portrait in a cap, open-mouthed*, 1630; and so on. Looking at this range of expressions makes you realise that Frans Hals's *The laughing cavalier*, 1624, is a technical topos as well as a terrific portrait – a technical test like the spring of lemon peel or mother-of-pearl oyster shell in a still life, or Hockney's rendering of a bigger splash. Hals captures the laugh without confusing it with an angry grimace, for example. Catching an expression unambiguously is a painterly feat. Mueck, capturing an ambiguous expression – the man's determination to disclose nothing, while being exposed in every other possible way – raises the stakes wonderfully. We have an allegory in all its obviousness and the cancellation of that allegory by a pallid, ordinary figure in his contemporary quiddity, his irreducible particularity. The sculpture is all reach and its opposite: just sitting tight, hardly daring to think.

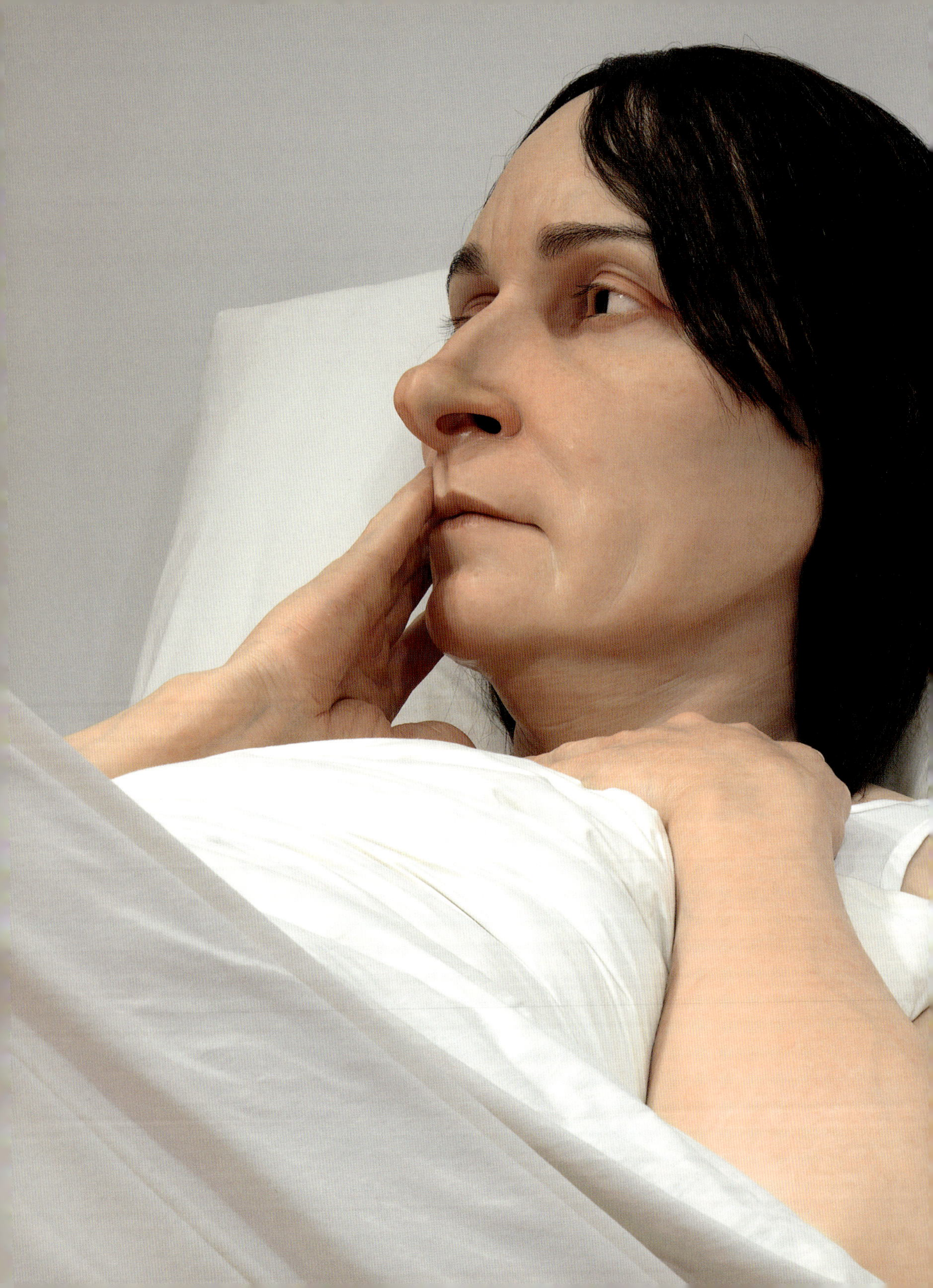

NICHOLAS CHAMBERS

THINKING SCULPTURES

In bed 2005 (detail)
Queensland Art Gallery, Brisbane

Portrayals of anonymous, solitary, introspective figures, where the activity of thinking could be said to be the subject of the work, are far from commonplace in the history of art. Certainly, there are countless portraits and busts of thinking writers and philosophers but the aim in these works is to portray a particular person rather than to convey the abstract notion of introspection. To take an example from the Victorian era, in Daniel Maclise's 1839 portrait of Charles Dickens the author is depicted at his desk, hand on a manuscript, looking ponderously upwards. The subject of this picture is undoubtedly thinking. Via the narrative elements of the composition we might even hazard a guess at what he is thinking about, but the purpose of the composition is to convey the persona of Dickens rather than to consider the nature of thought.

The most famous sculpture of introspection, Auguste Rodin's *The thinker*, 1880, undoubtedly depicts the act of thinking itself but as viewers we are cut off from what is going on inside his head. In Rodin's words:

> What makes my *Thinker* think is that he thinks not only with his brain, with his knitted brow, his distended nostrils and compressed lips, but with every muscle of his arms, back, legs, with his clenched fist and gripping toes.[1]

So, *The thinker* portrays introspection as a physical act and while this might prompt us to think about thinking, the character or content of the subject's thoughts is irrelevant.

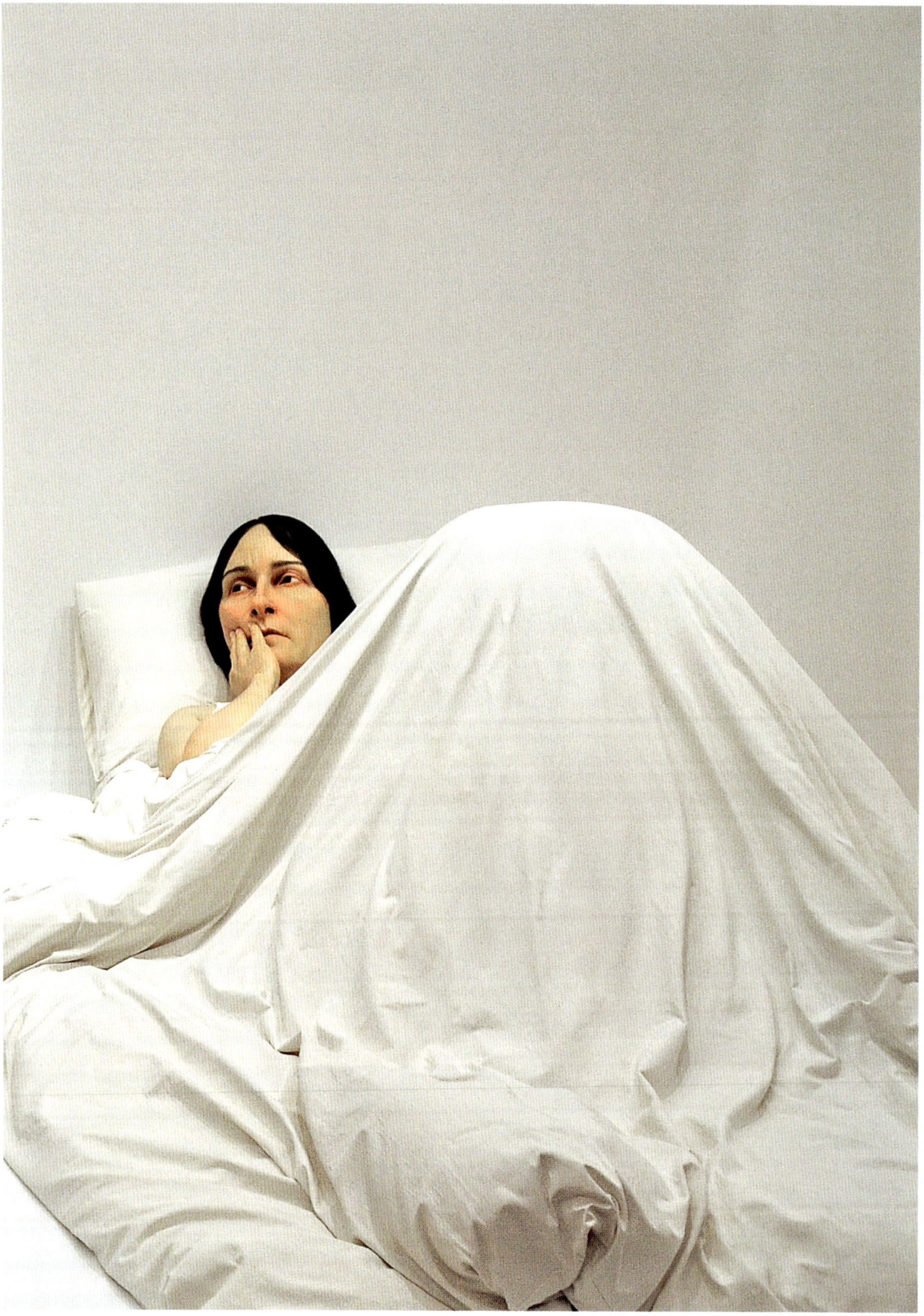

In a lecture presented at the University of Saskatchewan in 1968, British philosopher Gilbert Ryle posed a curious question: what is *The thinker* doing?[2] For a philosopher of language with behaviourist leanings, the answer was far from given. Following Ryle's argument, 'thinking' would constitute far too general and not terribly useful a response unless we were also able to describe the level of sophistication of his thought (silently counting passing cars, for example, being a less-sophisticated level than pondering a chess move or composing a piece of music) and to what specific end the thinking is directed.

Ryle's lecture was concerned with linguistics rather than art criticism but it illuminates the complexities involved in producing a plastic representation of introspection – what would an introspecting figure that gave us some access to the nature of their thoughts look like?

Solitary thinking figures have been a recurring subject in Ron Mueck's practice. *Ghost*, 1998; *Seated woman*, 1999; *Standing man*, 2000; and *In bed*, 2005; are key examples. The figures in these works all appear to be thinking about something: each is captured in a moment of solitary reflection, eyes open but focused inwards, apparently disengaged from the world around them. Each, however, has the uncanny ability to communicate to the viewer a far richer and more complex picture of what is taking place inside the subject's head than the unqualified idea of 'thinking'. As Heiner Bastian wrote of *Ghost*, 'the sculpture ... perfectly reflects the psychological state of embarrassment, shame, discomfort and withdrawal'.[3] Most importantly, it does so without narrative elements guiding us to this conclusion. The insight we have into this thinking subject's mind is due entirely to observable physical characteristics of her face and body.

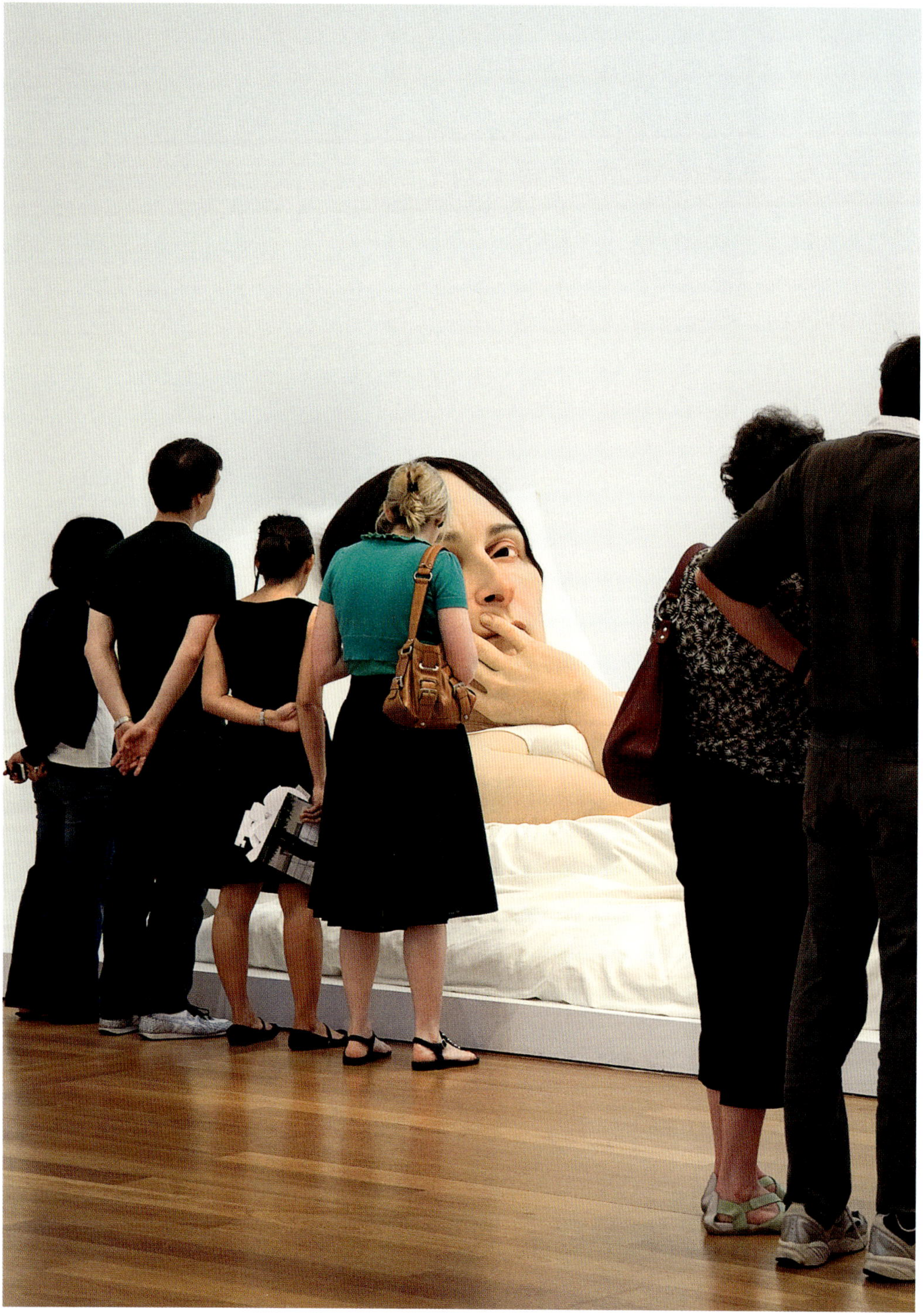

The monumentally scaled middle-aged subject of *In bed* sits with her knees drawn up beneath the bedclothes; only her head and arms are exposed. Posed in a reclining position and with her eyes at 150.0 cm high (approximately eye level for the average standing adult), viewers are given the ideal vantage from which to study her expression and think about what she's thinking. She is stripped of any context that might suggest the events that have led to her present situation, yet we have a clear impression of her mental state. Her hand partially covering her mouth and her upwards gaze focusing on nothing in particular, her slumped posture, slightly furrowed brow and countless other nuanced details are masterfully orchestrated to sharply convey the subject's ponderous and moderately troubled state of mind. We could go further, in fact, and analyse particular elements of her body language – the direction of her glance and involuntary covering of her face with her hand, for example, suggesting the formation of an image in her mind that she is not altogether comfortable with. Significantly, this reading of *In bed* does not rely on reference to a social type – a 'worrier', for example. The feeling that we have access to the tenor of the subject's thoughts starts with the artist's virtuosic study of body language but is ultimately brought about by a process of identification and transference. Our initial shock at the sculpture's viscerally naturalistic appearance and monumental scale is subsequently tempered by the prosaic nature of the subject – her resolute 'everydayness' – and our identification with what is taking place. We recognise ourselves frozen in similar moments of solitary introspection.

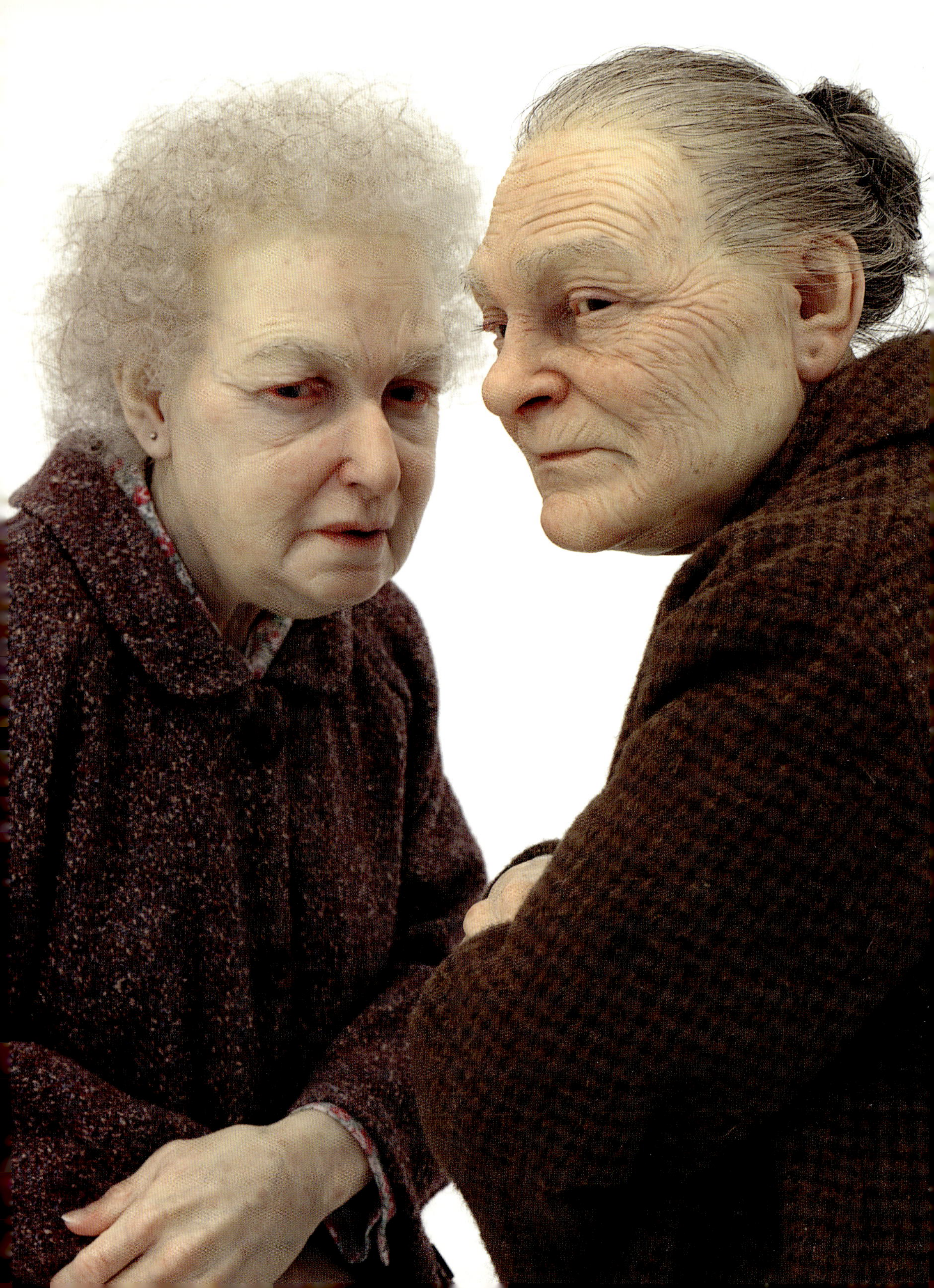

KELLY GELLATLY

TWO WOMEN

Two women 2005 (detail)
National Gallery of Victoria, Melbourne

Ron Mueck's *Two women*, 2005, undercuts the distinct stereotypical categories into which the depiction of old women tends to fall: that of the warm, loving and cuddly grandmother-type, who is wise, generous and consistently jolly, or the wizened old crone of fairytale fame – a manipulative, evil and ugly child-eater. Part of the shock of Mueck's women is the fact that they are so everyday, from their ashen faces, thinning hair and osteoporosis-ridden backs, through to their slip-on shoes and the bunched, wrinkly tights collected at their ankles. There is a conspiratorial, gossipy and decidedly critical air to their encounter, which creates the very distinct feeling, as we viewers approach them, that we may be the subject of their speculation and censure.

With this slight and very discreet turn of hand, Mueck confounds our sense of unease at experiencing the ravages of age by heightening the awareness of our own insecurities, which are seemingly now on the receiving end of the combined disapproval of these diminutive women. By skilfully turning the close scrutiny that is so central to an appreciation of his work back onto the viewer, Mueck reveals his extraordinary ability to create sculptures that subtly open up the audience to quiet, and at times confronting, moments of introspection and self-examination.

There is no doubt that a journey through Ron Mueck's oeuvre challenges and intrigues us with the full cycle of life – an enormous and quite obviously over-it, heavily pregnant woman (*Pregnant woman*, 2002),

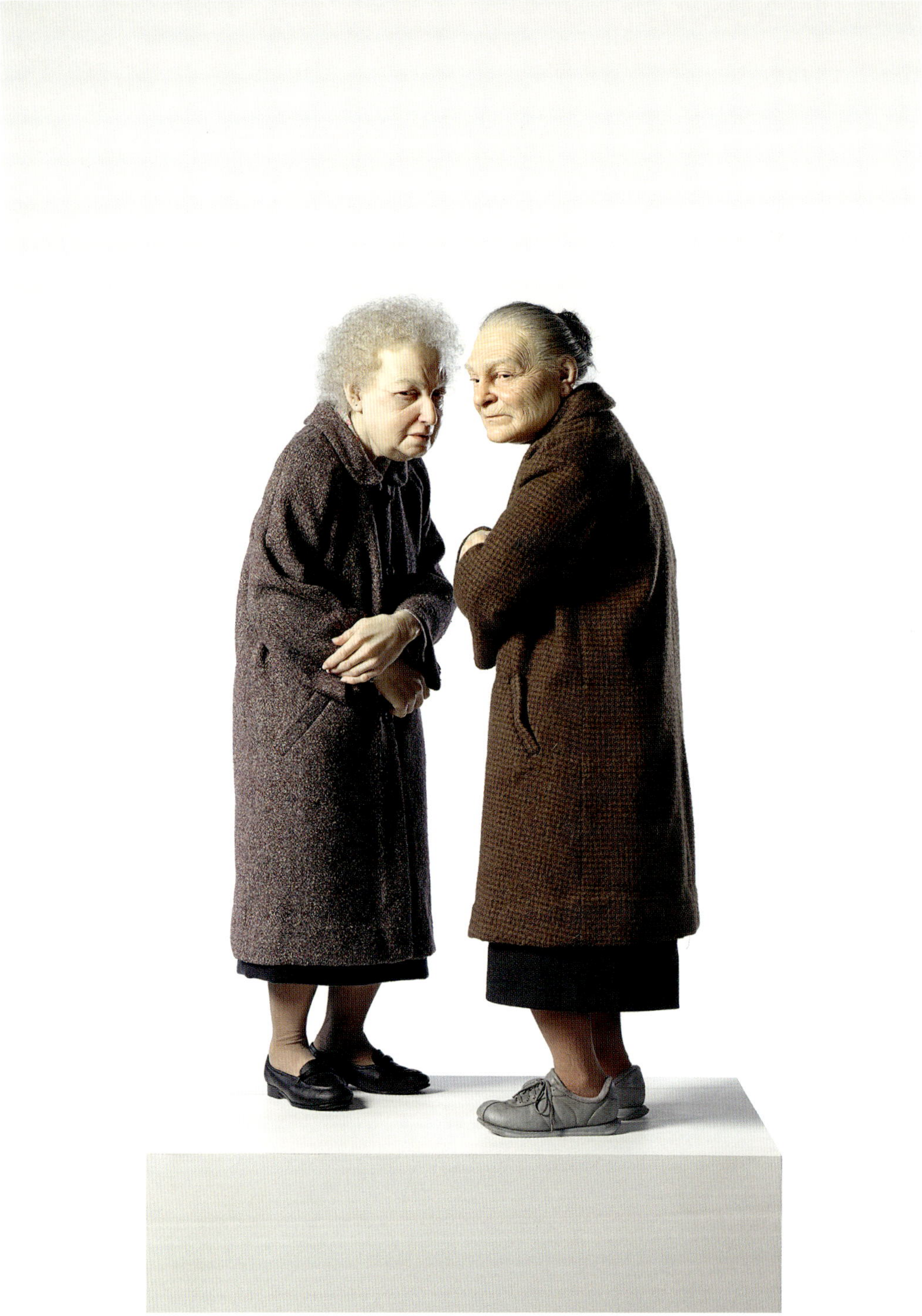

newborn babies whose squished faces and viscera-covered bodies reveal both the trauma and wonder of their recent births (*A girl*, 2006), and middle-aged men and women who appear to contend with an array of anxieties and concerns (*In bed*, 2005, and *Wild man*, 2005) or who undertake strange, metaphorical journeys that suggest ventures into unknown, uncharted waters (*Man in a boat*, 2002).

The aged, however, do not come off well in Mueck's work. Invariably wrinkled and grey, world-weary and withered, the encroaching years press upon them like the weight of the heavy fabrics of their sensible clothes, which cover their fragile, shrunken frames more for practicality or out of habit than for any sense of adornment, personal style or desire to present a certain persona or 'look'. Those days are long gone. In fact, there is a pervading sense among Mueck's elderly subjects of having almost given up; indeed, for some, this has occurred (*Dead Dad*, 1996–97) or seems perilously close (*Old woman in bed*, 2002).

The passing of the years in Mueck's work seems especially unkind to women. This may be just my own fear of ageing and the bias of my gender talking (and I am happy to admit this), but my conclusion is not, I hope, based on personal misgivings alone. While I, like many, cling desperately to the notion of 'growing old gracefully' as I reach every morning for yet another brand of miracle-producing face cream, I too can occasionally fall victim to the assumption (before I correct myself) that men become distinguished with age and women, well, just age. As American newspaper editor G. Norman Collie supposedly quipped: 'Grandchildren don't make a man feel old; it's the knowledge that he's married to a grandmother.'[1]

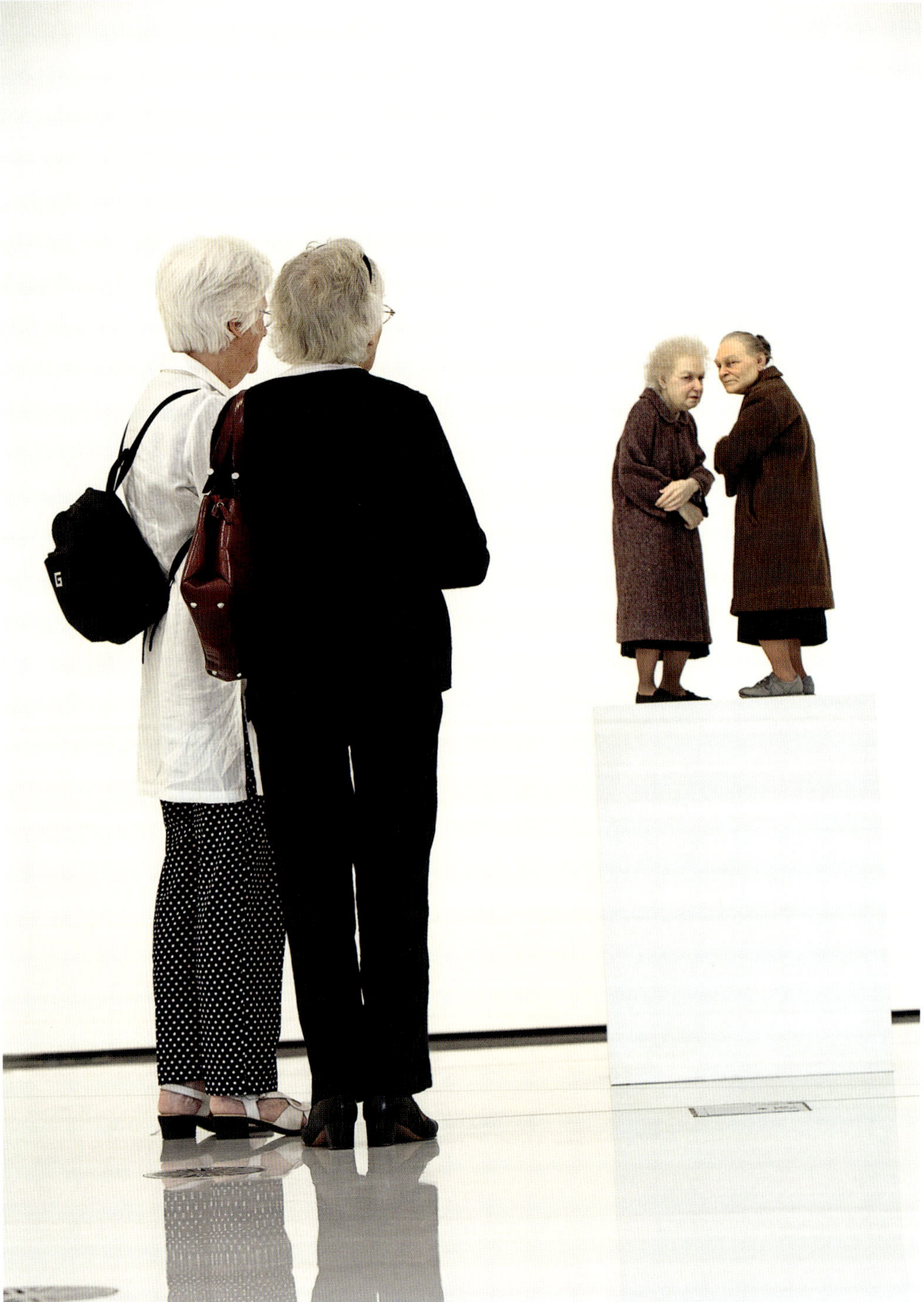

Through their very public presence, the female sitters of *Two women* confront us with the realities of the ageing process and remind us in turn of the rather suspect absence of the representation of advanced age in contemporary culture. The push/pull fascination/repulsion of Mueck's technical virtuosity denies us any form of escape here, and almost physically prevents us from simply ignoring, or pretending we do not see, his geriatric subjects. Like all of Mueck's work, the 'wow factor' of experiencing *Two women* is accompanied by an intoxicating mix of fascination and a kind of train-wreck voyeurism, as we are unwillingly and most definitely uncomfortably forced to focus on each tiny detail and marker of the women's old age.

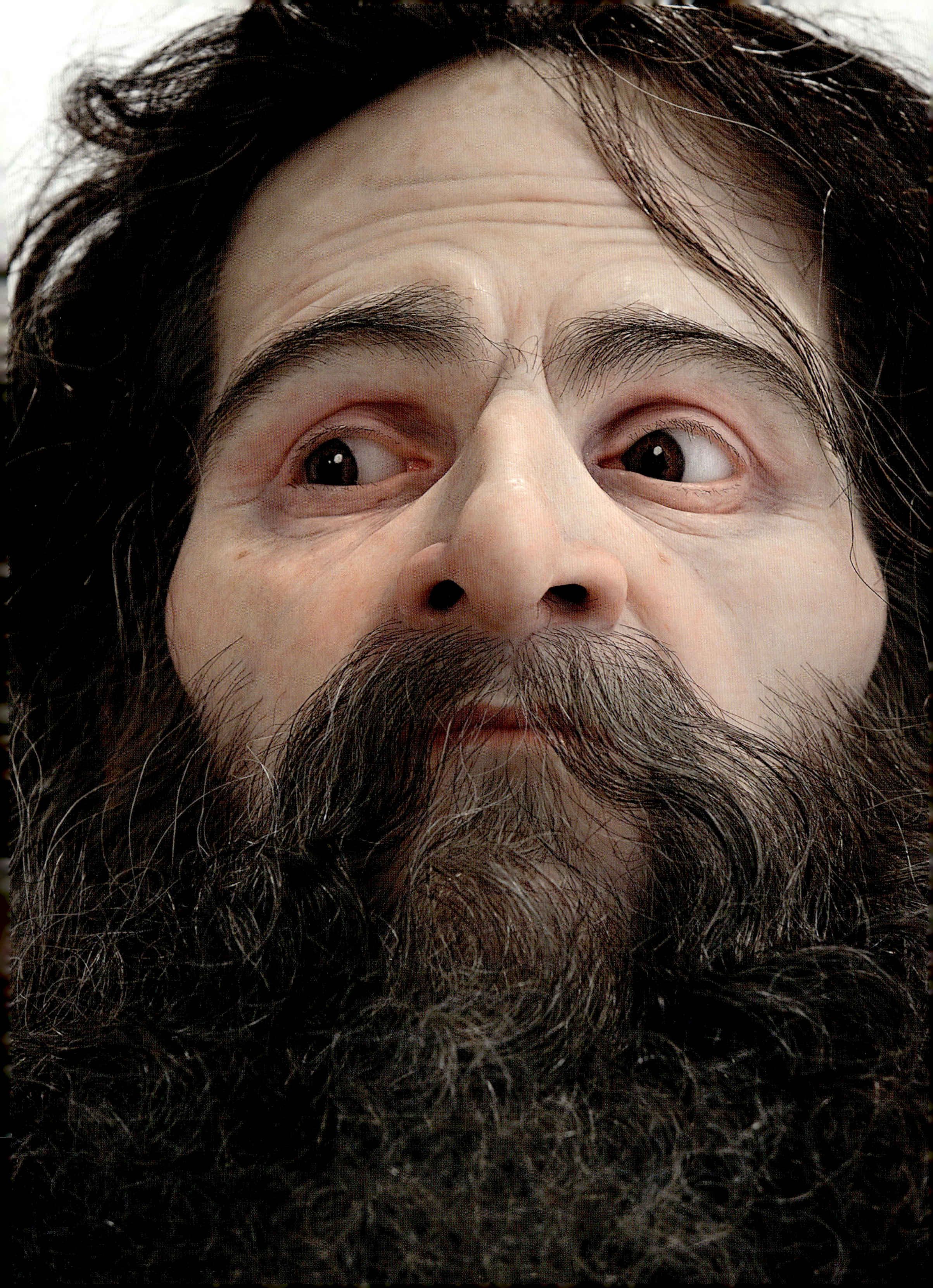

TED GOTT

WILD MEN OF THE WOODS

Wild man 2005 (detail)
McClelland Gallery +
Sculpture Park, Langwarrin

Rumours of wild men lurking deep in the forests of the world have recurred across millennia. In the fifth century BC, during a colonising expedition to southern Africa, Hanno of Carthage encountered the 'gorillae' – savage hairy men and women who climbed to safety when attacked, defending themselves with stones. Hanno's men captured, killed and flayed three females; their skins were brought back to Carthage and displayed as trophies in the Temple of Tanit. Numerous other authors in antiquity, such as Aristotle (fourth century BC), Pliny the Elder (first century AD) and Galen (second century AD), also wrote accounts of anthropoid, or human-behaving, hairy creatures inhabiting distant lands.

An understanding of the smaller monkeys was developed in the Western world from the twelfth century onwards, and they were imaged frequently in medieval art (albeit in mostly negative symbolic contexts). At the same time, the incredibly hirsute and club-bearing *woodwose* or 'wild man of the woods' appeared as a threatening bogeyman in painting and sculpture produced throughout medieval northern Europe.

In the mid 1500s, Konrad Gesner sought to synthesise knowledge of the larger, human-like and tailless forest-dwelling creatures described by the ancient writers, with mythical tales of the hairy wild men (the so-called *Homo sylvestris* or 'forest man') who were reported to lurk on the fringes of the 'civilised' world. While appearing bizarre and comical to modern eyes, the illustration of a strange lion-headed, pendulous-breasted and baboon-bottomed *Homo sylvestris* that appeared in Gesner's *Historiae*

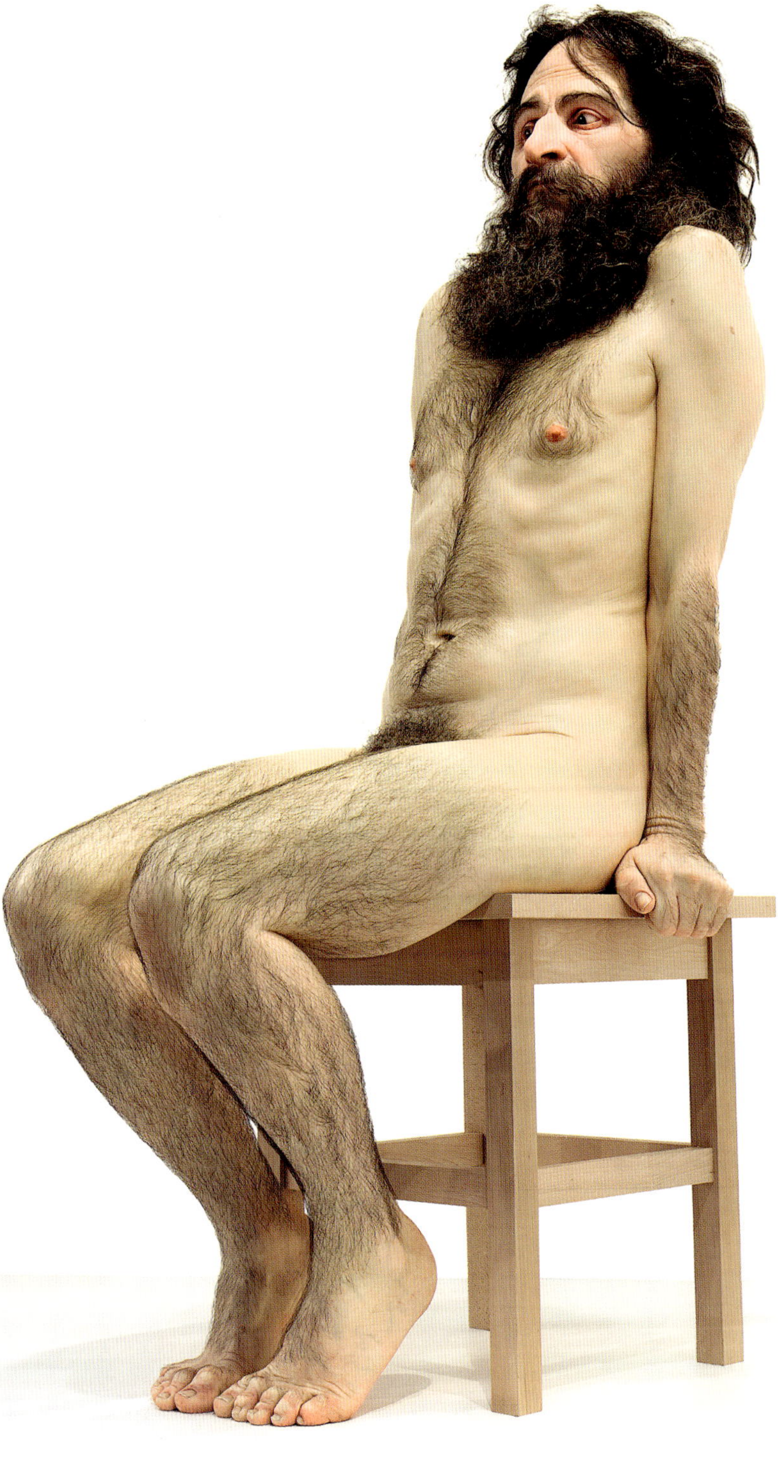

Animalium of 1551 married notions of mythical wild peoples with genuine, if primitive, observations of primate species. According to biblical authority, since god-fearing humans alone lacked a tail and walked upright, any other creature behaving in this fashion was deemed to be morally problematic and culturally threatening.

Wild men have always received bad press, as hirsute men still do today in a world obsessed with buffed youth and laser hair removal. Numerous editions of the *History of Four-footed Beasts and Serpents* by Edward Topsell combined a woodcut after Konrad Gesner's exotic *Homo sylvestris* with a wonderfully florid description of

> another kind of Munkey, for stature, bignesse and shape like a Man, for by his knees, secret parts and face, you would judge him a wilde man, such as inhabit *Numidia*, and the *Lapones*, for he is altogether overgrown with hair ... no creature, except a man can stand so long as he; he loveth women and children dearly, like other of his own kind, and is so venereous that he will attempt to ravish women.[1]

Throughout the seventeenth and eighteenth centuries, lurid tales of lustfully marauding primates were to parallel serious investigation of the existence of chimpanzees, orang-utans and gorillas (the latter being 'discovered' by Western science only in 1847).

While distinctions between the larger primates and humanity remained blurred, 'wild men' were consistently typecast as both violent and libidinous, and became associated with the randy and mischievous satyrs of ancient Greece. They also provided a good excuse to lock up wives and daughters. In 1658, at a time when knowledge of human reproduction was still in its infancy, Jacob Bontius noted in his *Historiae Naturalis* that the

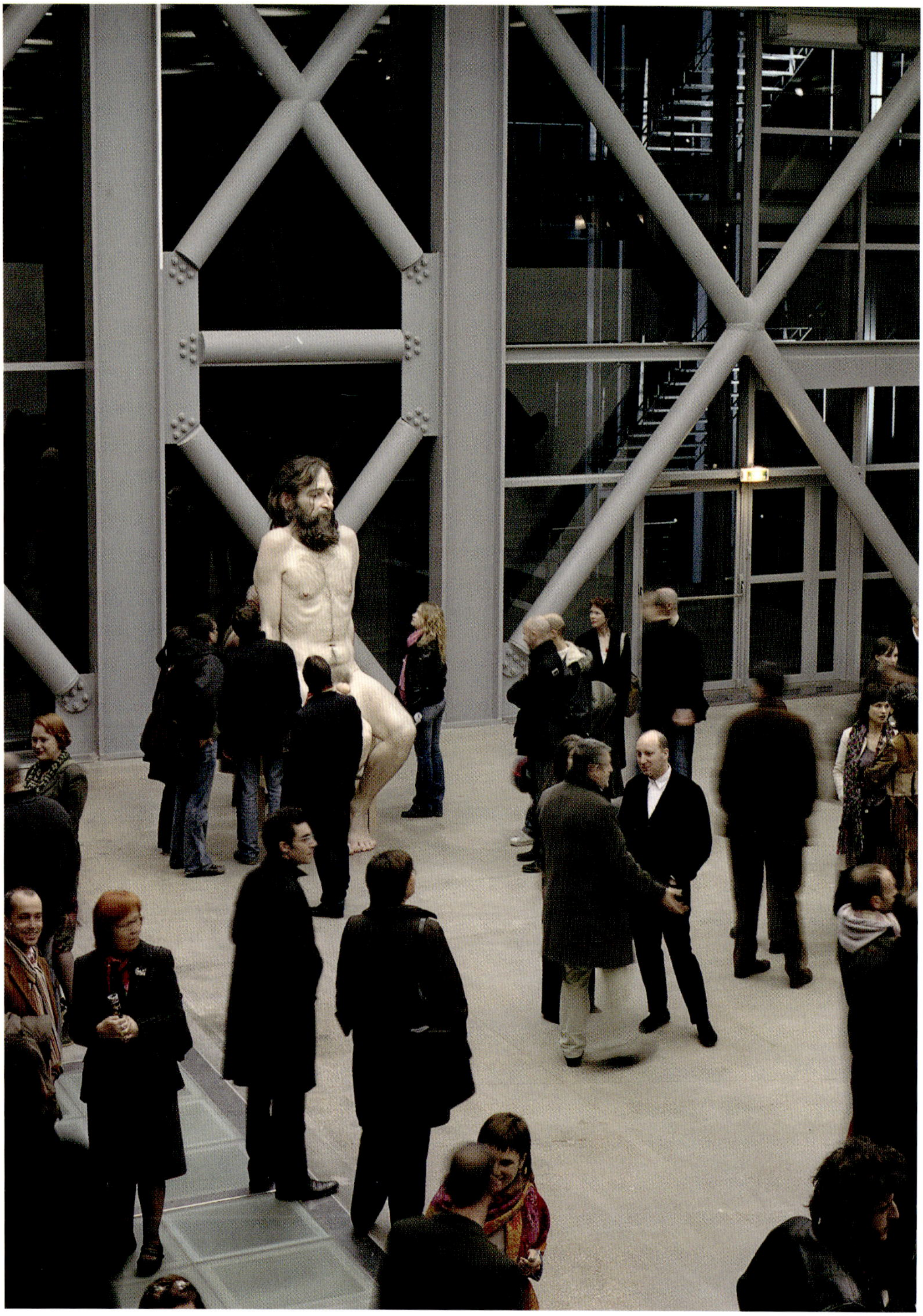

term orang-utan meant 'a man of the woods' in Indonesian and that it derived from the spurious belief of Javanese natives that these creatures were born from dissolute local women 'who mix with apes and monkeys with detestable sensuality'.[2]

Such stories of mysterious apes ravishing African or Indonesian women were commonplace in the seventeenth century. In the fourteenth volume of his monumental *Histoire Naturelle*, published in 1766, the celebrated French naturalist Comte de Buffon cited accounts (penned sixty years earlier by the Dutch voyager Schoutten) of orang-utans that 'lust after women, for whom there is no safety in travelling through the forests, for they might at any moment be attacked and ravished by these creatures'.[3] Similarly, Dr Gautier-Laboulaye, a surgeon working for the French navy in the Gabon who shipped the first gorilla remains to be seen in France to Paris's Muséum d'Histoire Naturelle in 1849, wrote of how male gorillas were apparently prone to 'slaking their lust by ravishing Negro women who wander carelessly in the woods'.[4] Fed by preposterous tales like these, for another century writers and film-makers were to image hairy apes as either maniacally homicidal (the 'butchery without motive' of the orang-utan in Edgar Allan Poe's *Murders in Rue Morgue*, 1841) or curiously licentious (the Fay Wray–sniffing Kong in RKO's legendary *King Kong*, 1933).

Locus for humanity's fears of its own repressed tendencies to violence and lust, 'wild men of the woods' have been demonised, hunted, despoiled and depilated throughout history – the anthropoid primates pushed to the brink of extinction in the wild, and bearded men throughout Westernised society branded nonsensically by marketing and fashion stylists as somehow unattractive to women. Small wonder that Ron Mueck's *Wild man*, 2005, wherever he comes from, looks more afraid of us than we can any longer be of him.

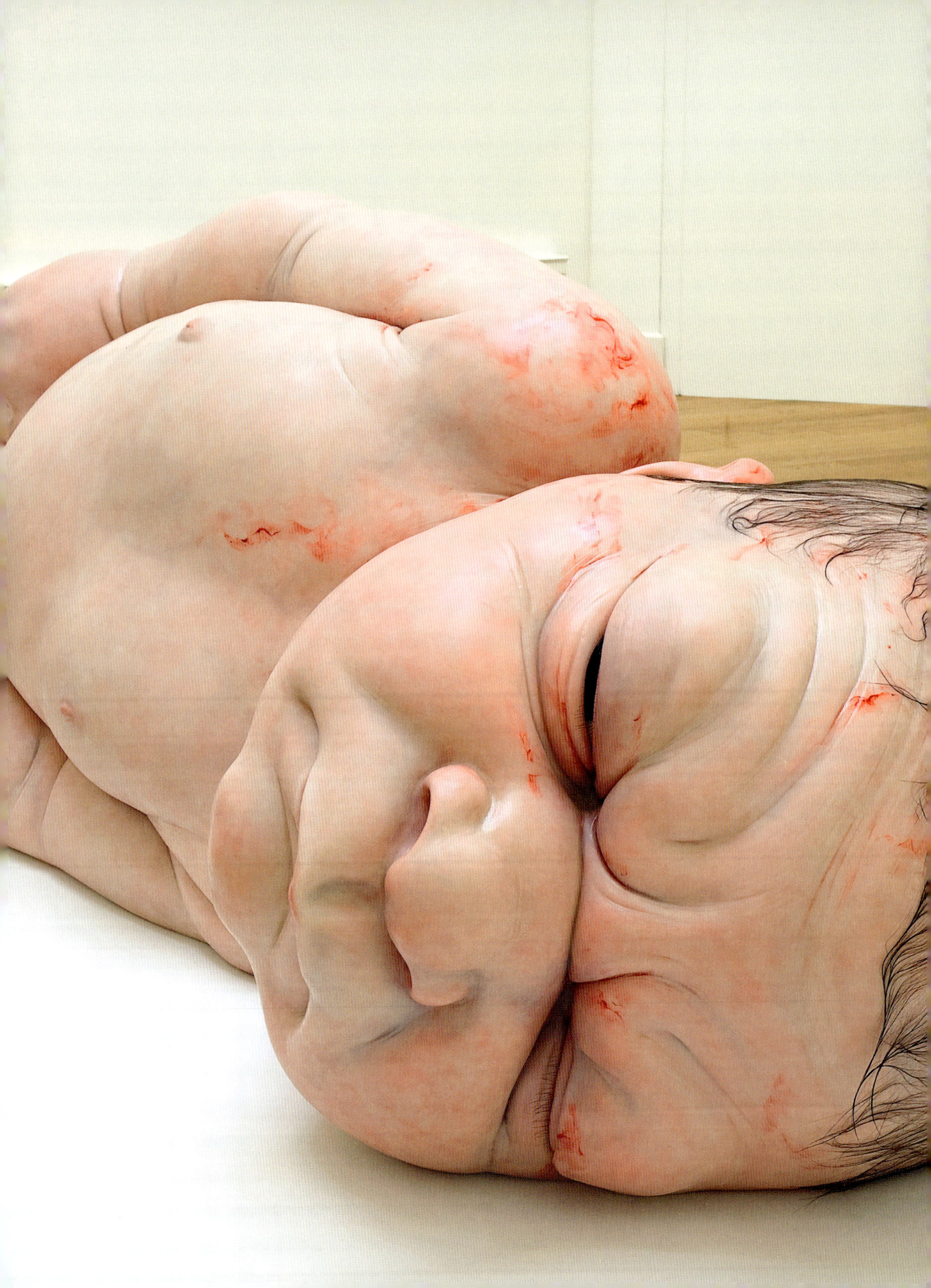

PHILIP LONG

FIRST SIGNS OF MOVEMENT

A girl 2006 (detail)
National Gallery of
Scotland, Edinburgh

Since Ron Mueck began working as an independent sculptor, a major preoccupation has been the subject of the child. A series of three larger-than-life-size babies made in 1996–97 were followed by several works dating from 2000 onwards, which dealt intensively with the subjects of giving birth and new life. Produced during the period Mueck was artist-in-residence at the National Gallery in London, where he was surrounded by centuries of artistic representation of the infant as an image of sanctity, Mueck's resulting exhibition in 2003 featured work representing pregnancy and the newly born. Executed with his typically veracious technique, the naked presence of an eight-foot tall pregnant woman, a half-life-size mother with a just-born child nestled on her belly and a swaddled baby, brought to the National Gallery a human realism on the miraculous subject of birth that no Old Master painting could achieve.

Three years later, Mueck put the finishing touches to *A girl*, 2006, a massively over-scale representation of a newly born baby, five metres in length. Lying with its umbilical cord still partly in place and marked all over with blood from the process of birth, the figure's scale and the sheer virtuosity of Mueck's technique transfixes the viewer. The child seems real, and this illusion grows the closer we get, such is Mueck's ability to replicate without trace of his hand the perfect imperfections of the new child's features. The overwhelming size tells us immediately that the figure is not real, but at the same time it has the effect of magnifying the illusion of reality. The work shocks when first viewed, but the more profound emotion that is imparted is one of vulnerability and a sense

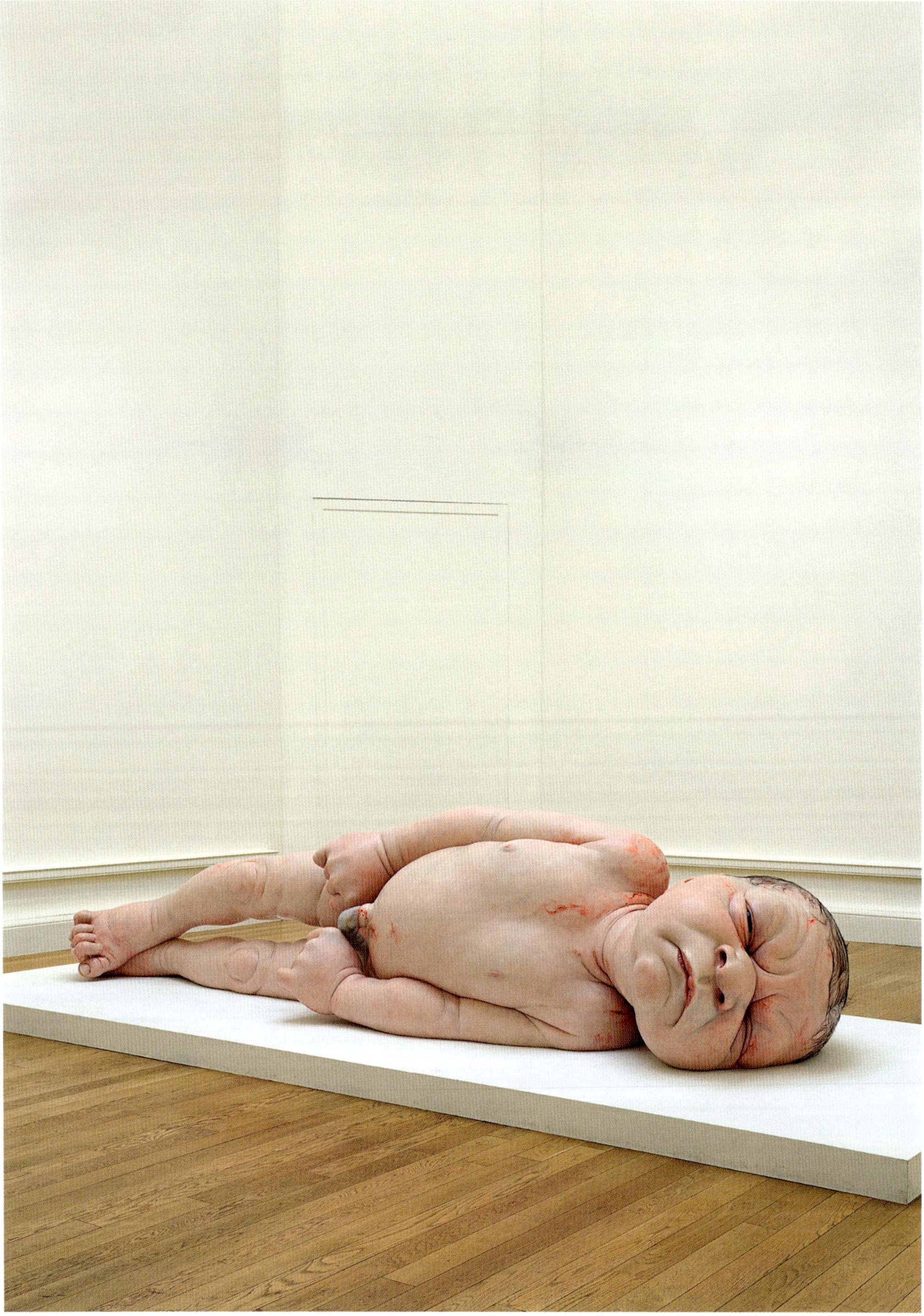

that we have intruded. This is common throughout Mueck's art. His figures often appear introverted and self-conscious, as a consequence of their personal state of being. Almost always they are still in pose. This adds to their illusion of reality. We know that, being sculptures, they cannot move, but their arrested positions suggest that they might do so – an enjoyable and eerie deception.

Mueck has commented that he prefers his works not to be seen in close relationship to each other, for fear of setting up a narrative between them. There is no personal story to be gathered from *A girl*, other than the profound one of a viewer's related experience. Mueck has two daughters and was present at their births. He has only occasionally worked from life, and is informed instead by photographs, images in books, what he sees in the street (enormous photographs of people on hoardings make a constant impression), and his memory and imagination.

A girl was first sculpted in clay on a much smaller scale. A cast was sliced into sections, which were then scaled up to form a core for the full-size figure, over which wire and plaster were laid. This provided the support for the final layer of clay, laboriously modelled, and the original sculpture was close by for the artist's reference. On completion, a mould was taken and the figure cast. The work was then painted, eyes made and hair inserted, all with extraordinary complexity and care.

A girl's pose does not seem to be the natural curled position of a newborn. The child appears to stretch out and stiffen her limbs, showing the first signs of movement she will make as an independent force of life, away from her mother. The hyperreality of Mueck's workmanship eludes our vision, which seems sharper as a consequence and more comprehending. With this sense of heightened awareness, our

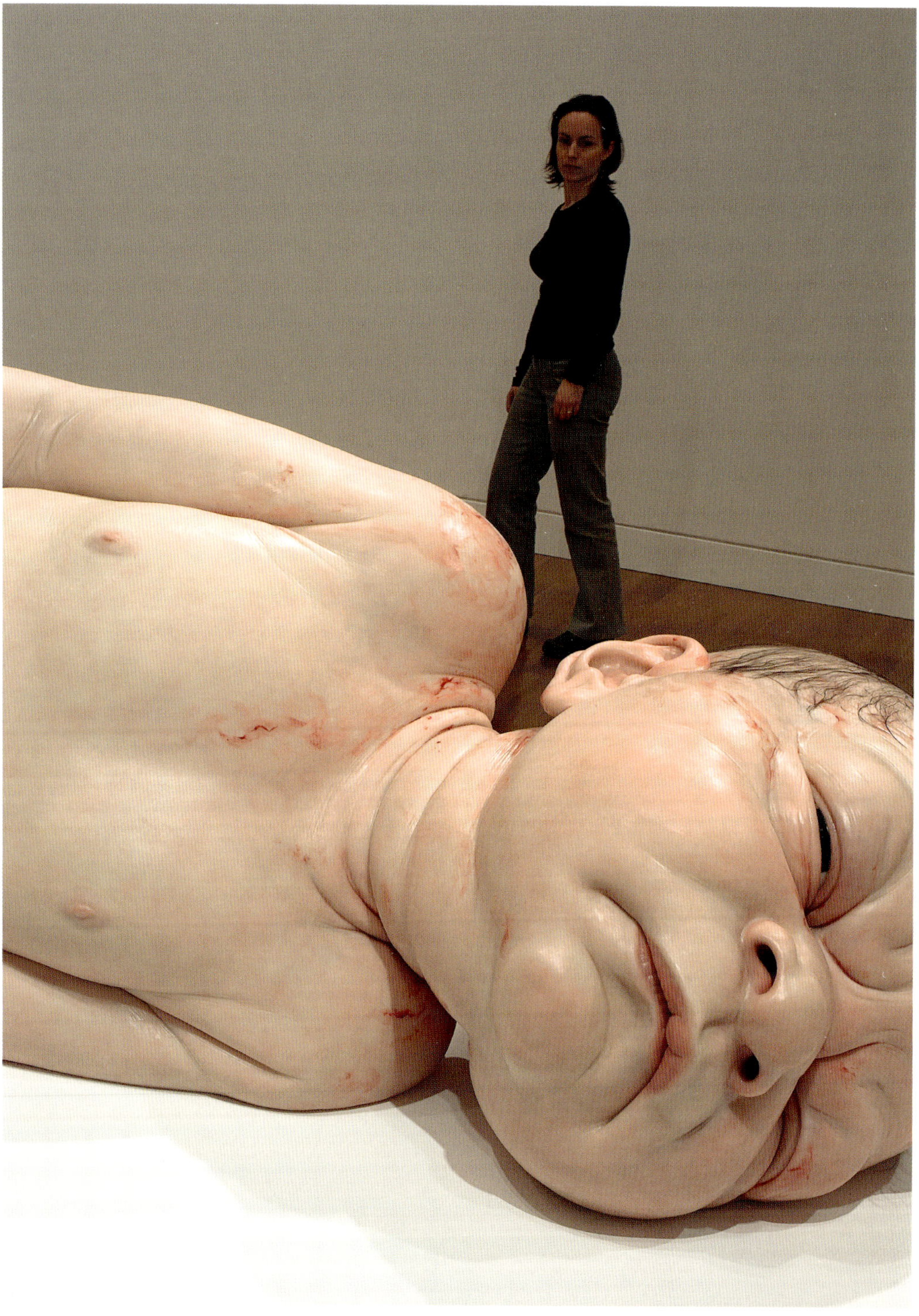

compulsion to look is increased, but the more our eyes shift backwards and forwards across the figure, attempting to take it in, the more she seems to resist our desire to scrutinise and understand. Her mystery lies in the fact that she is no more than what Mueck has made her to be – an extraordinarily lifelike representation of a profound human moment, which cannot be simply explained.

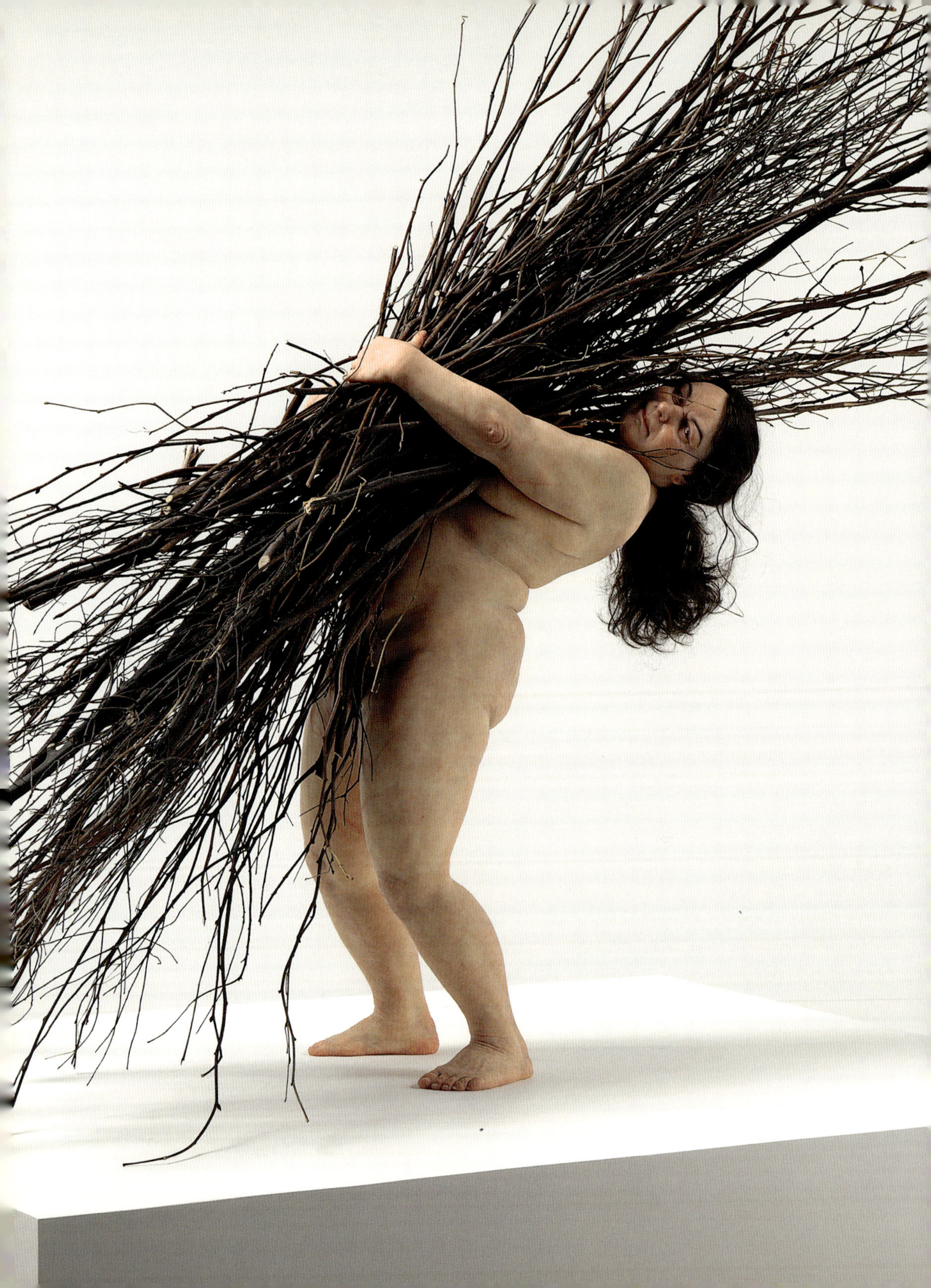

SUSANNA GREEVES

THE DREAM OF LIFE

Woman with sticks
2008
Anthony d'Offay, London

Ron Mueck's figures often seem to brood; they are inward-looking and sunk in private reveries. However, the subject of *Woman with sticks*, 2008, is intent and purposeful, focused on the task of containing the huge bundle of sticks that she can barely encircle with her arms. Her pose is active, feet sturdily planted and stocky body arched in a surprisingly supple backbend as she strains to hold her load clear of the floor, pressing the bundle firmly into her ample flesh and disregarding the twigs that have traced fine scratches on her arms and torso.

The physical presence of this woman is utterly convincing. Her scattering of grey hairs, the deep furrows of her forehead, the calluses on her elbows, the mottling of flesh on her thick calves and the flattened arches of her feet: every detail is minutely observed. Mueck so successfully creates the impression of life that his works tend to provoke an emotional, subjective response to the 'person' depicted, and criticism often moves directly to the question of character, narrative and meaning. Nevertheless, surely this subject was inspired at least in part by the artist's absorption in the properties of surface and form, anatomy and gravity; the rough, woody texture and long, angular shape of the sticks providing the perfect foil for Mueck's virtuoso rendering of soft, rosy flesh. The twigs are incontrovertibly real – that is, of our world – but the realism of the figure challenges us to afford her any lesser status. In fact, such is the hallucinatory exactness of detail that she almost makes the twigs seem more 'real', more clearly and exaggeratedly twig-like. By making his figure smaller than life-size, Mueck effects a kind of concentration or distillation of life force, packing more 'reality' into this condensed form, bringing it into sharper focus.

But what a strange reality this is. Countless 'women with sticks' have trudged their way across the world, bearing their daily burden in vast bundles on their heads or backs, and do today, but this woman does not belong to their number. Besides being white and well fed, she is barefoot and inexplicably naked, though her soft, prawn-pale body is most definitely accustomed to clothes. Her bundle is most impractically left unbound, and seems too long and awkward to allow her to walk with it. Somehow she has gathered the twigs, and just manages to contain them in her laced fingers, but what does she plan to do next? In an early sketch, Mueck had her eyeing one last twig lying on the ground, as if puzzling over how to pick it up without dropping the rest, though in the final work the artist apparently rejected this too-neat narrative.

The reality invoked here is the reality of a dream: crystal clear and possessing its own logic, which would seem senseless to the waking world. Her task is one you might face in a dream: a dream in which you find yourself naked, but know somehow and with absolute certainty that it is vital to collect every twig and not let any fall. There is something, too, about her sturdy peasant frame, the whisper of witchiness in her wild hair and broom-like twigs that suggests a northern forest of folklore and fairytale. Near-impossible tasks are set in fairytales – gather the thistles to make shirts, spin straw into gold – and perhaps she is engaged in some such magical chore (... 5, 6, pick up sticks). Just as, in empathy with this convincingly human body, we 'feel' the prick of twigs against tender flesh, in her odd task we recognise a familiar emotional experience. Her predicament is a metaphor for picking up more than you can hold, or taking on more than you can manage, grappling with a thorny issue and feeling under-equipped for a challenge.

Mueck's figures are convincingly specific, individual portraits down to the last mole, but at the same time each taps into something universally human. The power of his work arises out of this coexistence of the particular and the archetypal. While in many cases this is achieved by evoking familiar emotional states and fundamental human experiences (childhood, pregnancy, birth, ageing and death), *Woman with sticks* instead draws on a subconscious realm. Perhaps her closest counterpart is *Man in a boat*, 2002. As well as being of a similar scale, he is still and yet active, tensed and focused. His boat, like her sticks, provides an evocative but enigmatic prop in the mysterious narrative that is part-metaphor, part-allegory. Dreams, allegory, fable and fairytales are other means of accessing the universal truths and experiences of the subconscious, and it is from this powerful reserve of common understanding that these works speak to us.

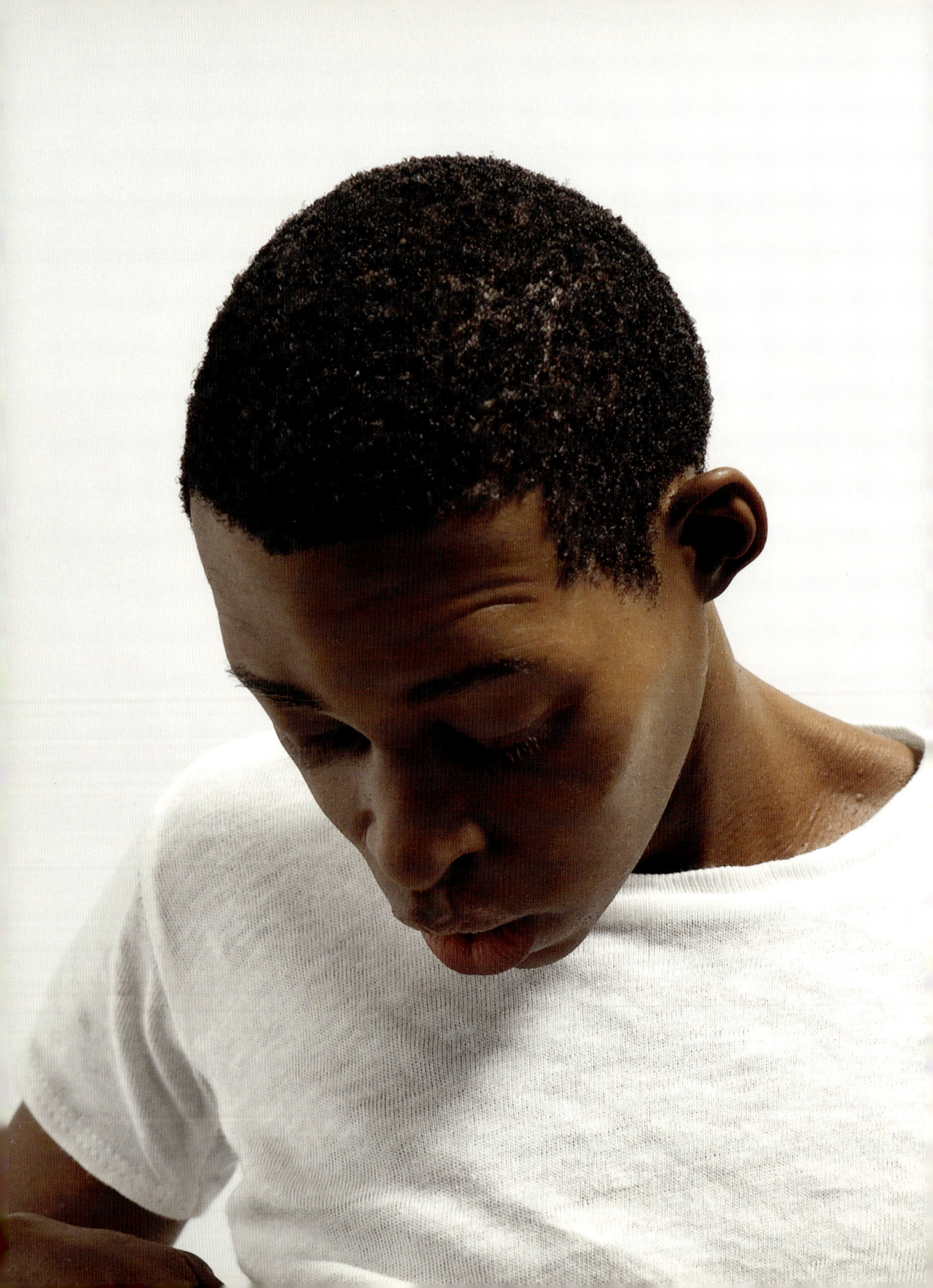

ANGELA NDALIANIS

BOY WONDER

Youth 2009 (detail)
Anthony d'Offay, London

In his book *Wonder, the Rainbow, and the Aesthetics of Rare Experiences*, Peter Fisher explores the wonder-evoking capacity of art. He explains that wonder is reliant on the visual and on the 'aesthetics of rare experiences' that are not common to the everyday.[1] Fisher explains that the definition of the word 'wonder' signifies both interrogation ('I wonder why?') and exclamation (the 'aha' moment of 'getting it') once the source of the wonder is unveiled. The aesthetics of wonder exist at the border between sensation and thought. A viewer confronted with the object of wonder is drawn into a problem-solving experience that can lead to a wonder-inducing journey, and it is precisely such a journey that Ron Mueck takes us on in his work *Youth*, 2009. However, this is a dual journey of wonder. The first involves us as spectators who marvel at the intricacy, detail and mastery that has given life to this three-dimensional image of a teenage boy, his underwear fashionably peeking out from underneath his low-cut, baggy jeans. The second involves the boy himself who, as he lifts his T-shirt and looks intently at his midriff, appears to be caught in the state of interrogation that is integral to the experience of wonder. His gaze and look of hesitant confusion-come-realisation forces the viewer to also participate in this second journey by adopting a similar response as we too wonder about what has caught his attention. Unlike the wonder-inducing experience that fills us with delight and astonishment as we acknowledge the skill and artistry that has evoked every detail of this figure – from the lines and textures of the folding skin on the boy's feet to the delicate and detailed actions of the agile fingers as they search the torso that

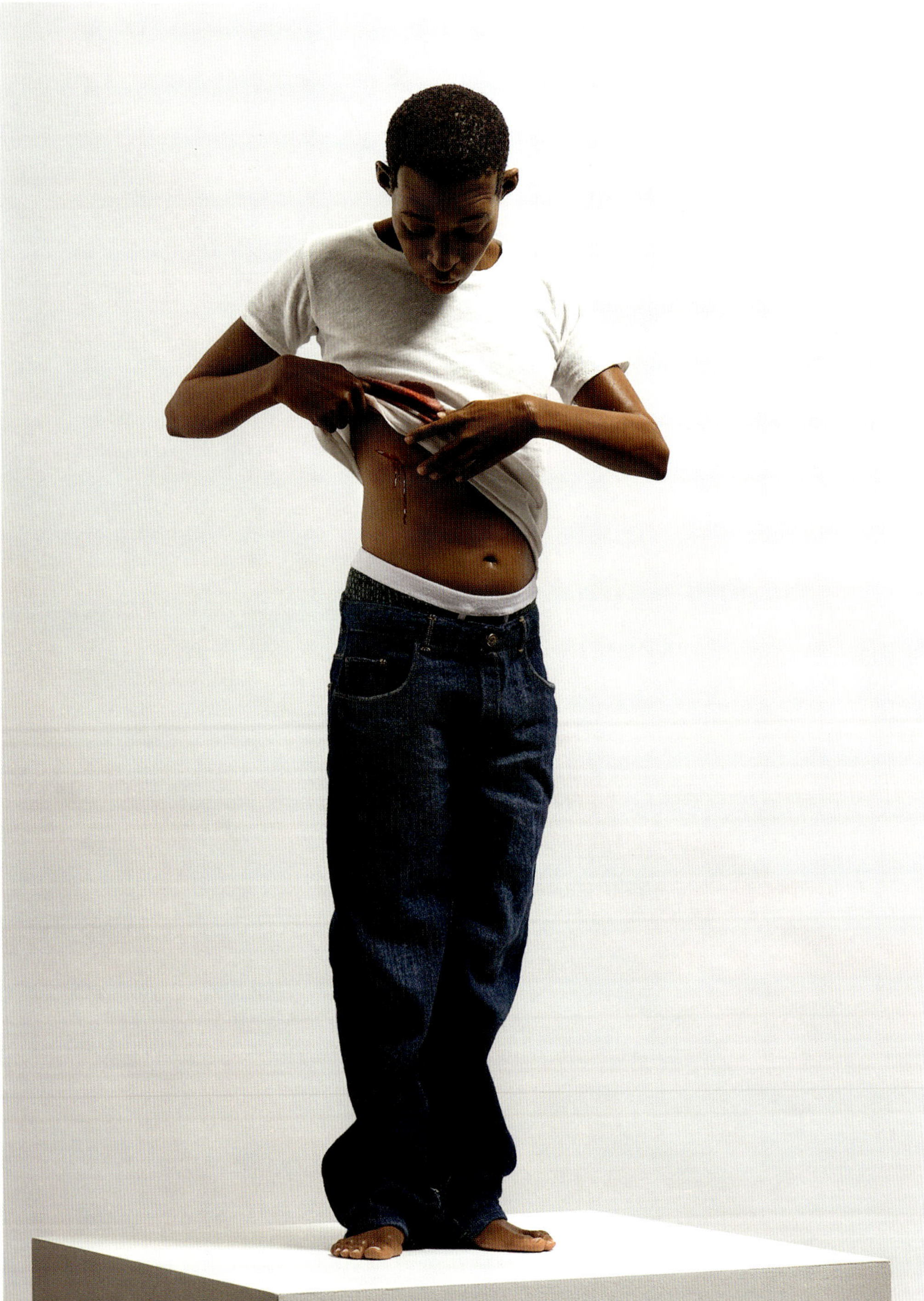

lies beneath the fabric of the T-shirt – our engagement with the boy's sight and dawning awareness draws us into a drama that exposes a narrative of horror. Whereas wonder normally leads to a state that generates delight and amazement – the 'aha' moment – in this instance it incites dread and shock. An open wound reveals itself between the boy's hands, both to the viewer and the boy, and the realisation finally hits home. It is this realisation that the boy is only just beginning to acknowledge in his facial expression: he has been stabbed.

But while the boy is frozen in the liminal space that exists between interrogation and exclamation, the audience moves in time and explores the event that unravels before them through further exploration of the work in its three dimensions. The rare experience that is embodied by this artwork suddenly shifts to also become what, unfortunately, has become anything but a rare experience among young adults in urban societies across the Western world – in this case, specifically in the United Kingdom urbanscape. Discussing Alex Ross's virtuosic paintings of comic book superheroes, Martyn Pedler has stated that Ross embraces a realism in his artwork that makes his superhero subjects appear to be frozen in time. Mueck's sculptures and Ross's paintings have much in common: while bodies appear to succumb to an eerie stillness or stasis, they in fact invoke a synchronic logic that 'synthesize[s] a photographer's eye'.[2] *Youth* expresses itself almost as a panel of a comic book would, containing within its stillness the brutal violence of the moments that occurred before the event that is captured, and the horrific realisation of an innocent life that is under threat in the moments that follow. The miniature dimensions of this boy evocatively capture a sense of innocence and fragility, but this is soon also merged with a sense of tragedy and plain old stupidity as we realise that it is this very innocence and naivety that gave rise to a

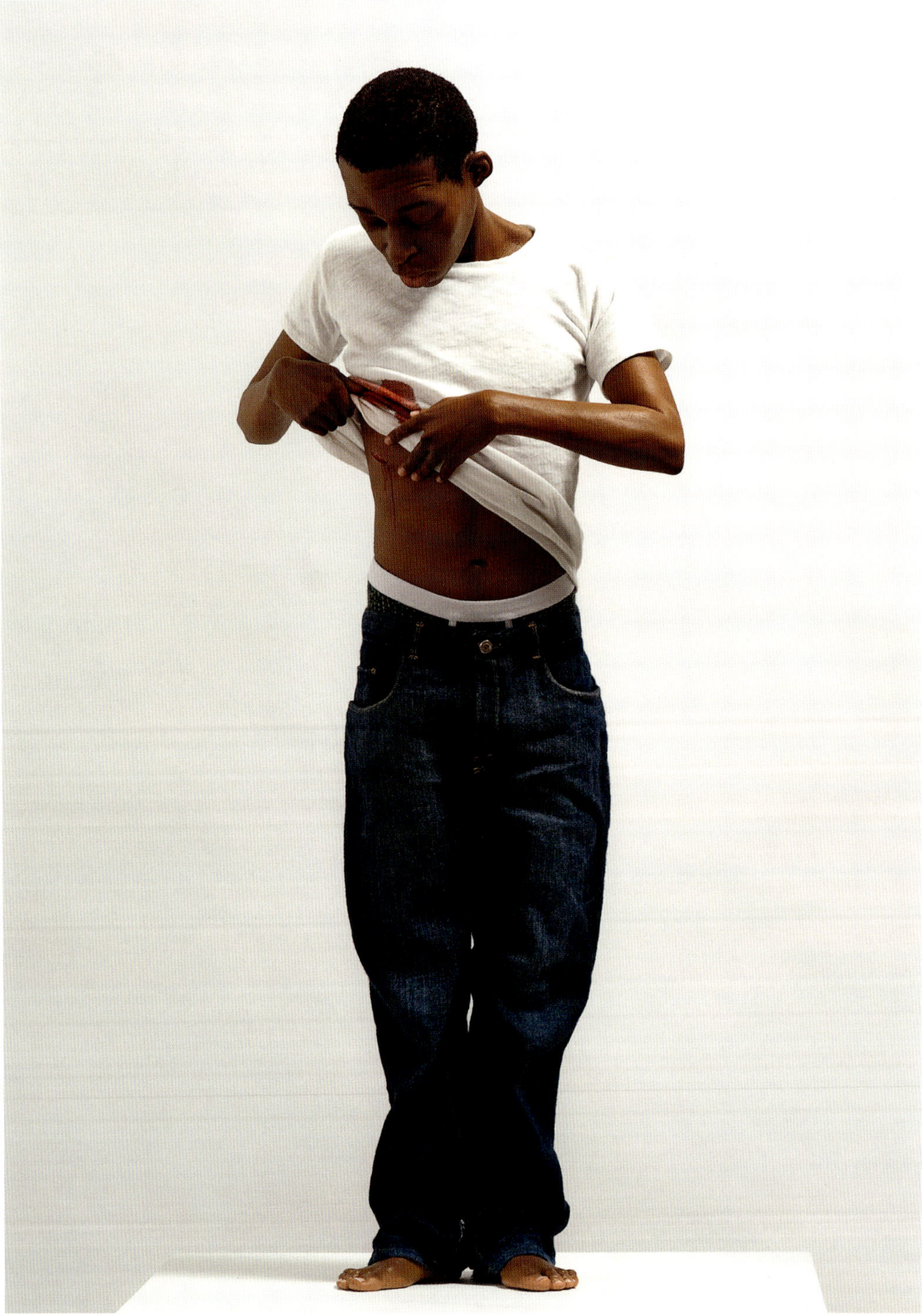

violent action that now threatens to transform a state of life into one of death; an action that fails to understand or acknowledge the reality and fragility of human mortality.

In his work Mueck always uses scale for emotive and expressive effect, and *Youth* is no exception. Wendy Haslem has convincingly argued that the miniature can have the effect of transporting us into the space of the uncanny, a space that tends to both defamiliarise the familiar and reject linear time and cohesive space. In *Youth* Mueck does both. Time stands still at the moment of realisation. Yet space also plays a crucial role in our interaction with this work and the action it represents. The boy can only be understood as miniaturised – and therefore defamiliarised – when it is understood that he has been wrenched from the social context and urban environment that brought about the violent act that leaves a mark on his body. That context, which would render his body 'normal' size, has been removed and is replaced instead with the context of the gallery space in which he is exhibited. It is this context that miniaturises the boy's body, in the process rendering the subject matter uncanny. As outlined by Haslem, when adopting 'miniature thinking', 'One must go beyond logic in order to experience what is large in what is small'.[3] The large, in this instance, is found in the moment of exclamation and revelation – the point where the spectator wonders in dread and disbelief at the social reality that gives rise to and nurtures such teen violence, rendering stabbings and street fights into an everyday occurrence that is anything but the rare experience that it ought to be.

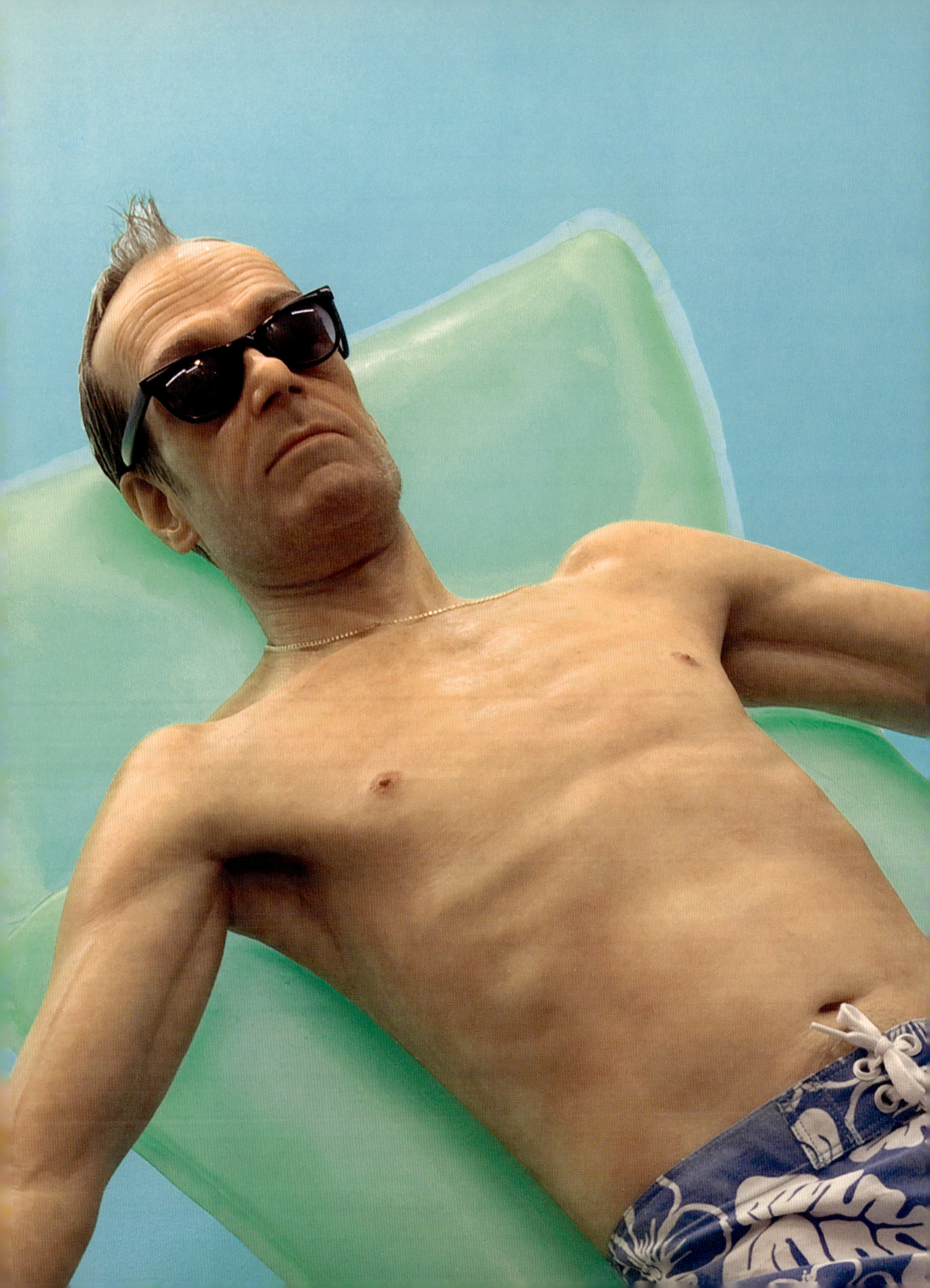

JUSTIN PATON

A MAN IN TIME

Drift 2009 (detail)
Anthony d'Offay, London

Do you have the time? I'm not asking you what time of day it is. I'm asking you how much time you have, period, and how you want to spend it.

The question bears down on us, here at the sped-up start of the twenty-first century. Things go faster and time seems thinner. There is something almost boastful about our responses when asked how things are going: I'm swamped, snowed under, absolutely flat-tack. This urgency has spawned its own workplace doctrine, known as time management – a regime of schedules and updates that often seem to leave you spending all of your time managing your time. Worse still is the phenomenon of organised leisure – 'time off' that is managed so fiercely it becomes another kind of work. The result is a world in which everyone seems to be racing against time, and no one is simply *in* it.

But imagine for a minute that you find yourself in a city with time on your hands. Perhaps you have missed an appointment or a plane has been delayed. Either way, something has fallen through, leaving a hole in your day, and you decide to visit a gallery. And in there, wandering with no special purpose, you turn a corner and see something remarkable up ahead. A man afloat on the wall – middle-aged, lightly tanned, in cheerful blue swim shorts, on a lilo. His arms are flung wide and his fingertips might be trailing in water. There is not even a book or a drink to distract him. Hovering there, he strikes you immediately as a figure to admire and even envy. He is doing what you

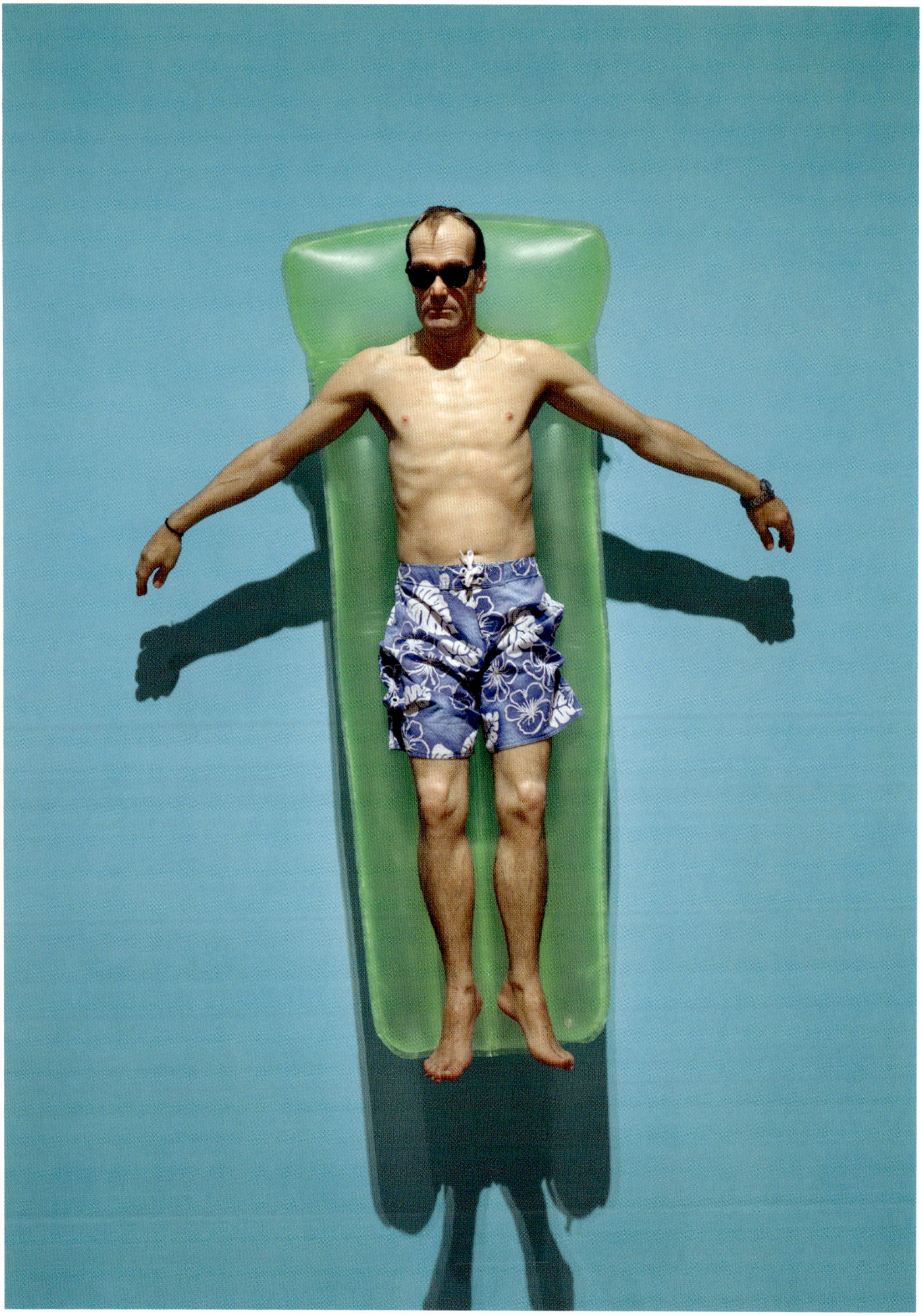

have been dreaming of doing – winding down, doing nothing, resisting the compulsion to rush. He is a man with all the time in the world.

Spend a little longer with this sculpture, though, and things become more complicated. Up close, you start to see the claims time has made on him: the fine web of wrinkles at his wrists and ankles, the pouching under his chin, and the suggestion of exhaustion in his downturned mouth. There is grey in his hair; you guess he might be fifty. Ron Mueck is well known as a sculptor of the extremities of human life, of the big dramas of birth and death. But in this work he is also a supremely attentive sculptor of middle age, of that stretch of life between the forties and the sixties when the body starts to show signs of wear. And what brings home this vulnerability with special force is not any one detail within the sculpture but the space Mueck leaves around it. This figure is not floating on his back within the confines of a pool but is hung high on the vast, white gallery wall, as if pulling away from us on an upward current. The effect is compounded by the size of the sculpture, which is about two-thirds the height of a human. The result is a figure who is always farther away than you expect – a figure who seems, even when you go in close, to be floating up and away.

Standing there and looking up at the sculpture, something else becomes impossible to ignore: whenever we look up at a nearly naked male figure with arms flung wide, we cannot help but think of carvings of the crucifixion afloat on church walls. The power of those sculptures lies in the way they make the story of the Passion physical, placing us at the foot of the cross staring up at Christ's sorrowing eyes. The power of Mueck's sculpture, by contrast, flows not from directness but uncertainty, because the exact feelings of his figure are hidden behind dark sunglasses. Something in the angle of his

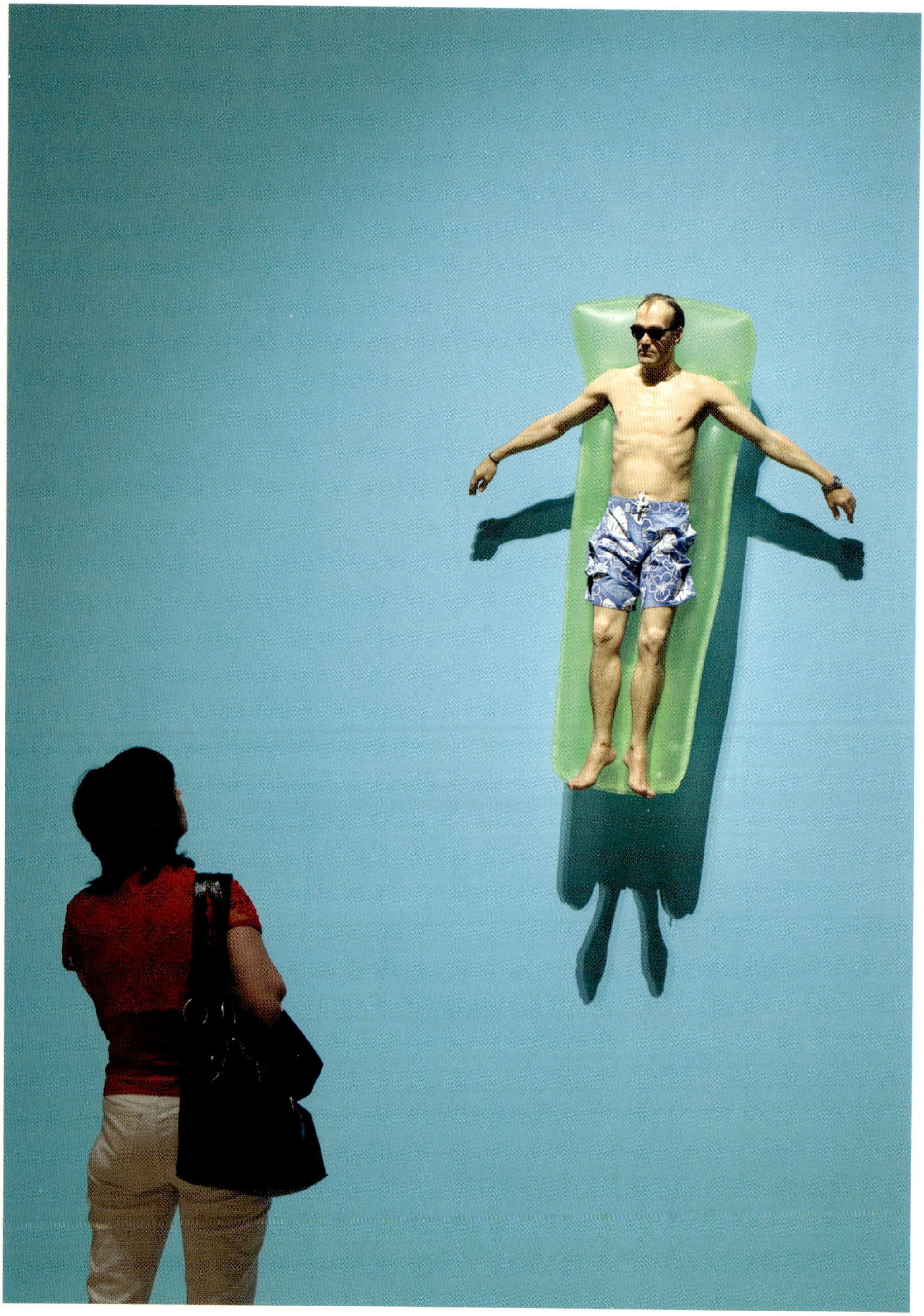

head creates a feeling of farewell, as if he is looking back towards us with resignation while the current carries him to some other place. However, at the same time it seems equally plausible that he is just a guy asleep in a pool.

So what will it be? How will you leave it with this figure? The day is passing, other exhibits are waiting, and your mobile phone keeps buzzing with fresh messages. The natural impulse at this point is to tie this sculpture to one interpretation or another. Is this man bobbing around sleepily in a backyard pool or approaching the end of his life? Is he taking his time or running out of it? The sculpture very quietly and forcefully refuses to provide an answer. Or, rather, it answers yes to both possibilities. Life, Mueck seems to be saying, cannot be divided up into minor moments and grand ones. We are on the journey even when – especially when – we appear to be doing nothing. We are all profoundly adrift.

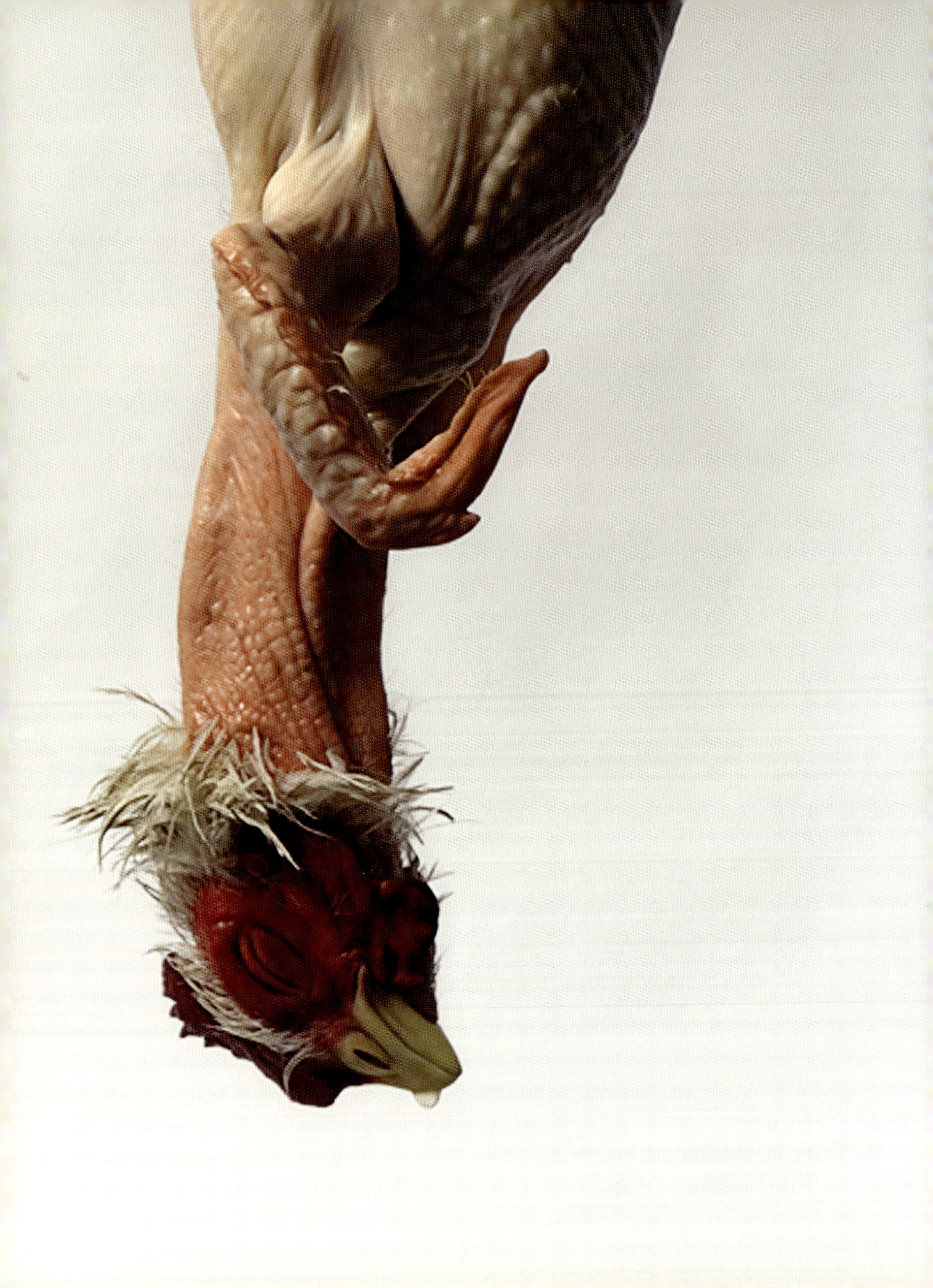

SUSANNA GREEVES

THINGS OF THE FLESH

Still life 2009 (detail)
Anthony d'Offay, London

The rubber chicken, a joke shop staple and instrument of buffoonery: Mueck's version of the beast is as remote from its flaccid, comic cousin as his figures are from shop window mannequins, but the work delivers a slap in the face nevertheless. How can we understand the presence of this outsized carcass among the human figures that Mueck so successfully imbues with life, sensibility and an interior narrative?

In genre terms, this is a shift from portraiture to still life. Plucked poultry and game is a frequent subject of the still-life tradition, and Mueck's version in particular recalls the near hyperrealism of the seventeenth-century golden age of the Dutch still life, when kitchen and market scenes were identified as a particular subdivision of this favourite genre. Pallid, puckered flesh was, like fur, fine crystal, dewy petals or burnished metal, an opportunity for the artist to display the breadth of his skill in the virtuoso imitation of nature. For Mueck, too, the subject presents a technical challenge and a formal exercise in the description of scaly and clammy textures, in a bruise-toned palette of pinks, blues and purples with livid highlights in fresh blood-red. *Nature morte, natura morta* – the Romance languages give it a more fitting name, one which also acknowledges the close relation to the *vanitas* tradition. Where Mueck usually seeks to convince us of life, here he creates true-to-life dead flesh. At this scale, Mueck's chicken overwhelms us with the undeniable fact of mortality: living matter becomes dead, cold meat.

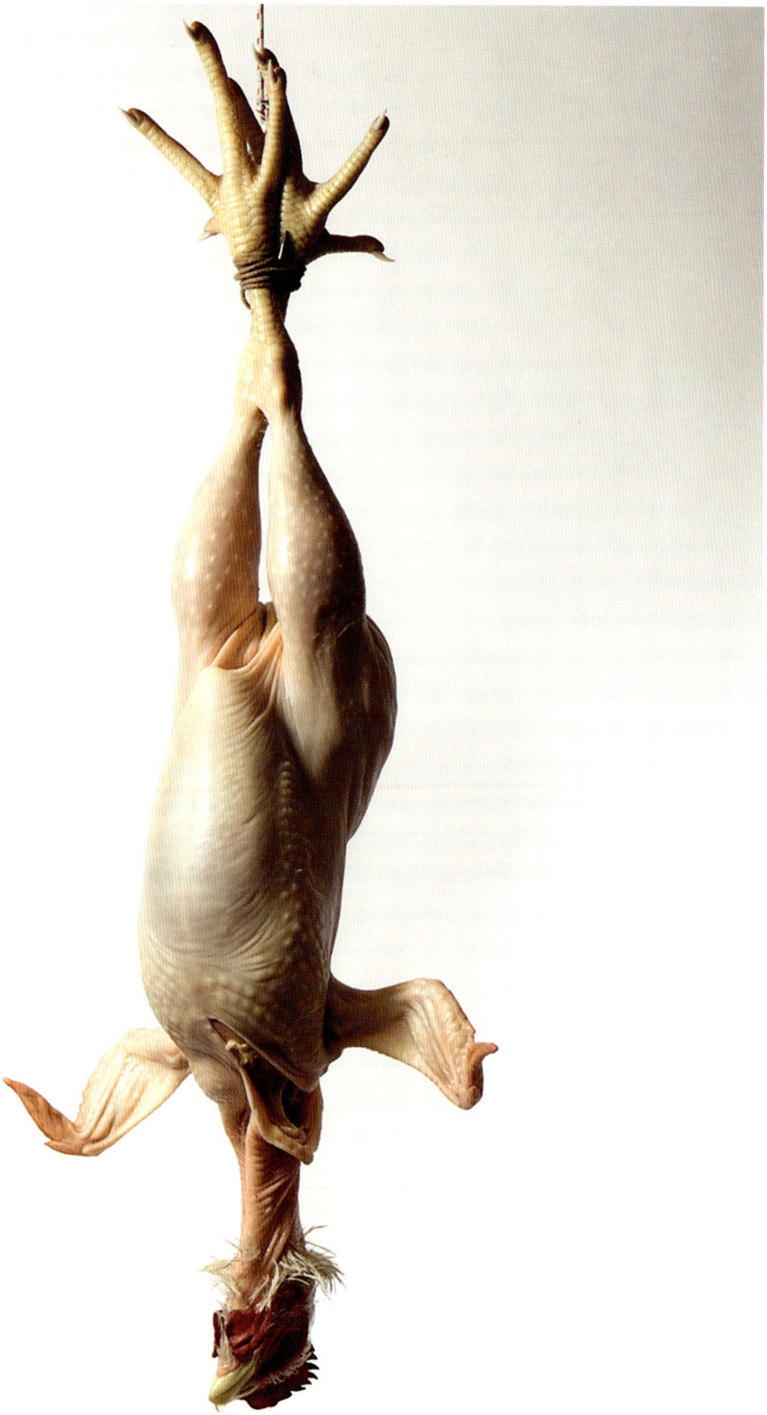

But to call this a still life is to deny the pathos and strange anthropomorphism of the creature, now made human-sized. Certainly it is – or was – a bird, and now stripped of its feathers it becomes strangely reptilian (betraying its prehistoric ancestry), yet there is much that is undeniably and expressively human in its almost serene expression, pathetic stubby arms spread in surrender, bunched haunches and splayed finger-like toes. It is an impression underlined by the echoes between this pose and other works of Mueck's – the tiny *Baby*, 2000, in particular, whose cocked elbows echo these wings and whose pose was taken, inverted, from an image of a newborn hoisted aloft by the feet exactly as this chicken is suspended. Baby and chicken are both equally incongruously pinned out, cruciform, beneath our gaze. Four hundred years earlier, Rembrandt painted his hanging, crucifix-like *Flayed ox*, 1655, later inspiring Chaïm Soutine's more human and tortured carcass of beef, and in turn the hanging carcasses flanking Francis Bacon's Pope Innocent in *Figure with meat*, 1954. This historical sequence of works brings together the imagery of slaughtered flesh with Christ's sacrifice in meditations on humanity and mortality of deepening despair and cynicism.

Not only does Mueck's creature seem human, but it is nakedly and obscenely so, from the phallic shaft of the neck to the scrotal puckering of the flesh, the gaping cavity between the thighs and the raw lips of the gash at the neck. Throughout his oeuvre Mueck has shown us his subjects in their most vulnerable and exposed states – naked, newly born, in bed, after giving birth and in the terrible intimacy of death – but how more exposed could one be than this poor creature, which has been stripped, plucked, pierced and eviscerated. The artist gives them all the same careful scrutiny, which is not harsh or cold because it involves a kind of deep physical and emotional empathy, but simply

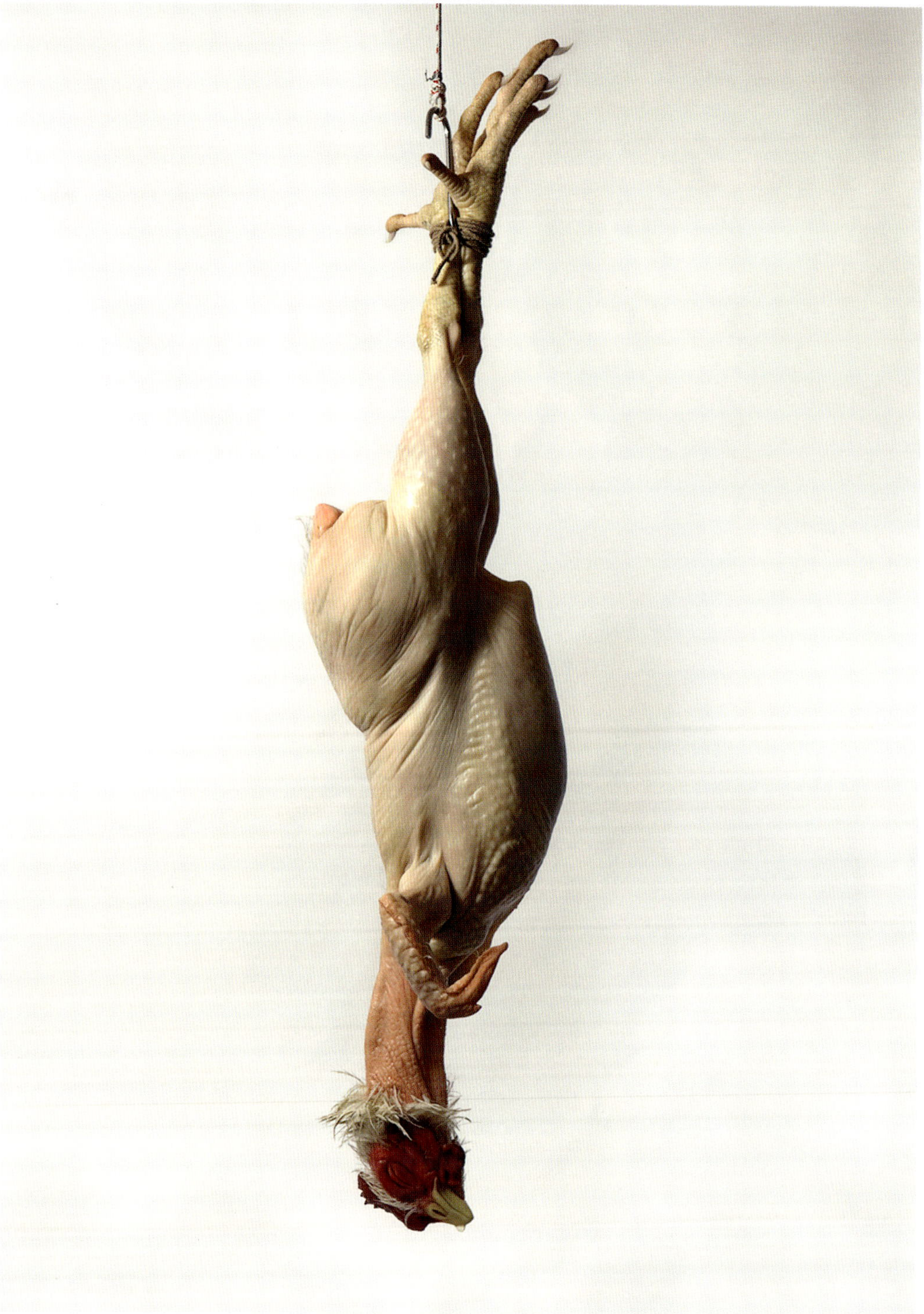

matter-of-fact, unflinching and unsentimental. A charge that has been levelled at Lucian Freud, for all his brilliance, is that he renders his nudes so like meat. Perhaps we might say the reverse here – that Mueck has modelled dead meat and given it a kind of humanity.

CHRONOLOGY

1958 Born Melbourne, Australia

1978–83 Works as creative director in Australian children's television

1984 Travels to US then to UK to work in film industry

1986 Establishes himself in London and sets up company creating models for film, television and advertising industries

1996 Asked by painter Paula Rego (mother-in-law) to create figure of Pinocchio to include in her tableau for *Spellbound: Art and Film*, held at Hayward Gallery (22 February – 6 May 1996)

Pinocchio, 1996, seen by prominent art collector Charles Saatchi, who commissions him to make three new sculptures for his collection: *Dead Dad*, 1996–97; *Angel*, 1997; and *Mask*, 1997

1997 *Dead Dad* included in exhibition *Sensation: Young British Artists from the Saatchi Collection*, which opens at London Royal Academy of the Arts (18 September – 28 December 1997). Exhibition also travels to Nationalgalerie im Hamburger Bahnhof, Museum für Gegenwart, Berlin (30 September 1998 – 17 January 1999), and to Brooklyn Museum, New York (2 October 1999 – 9 January 2000)

1998 Starts working with Anthony d'Offay and has first solo exhibition at the d'Offay Gallery, London (29 April – 18 June 1998)

1999 Completes his 4.9-metre high sculpture *Boy*, 1999, which is installed in *The Mind Zone* at London's Millennium Dome

2000 Holds second solo exhibition with Anthony d'Offay Gallery (15 September – 9 December 2000)

Granted two-year residency as Associate Artist, National Gallery, London. Produces works including *Mother and child*, 2001; *Man in a boat*, 2002; *Pregnant woman*, 2002; and *Swaddled baby*, 2002

2001 *Boy*, 1999, exhibited at *la Biennale di Venezia 49* – the 49th Venice Biennale (10 June – 4 November 2001)

Holds solo exhibition in US with James Cohan Gallery, New York (12 May – 16 June 2001)

2002 First solo exhibition in Australia held at Museum of Contemporary Art, Sydney (19 December 2002 – 2 March 2003). The exhibition, based on works produced during residency at the National Gallery, London, also includes *Crouching boy in mirror*, 1999–2002; *Old woman in bed*, 2000; and *Mask II*, 2001

Directions: Ron Mueck opens at Hirshhorn Museum and Sculpture Garden, Smithsonian Institution, Washington DC (18 July – 27 October 2002)

2003 *Ron Mueck: Making Sculpture at the National Gallery* opens at National Gallery, London (19 March – 22 June 2003)

Ron Mueck: Hyperreal opens at Nationalgalerie im Hamburger Bahnhof, Museum für Gegenwart, Berlin (10 September – 2 November 2003)

Ron Mueck opens at Frans Hals Museum, Haarlem, Netherlands (15 November 2003 – 18 January 2004)

2005 *Pregnant woman*, 2002, exhibited at National Gallery of Victoria, Melbourne (29 January – 27 February 2005), and Queensland Art Gallery, Brisbane (12 March – 5 June 2005), in *Ron Mueck: The Making of* Pregnant Woman *2002*, a travelling exhibition organised by National Gallery of Australia, Canberra

Fondation Cartier pour l'Art Contemporain, Paris, presents *Ron Mueck* (19 November 2005 – 19 February 2006), which includes five new sculptures: *In bed*, 2005; *Mask III*, 2005; *Spooning couple*, 2005; *Two women*, 2005; and *Wild man*, 2005

2006 Versions of the Fondation Cartier exhibition travel to the National Galleries of Scotland, Edinburgh, where the new sculpture *A girl*, 2006, is added (5 August – 8 October 2006); Brooklyn Museum, New York (3 November 2006 – 4 February 2007); National Gallery of Canada, Ottawa (2 March – 6 May 2007); Modern Art Museum, Fort Worth, Texas (24 June – 21 October 2007); Andy Warhol Museum, Pittsburgh (13 December 2007 – 30 March 2008) and the 21st Century Museum of Contemporary Art, Kanazawa (26 April – 8 August 2008) – the artist's first major exhibition in Japan

2007 Special exhibition held for *A girl*, 2006, at the Centro de Arte Contemporáneo de Málaga, Spain (30 March – 17 June 2007)

2008 McClelland Gallery + Sculpture Park, Langwarrin, exhibits newly acquired *Wild man*, 2005, together with *Two women*, 2005, and *Pregnant woman*, 2002, in *Ron Mueck @ McClelland* (24 August – 2 November 2008)

Mask II, 2002, included in *Statuephilia: Contemporary Sculptors at the British Museum*, British Museum, London (4 October 2008 – 25 January 2009)

2009 *Mask III*, 2005; *Spooning couple*, 2005; and *Wild man*, 2005; featured in *ARTIST ROOMS: Ron Mueck* at Aberdeen Art Gallery and Museums, Scotland (29 August – 31 October 2009).

RON MUECK'S SCULPTURES ARE HELD IN THE FOLLOWING PUBLIC COLLECTIONS:

Århus Kunstmuseum, Denmark
Art Gallery of New South Wales, Sydney, Australia
Hirshhorn Museum and Sculpture Garden, Smithsonian Institution, Washington DC, United States
Kunstsammlung Nordrhein-Westfalen, Dusseldorf, Germany
McClelland Gallery + Sculpture Park, Langwarrin, Australia
Modern Art Museum of Fort Worth, Texas, United States
Museum Brandhorst, Munich, Germany
National Galleries of Scotland, Edinburgh, Scotland
National Gallery of Australia, Canberra, Australia
National Gallery of Canada, Ottawa, Canada
National Gallery of Victoria, Melbourne, Australia
Queensland Art Gallery, Brisbane, Australia
San Francisco Museum of Modern Art, California, United States
Tate, London, United Kingdom
Towada Art Center, Towada, Japan

NOTES

INTRODUCTION

1 Paula Rego, quoted in Drusilla Beyfus, 'Body of work', *Telegraph*, 29 July 2006, reproduced at <www.telegraph.co.uk/culture/art/3654109/Body-of-work.html>.

2 Young British Artists is the name given to a group of artists who were active in the United Kingdom from the late 1980s. Originating from Britain's Goldsmith College, the group included artists such as Christine Borland, Tracey Emin, Damien Hirst, Sarah Lucas and Cornelia Parker. The group was identified by an openness towards materials and processes used in their practice and the form their art took.

3 Exhibition dates: Royal Academy of Arts, London, 18 September – 28 December 1997; Hamburger Bahnhof Museum für Gegenwart, Berlin, 30 September 1998 – 17 January 1999; Brooklyn Museum, New York, 2 October 1999 – 9 January 2000.

4 A press statement issued on the 26 November 1999 by the National Gallery of Australia stated:

> The Director and Council of the National Gallery of Australia have taken the decision not to show the exhibition *Sensation: Young British Artists from the Saatchi Collection* at the National Gallery of Australia next year.
>
> As a publicly funded institution, the Gallery will not proceed with a show which has been the centre of a furore in New York over issues which have obscured discussion of the artistic merit of the works of art.

The Director and Council had wished to bring this much discussed exhibition of Contemporary British Art to the Australian public. The Gallery had looked forward to engaging the Australian public about issues in contemporary art and will now seek other avenues in which to do so. Reproduced at <www.nga.gov.au/AboutUs/press/preY2k2.cfm>.

5 When *Sensation* opened in London on 18 September 1997, the public controversy surrounded Marcus Harvey's work *Myra*, 1995, which depicted convicted child murderer Myra Hindley by using children's handprints. The exhibition was picketed by the Mothers Against Murder and Aggression who, with the mother of one of Hindley's victims, fought unsuccessfully to have the work removed. The piece was subsequently vandalised with ink and eggs but it was returned to display following conservation treatment.

Upon opening in New York, the exhibition was met with an immediate protest that centred on Chris Ofili's work *The Holy Virgin Mary*, a painting of a black Madonna with collaged images of female buttocks and genitalia, and pieces of resin-covered elephant dung. The exhibition was also criticised for the funding arrangements, which involved Saatchi, along with the auction house Christie's, providing much of the financial backing for the project.

6 Sean O'Hagan, 'Ron Mueck: from Muppets to motherhood', *Observer*, 6 August 2006, reproduced at <www.guardian.co.uk/artanddesign/2006/aug/06/art2>.

7 Ron Mueck, conversation with the author, 3 August 2009.

8 *Shirl's Neighbourhood* was an afternoon children's series that was aired on Australian television between 1978 and 1983. The half-hour program was hosted by Graeme 'Shirley' Strachan, the former

lead singer from the band Skyhooks. It included a cast of puppet characters, such as Norm the Kangaroo, Claude the Crow and Stanley the Snake. Ron Mueck was the Creative Director and was responsible for the creation of many of the puppets.

9 Mueck worked on several of Jim Henson's productions, most notably *Labyrinth*, where he worked as one of the puppeteers and was the voice of the character Ludo.

10 Ron Mueck, conversation with the author, 3 August 2009. Mueck also acknowledges the role Charles Saatchi played in his shift into a purer form of sculpture and to his recognition as an artist.

11 Ron Mueck, email correspondence with the author, 15 October 2009.

12 Anthony d'Offay ran his Dering Street gallery in London from 1980 until 2001. During this time he represented artists such as Joseph Beuys, Gilbert and George, Anselm Kiefer, Jeff Koons, Richard Hamilton, Gerhard Richter and Bill Viola. In the early 1990s he was involved in exhibiting the work of some of the Young British Artists. Anthony d'Offay continues to represent Ron Mueck and operates as Anthony d'Offay Limited.

13 Susanna Greeves, 'Ron Mueck: a redefinition of realism', in Heiner Bastian (ed.), *Ron Mueck* (exh. cat.), 2nd edn, rev., Hatje Cantz Publishers, Ostfildern-Ruit, 2005, p. 31.

14 Ron Mueck, email correspondence with the author, 15 October 2009.

THE ART OF EXCESS: FIVE MOVEMENTS

1 Roland Barthes, *Camera Lucida: Reflections on Photography*, McGraw-Hill Ryerson, Toronto, 1980. In *Camera Lucida*, Barthes developed this term to refer to the conflation of the familiar and unfamiliar. He created the term after his mother's death, when he found a photograph of her, which he described as being invested with vivifying qualities missing from her familiar image.

2 Patti Smith, in *Still Moving/Patti Smith*, 16 mm film by Robert Mapplethorpe, 1978.

MASK II AND THE CURSE OF NARCISSUS

1 *Mask II* was displayed as part of the exhibition *Statuephilia: Contemporary Sculptors at the British Museum* held at the British Museum, London, from 4 October 2008 to 25 January 2009.

TAKING THE WEIGHT

1 Brian Kennedy, 'Ron Mueck: the making of *Pregnant woman*, 2002', National Gallery of Australia, 23 March 2004, reproduced at <www.nga.gov.au/mueck/director.cfm>.

INVITATION AU VOYAGE

1 Oscar Wilde, *The Critic as Artist*, Mondial Books, New York, 2007, p. 44.
2 ibid, p. 46.
3 James Joyce, *Ulysses*, Penguin Books, London, 2000, p. 125.
4 'The art of fiction', interview no. 39 with Jorge Luis Borges, *Paris Review*, no. 40, 1967.

THINKING SCULPTURES

1 Auguste Rodin, cited in John L. Tancock, *The Sculpture of Auguste Rodin*, Philadelphia Museum of Art, Philadelphia, 1976, p. 112.
2 Gilbert Ryle, 'The thinking of thoughts: what is "Le Penseur" doing?', *University Lectures*, no. 18, University of Saskatchewan, Saskatoon, 1968.
3 Heiner Bastian, 'On several sculptures by Ron Mueck', in Heiner Bastian (ed.), *Ron Mueck* (exh. cat.), 2nd edn, rev., Hatje Cantz Publishers, Ostfildern-Ruit, 2005, p. 60.

TWO WOMEN

1 'Quotations about age', The Quote Garden, reproduced at <www.quotegarden.com/age.html>.

WILD MEN OF THE WOODS

1 Edward Topsell, *The History of Four-footed Beasts and Serpents: Describing at Large their True and Lively Figure, their Several Names, Conditions, Kinds, Virtues (Both Natural and Medicinal) Countries of their Breed ... / Collected Out of the Writings of Conradus Gesner and Other Authors*, G. Sawbridge, T. Williams and T. Johnson, London, 1658, p. 8.

2 Jacob Bontius (1658), quoted in Robert M. Yerkes and Ada W. Yerkes, *The Great Apes: a Study of Anthropoid Life*, Yale University Press, New Haven, 1929, p. 1.

3 Georges-Louis Leclerc, Comte de Buffon, *Histoire Naturelle, Générale et Particulière, avec la Description du Cabinet du Roi*, Paris, l'Imprimerie royale, vol. xiv, 1766, p. 50. Ron Mueck provided the voice for the much more benign, hairy, orang-utan-like creature Ludo in Jim Henson's film *Labyrinth* in 1986.

4 Gautier-Laboulaye, quoted in M. Dureau de la Malle, 'Mémoire sur le grand gorille de Gabon, *Troglodytes Gorilla*, déterminant la limite de la navigation d'Hannon, le long des côtes de l'Afrique occidentale', *Annales des Sciences naturelles, Zoologie*, series 3, vol. 16, Victor Masson, Paris, 1851, p. 191.

BOY WONDER

1 Peter Fisher, *Wonder, the Rainbow, and the Aesthetics of Rare Experiences*, Harvard University Press, Cambridge, 1998.

2 Martyn Pedler, 'The fastest man alive: stasis and speed in contemporary superhero comics', *Animation: an Interdisciplinary Journal*, vol. 4, no. 3, pp. 1–15.

3 Wendy Haslem, 'Going places sitting down: micrographia and the triptych', *Computers in Entertainment*, vol. 7, no. 1, February 2009, pp. 1–14. Haslem in particular draws upon Gaston Bachelard's work on the miniature in his book *The Poetics of Space* (1958).

COMPILED BY
DEIRDRE CANNON
AND TRISH LITTLE
WITH ASSISTANCE
FROM HANNAH
BARRY

CATALOGUE RAISONNÉ

RON MUECK

born Australia 1958,
lived in England 1986–

✦ ✦ ✦

NOTES TO THE READER

This catalogue raisonné is ordered chronologically by production date except where two or more versions of a work exist. In these cases, entries for the subsequent versions appear immediately following the entry for the first version. Ron Mueck identifies the first version of a work as 1/1 and the second as artist's proof. In the case of *Mask*, 1997, and *Baby*, 2000, an edition in plaster was also produced. The exhibition history included with the entries identifies the relevant version (ed. 1/1 or A/P [artist's proof]) where this can be confirmed. Page references in italics indicate illustrations for all works in the exhibition *Ron Mueck*, 2010. Please note: *Pregnant woman*, 2002, exhibited Christchurch Art Gallery, New Zealand, only.

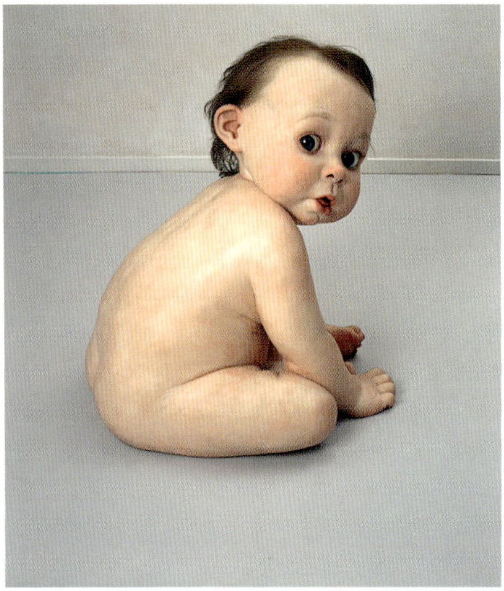

Big baby 1996
silicone, polyurethane, wood, synthetic hair, ed. 1/1
85.0 × 71.0 × 70.0 cm
Private collection

EXHIBITIONS: *Ant Noises at the Saatchi Gallery: Part 1*, Saatchi Gallery, London, 20 Apr. – 20 Aug. 2000.

LITERATURE: Adams et al. 1997, p. 203; Price 1998, unpaginated illus.; Hayward et al. (eds) 1999, p. 381 illus.; De Cruz 2000, unpaginated illus.; Ellis 2003, pp. 213, 157 illus.; Bastian (ed.) 2005, pp. 26, 70 illus.; Bevan, *Art Newspaper*, 2005, p. 41; Rosenblum 2005, pp. 58, 108 illus.; Greeves & Raine 2007, pp. 75, 59 illus.; Hill, *Art & Australia*, 2007, p. 248; Lindsay & Gott 2008, p. 2.

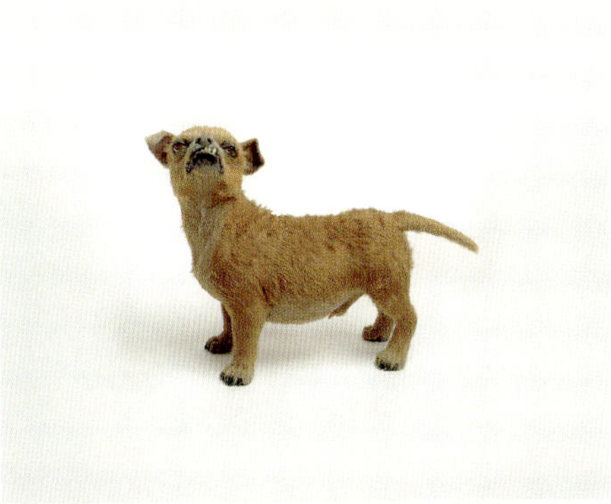

Mongrel 1996
polyester resin, fibreglass, synthetic fur, ed. 1/1
40.0 × 61.0 × 20.3 cm
Collection of Sheilagh Tennant, Edinburgh

EXHIBITIONS: *Best in Show: the Dog in Art from the Renaissance to Today*, Bruce Museum, Connecticut, 13 May – 27 Aug. 2006; touring: Museum of Fine Arts, Houston, 1 Oct. 2006 – 1 Jan. 2007; *Inspired*, Mitchell Library, Glasgow, 4 Apr. – 20 Sep. 2009.

LITERATURE: Bastian (ed.) 2005, p. 71 illus.; Rosenblum 2005, p. 109 illus.; Peters et al. 2006, pp. 97, 96 illus.; Greeves & Raine 2007, p. 72, 59 illus.; Mueck et al. 2008, p. 67.

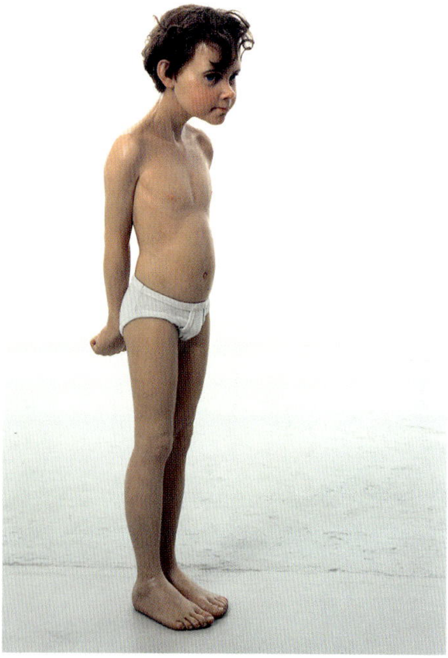

Pinocchio 1996
polyester resin, fibreglass, aluminium wire, synthetic hair, cotton, ed. 1/1
84.0 × 20.0 × 18.0 cm
John and Amy Phelan Collection, New York

EXHIBITIONS: *Spellbound: Art and Film*, Hayward Gallery, London, 22 Feb. – 6 May 1996, exhibited as part of Paula Rego's installation; *Ant Noises at the Saatchi Gallery: Part I*, Saatchi Gallery, London, 20 Apr. – 20 Aug. 2000.

LITERATURE: McEwen 1996; Adams et al. 1997, p. 203; Price 1998, unpaginated illus.; Hayward et al. (eds) 1999, p. 383 illus.; De Cruz 2000, unpaginated illus.; Wilson in Szeemann & Liveriero Lavelli (eds) 2001, p. 106; Lawrence 2002, unpaginated; National Museum of Modern Art, Tokyo 2002, p. 67 illus.; Ellis 2003, pp. 213, 156 illus.; Greeves & Wiggins 2003, pp. 43, 42 illus.; Musa, *Canberra Times*, 2004, p. 3; Banks, *West Australian*, 2005, p. 14; Bastian (ed.) 2005, pp. 26, 70, 10 illus.; Bevan, *Art Newspaper*, 2005, p. 41; Clair 2005, p. 492; Rosenblum 2005, p. 109 illus.; Hill, *Art & Australia*, 2007, p. 248; Mueck et al. 2008, p. 35 illus.

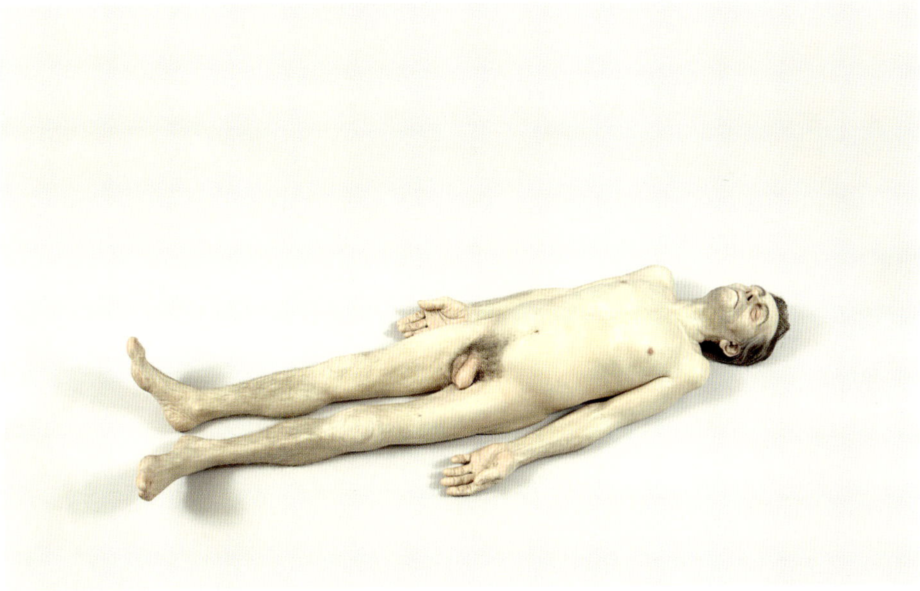

Dead Dad **1996–97**
silicone, polyurethane, styrene, synthetic hair, ed. 1/1
20.0 × 38.0 × 102.0 cm
Stefan T. Edlis Collection, Chicago

pp. 18, 36, 38, 40

EXHIBITIONS: *Sensation: Young British Artists from the Saatchi Collection*, Royal Academy of Arts, London, 18 Sep. – 28 Dec. 1997; touring: Nationalgalerie im Hamburger Bahnhof, Museum für Gegenwart, Berlin, 30 Sep. 1998 – 17 Jan. 1999; Brooklyn Museum, New York, 2 Oct. 1999 – 9 Jan. 2000; *SlowTech*, Museum of Contemporary Art, Taipei, 24 Jun. – 3 Sep. 2006; *Ron Mueck*, Brooklyn Museum, New York, 3 Nov. 2006 – 4 Feb. 2007; touring: Modern Art Museum of Fort Worth, Texas, 24 Jun. – 21 Oct. 2007.

LITERATURE: Adams et al. 1997, pp. 33, 203, 127 illus.; Barrett, *Artext*, 1998, p. 93; MacRitchie, *Art in America*, 1998, p. 37 illus; Myers, *Artext*, 1998, p. 84; Price 1998, unpaginated illus.; Raine 1998, pp. 21, 22, 20 illus.; Hayward et al. (eds) 1999, pp. 384–5 illus.; Rinder & Crowley 1999, pp. 7–8; Saltz, *Village Voice*, 2001, p. 61 illus.; Gerchow & Belting 2002, p. 182 illus.; Herd, *Weekend Australian*, 2002, p. 12; Lawrence 2002, unpaginated; Pearlman, *Sydney Morning Herald*, 2002, p. 4; Darwent, *Independent*, 2003, p. 8; Ebony et al. 2003, p. 150; Ellis 2003, pp. 212, 152–3 illus.; Etherington-Smith, *Art Review*, 2003, p. 64; Greeves & Wiggins 2003, pp. 20, 23, 43, 47, 53, 56, 60, 45 illus.; Hatton, *Art Monthly Australia*, 2003, p. 11; Leydier, *Art Press*, 2003, pp. 27–8, 28 illus.; Martin, *Art & Australia*, 2003, p. 568; Pietsch, *Art*, 2003, pp. 62, 63 illus.; Théberge 2003, p. 56; Chapman, *Artlook*, 2004, p. 9; Kennedy, *Antiques and Art in New South Wales*, 2004, p. 11; Banks, *West Australian*, 2005, p. 14; Bastian (ed.) 2005, pp. 7, 26, 32–3, 38–9, 62, 71, 61 illus.; Bevan, *Art Newspaper*, 2005, p. 41; Clair, *Art Press*, 2005, p. 13; Clair 2005, p. 492; Makin, *Herald Sun*, 2005, p. 89; Rosenblum 2005, pp. 46, 50, 64, 109, 42–3 illus.; Farine, 'Ron Mueck: corps surhumains', *L'Oeil*, 2006, p. 62; Lai & Yuan 2006, pp. 101, 102–6 illus.; Raine, *Guardian*, 2006, p. 12; Greeves & Raine 2007, pp. 70–2, 14 & 59 illus.; Hill, *Art & Australia*, 2007, pp. 248, 242–3 illus.; Prieto, *Arte y Parte*, 2007, p. 95; Spaid, *ArtUS*, 2007, p. 59; Art & Australia, 2008, p. 228; Chambers, *Art Lines*, 2008, p. 23; Collins 2007, p. 394 illus.; Grosenick (ed.) 2008, p. 198; Lindsay & Gott 2008, p. 2; Mueck et al. 2008, pp. 66–7, 80–1, 31 illus.; Heartney, 2008, pp. 201, 202 illus.

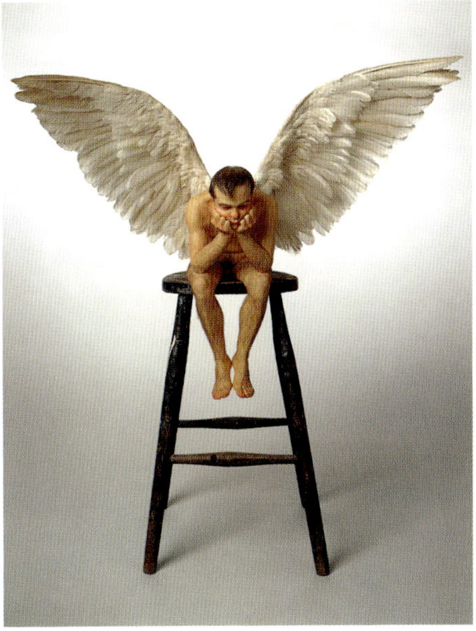

Angel 1997
silicone, aluminium, goose wings, synthetic hair, wood, ed. 1/1
110.0 × 87.0 × 81.0 cm (figure); 60.0 × 40.0 × 38.0 cm (stool)
Hoffman Collection, Dallas

EXHIBITIONS: *Ron Mueck*, Anthony d'Offay Gallery, London, 29 Apr. – 18 Jun. 1998; *Sensation: Young British Artists from the Saatchi Collection*; touring: Nationalgalerie im Hamburger Bahnhof, Museum für Gegenwart, Berlin, 30 Sep. 1998 – 17 Jan. 1999; Brooklyn Museum, New York, 2 Oct. 1999 – 9 Jan. 2000; *Ant Noises at the Saatchi Gallery: Part I*, Saatchi Gallery, London, 20 Apr. – 20 Aug. 2000.

LITERATURE: Myers, *Artext*, 1998, p. 84; Price 1998, unpaginated illus.; Raine, *Modern Painters*, 1998, p. 22; Hayward et al. (eds) 1999, pp. 387, 494 illus.; LeVitte-Harten 1999, p. 41; De Cruz 2000, cover illus.; Restorff, *Kunstzeitung*, 2000, p. 1 illus.; Wilson, *Art Monthly*, 2000, p. 9; Crone, *Art & Australia*, 2003, pp. 218, 219 illus.; Cumming, *Observer Review*, 2003, p. 10; Ellis 2003, pp. 159, 213 & cover illus.; Greeves & Wiggins 2003, pp. 19, 18 illus.; Pietsch, *Art*, 2003, p. 57 illus.; Bastian (ed.) 2005, pp. 13, 26, 72 illus.; Bevan, *Art Newspaper*, 2005, p. 41; Rosenblum 2005, p. 109 illus.; Hill, *Art & Australia*, 2007, pp. 248, 244 illus.; Lindsay & Gott 2008, p. 2; Mueck et al. 2008, p. 21 illus.

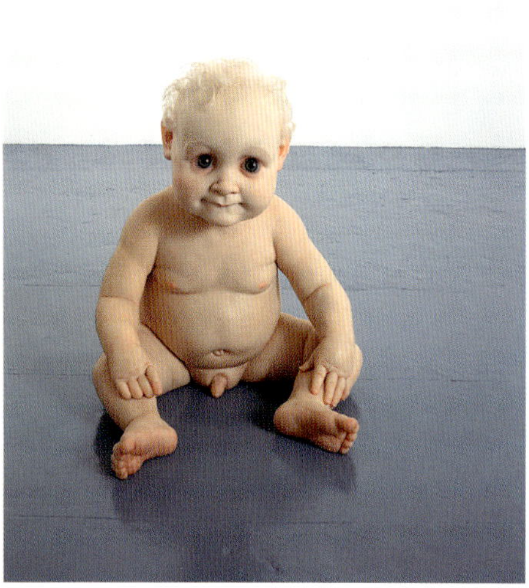

Big baby II **1997**
polyester resin, fibreglass, silicone, synthetic hair, ed. 1/1
85.0 × 71.0 × 70.0 cm
Caldic Collectie, Rotterdam

EXHIBITIONS: *Heaven*, Kunsthalle, Düsseldorf, 30 Jul. – 17 Oct. 1999; *Ant Noises at the Saatchi Gallery: Part I*, Saatchi Gallery, London, 20 Apr. – 20 Aug. 2000; *Imagine, You Are Standing Here in Front of Me: Caldic Collectie*, Museum Boijmans Van Beuningen, Rotterdam, 23 Nov. 2002 – 2 Feb. 2003; *Child in Time: Views of Contemporary Artists on Youth and Adolescence*, Gemeentemuseum Helmond, Netherlands, 24 May – 7 Sep. 2003; *Soul, Inspired Art*, Museum of Modern Art, PMMK, Oostende, 15 Jul. – 15 Sep. 2005; *De Overkant/Downunder*, Escher in het Paleis, The Hague, Netherlands, 1 Jun. – 9 Sep. 2007.

LITERATURE: Adams et al. 1997, pp. 203, 126 illus. (work in progress); Price 1998, unpaginated illus.; de Wavrin, *Beaux Arts Magazine*, 1999, pp. 108–9, 108 illus; Jocks, *Kunstforum International*, 1999, pp. 388–9; LeVitte-Harten 1999, pp. 41, 42 illus.; Guldemond (ed.) 2002, p. 190 illus.; Bastian (ed.) 2005, p. 72 illus.; Bevan, *Art Newspaper*, 2005, p. 41; Rosenblum 2005, p. 109 illus.; *Den Haag Sculptuur 2007* 2007, pp. 151–2, 153 illus.

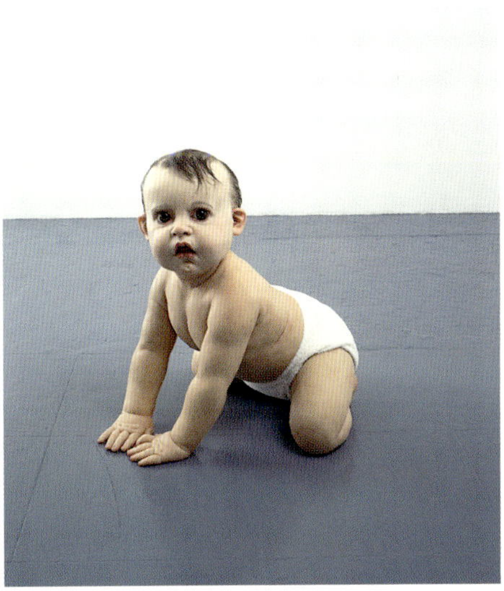

Big baby III 1997
polyester resin, fibreglass, silicone, synthetic hair, cotton, ed. 1/1
86.0 × 81.0 × 70.0 cm
Stefan T. Edlis Collection, Chicago

EXHIBITIONS: *Heaven*, Kunsthalle, Düsseldorf, 30 Jul. – 17 Oct. 1999; *Ant Noises at the Saatchi Gallery: Part I*, Saatchi Gallery, London, 20 Apr. – 20 Aug. 2000; *A Perspective on Contemporary Art: Continuity and Transgression*, National Museum of Art, Tokyo, 29 Oct. – 23 Dec. 2002; touring: National Museum of Osaka, Osaka, 16 Jan. – 23 Mar. 2003.

LITERATURE: Adams et al. 1997, pp. 203, 127 illus.; Price 1998, unpaginated illus.; Hayward et al. (eds) 1999, p. 382 illus.; LeVitte-Harten 1999, pp. 41, 43 illus.; De Cruz 2000, unpaginated illus.; Wilson, *Art Monthly*, 2000, p. 9; National Museum of Modern Art, Tokyo 2002, p. 65 illus.; Bastian (ed.) 2005, p. 72 illus.; Rosenblum 2005, p. 109 illus.

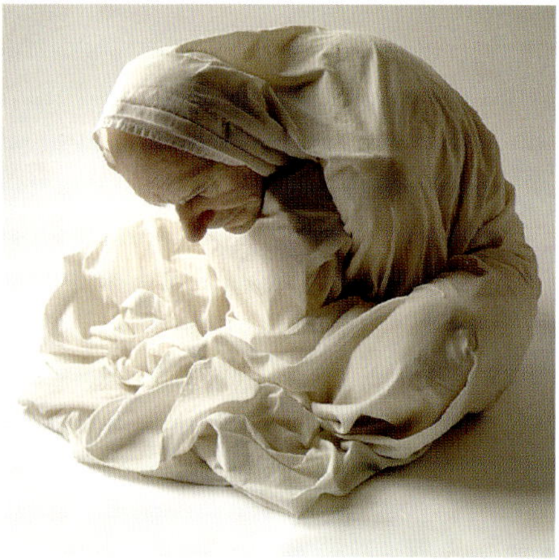

Man in a sheet 1997
polyester resin, fibreglass, silicone, polyurethane, aluminium wire, synthetic hair, cotton, ed. 1/1
34.0 × 48.5 × 50.0 cm
Olbricht Collection, Germany

EXHIBITIONS: *Unsichere Grenzen*, Kunsthalle zu Kiel, Kiel, 17 Jun. – 29 Aug. 1999; *Ohne Zögern: Without Hesitation: Die Sammlung Olbricht Teil 2*, Neues Museum Weserburg and Gesellschaft für Aktuelle Kunst, Bremen, 3 Jun. – 6 Sep. 2001; *Ebenbilder: Kopien von Körpen – Modelle des Menschen*, Ruhrlandmuseum, Essen, Germany, 6 Mar. – 30 Jun. 2002; *Gewissenlos – Gewissenhaft: Menschenversuche im Konzentrationslager*, Berliner Medizinhistorisches Museum, Berlin, 24 Apr. – 27 Jul. 2003; *Ron Mueck: Hyperreal*, Nationalgalerie im Hamburger Bahnhof, Museum für Gegenwart, Berlin, 10 Sep. – 2 Nov. 2003; *Ich Will, Dass du Mir Glaubst!, 9: Triennale Kleinplastik Fellbach*, Alte Kelter, Fellbach, 26 Jun. – 3 Oct. 2004.

LITERATURE: Schmidt & Ermacora 1999, pp. 20–1, 18–19 illus.; Schmidt in Schoppmann et al. (eds) 2001, pp. 182, 183 illus.; Gerchow & Belting 2002, p. 280 illus.; Nungesser, *Kunstforum International*, 2003, p. 265; Ammann & de Ligt 2004, p. 244, p. 99 illus.; Bastian (ed.) 2005, pp. 54–6, 43, 73 illus; Rosenblum 2005, pp. 63, 110 illus.

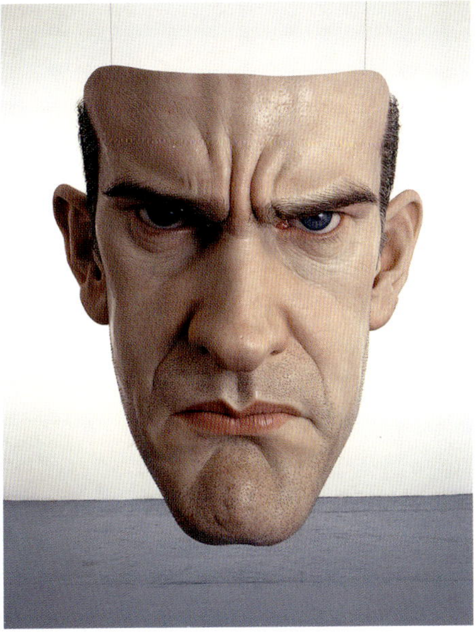

Mask 1997
polyester resin, fibreglass, synthetic hair, steel, ed. 1/1
145.0 × 137.0 × 106.0 cm
Collection of Mr and Mrs J. Tomilson Hill, New York

Untitled (Mask) 2000
plaster, edition of 12
10.5 × 14 × 13 cm
Various collections

EXHIBITIONS: *Ron Mueck*, Anthony d'Offay Gallery, London, 29 Apr. – 18 Jun. 1998; *Sensation: Young British Artists from the Saatchi Collection*, touring: Nationalgalerie im Hamburger Bahnhof, Museum für Gegenwart, Berlin, 30 Sep. 1998 – 17 Jan. 1999; Brooklyn Museum, New York, 2 Oct. 1999 – 9 Jan. 2000; *Ant Noises at the Saatchi Gallery: Part I*, Saatchi Gallery, London, 20 Apr. – 20 Aug. 2000; *New at the Nasher*, The Nasher Museum of Art at Duke University, North Carolina, 19 Jul. 2007 – 6 Jul. 2008.

LITERATURE: Myers, *Artext*, 1998, p. 84; Price 1998, unpaginated illus.; Raine, *Modern Painters*, 1988, p. 22 cover illus.; Hayward et al. (eds) 1999, p. 495 illus.; LeVitte-Harten 1999, p. 41; De Cruz 2000, p. 1, unpaginated illus.; Ingram, *Australian Financial Review*, 2001, p. 39; National Museum of Modern Art, Tokyo 2002, p. 71 illus.; Ellis 2003, pp. 212, 155 illus.; Greeves & Wiggins 2003, p. 62; Hatton, *Art Monthly Australia*, 2003, p. 11; Majendie, *Age*, 2003, p. 12 illus.; Thompson, *Herald Sun*, 2003, p. 29 illus; Bastian (ed.) 2005, pp. 40, 73 illus.; Bevan, *Art Newspaper*, 2005, p. 41; Rosenblum 2005, pp. 109, 77 illus.; Farine, 'Les grandes personnes de Ron Mueck', *L'Oeil*, 2006, p. 65 illus.; Hartley 2006, p. 11; Raine, *Guardian*, 2006, p. 12; Mueck et al. 2008, p. 80.

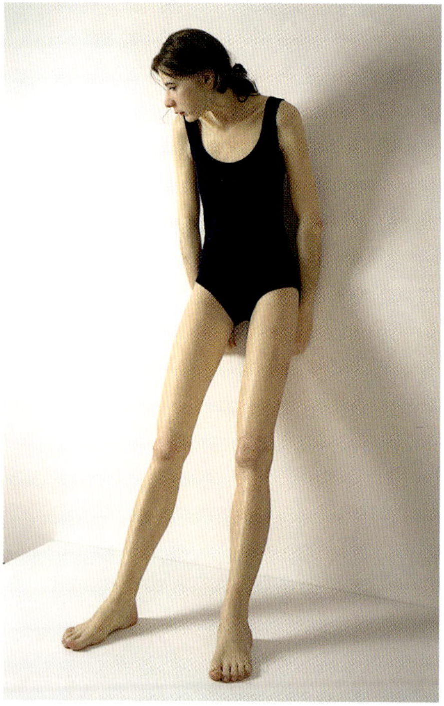

Ghost 1998
polyester resin, fibreglass, silicone, synthetic hair, cotton, ed. 1/1
202.0 × 65.0 × 99.0 cm
Tate
Purchased, 1998 (T07445)

EXHIBITIONS: *Ron Mueck*, Anthony d'Offay Gallery, London, 29 Apr. – 18 Jun. 1998; *The Uncanny*, Tate Liverpool, England, 20 Feb. – 3 May 2004; touring: Museum Modener Kunst Stiftung Ludwig Wien, Vienna, 15 Jul. – 31 Oct. 2004; *The Human Figure in British Art from Moore to Gormley*, Millennium Galleries, Sheffield, 22 Jan. – 17 Apr. 2005; *Ron Mueck*, Scottish National Gallery of Modern Art, Royal Scottish Academy Building, Edinburgh, 5 Aug. – 8 Oct. 2006.

LITERATURE: Myers, *Artext*, 1998, p. 84; Raine, *Modern Painters*, 1998, pp. 21–2, 23 illus.; Wilson in Szeemann & Liveriero Lavelli (eds) 2001, p. 106; Cumming, *Observer Review*, 2003, p. 10; Greeves & Wiggins 2003, pp. 59, 61 illus.; Kelley et al. 2004, p. 93 illus.; Bastian (ed.) 2005, pp. 60–1, 23 & 74 illus.; Clair, *Art Press*, 2005, p. 13 illus.; Rosenblum 2005, pp. 58, 68, 55 & 110 illus.; Hartley 2006, p. 8, pl. 8 illus.; Raine, *Guardian*, 2006, p. 12; Greeves & Raine 2007, pp. 72, 18 & 61 illus.; Hill, *Art & Australia*, 2007, p. 251; Grosenick (ed.) 2008, p. 198; Mueck et al. 2008, pp. 67, 33 illus.

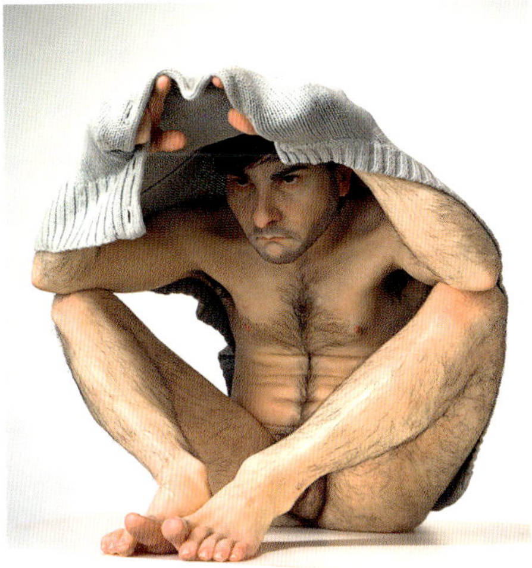

Man under cardigan 1998
silicone, polyurethane, polyester resin, aluminium wire, wool, ed. 1/1
44.0 × 47.0 × 63.0 cm
Vicki and Kent Logan Collection

EXHIBITIONS: *Ron Mueck*, Anthony d'Offay Gallery, London, 29 Apr. – 18 Jun. 1998; *Spaced Out: Late 1990s Works from the Vicki and Kent Logan Collection*, California College of Arts and Crafts, San Francisco, 17 Apr. – 5 Jun. 1999; *Supernova: Art of the 1990s from the Logan Collection*, San Francisco Museum of Modern Art, San Francisco, 13 Dec. 2003 – 23 May 2004; *In Limbo*, Victoria H. Myhren Gallery, Denver University, Denver, 13 Jan. – 11 Mar. 2005.

LITERATURE: Myers, *Artext*, 1998, p. 84 illus.; Rinder & Crowley 1999, pp. 7–8, pl. 5 illus.; Grynsztejn 2003, p. 95 illus.; Bastian (ed.) 2005, pp. 74, 65 illus.; Chanzit 2005, pp. 40, 41 illus.; Clair, *Art Press*, 2005, p. 12 illus.; Rosenblum 2005, pp. 63, 59 & 110 illus.; Mueck et al. 2008, p. 37 illus.

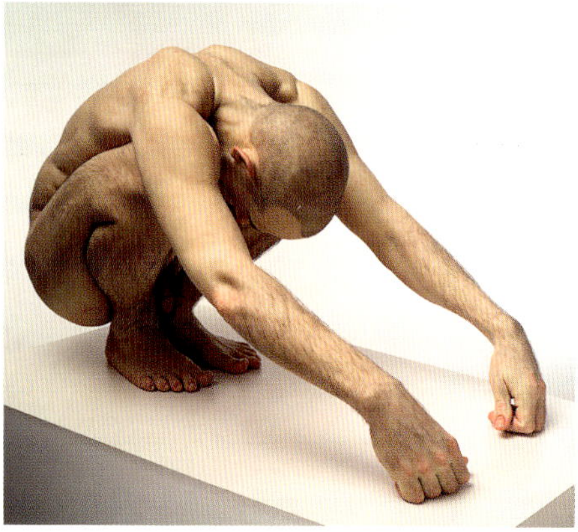

Shaved head 1998
silicone, polyurethane, aluminium wire, synthetic hair, ed. 1/1
49.5 × 36.7 × 83.8 cm
Hoffman Collection, Berlin

EXHIBITIONS: *La Biennale di Venezia, 49: Esposizione Internazionale d'Arte: Platea dell'Umanità/Plateau of Humankind*, Corderie, Venice, 10 Jun. – 4 Nov. 2001; *Ron Mueck: Hyperreal*, Nationalgalerie im Hamburger Bahnhof, Museum für Gegenwart, Berlin, 10 Sep. – 2 Nov. 2003.

LITERATURE: Szeemann & Liveriero Lavelli (eds) 2001, p. 108 illus.; Acret, *ART AsiaPacific*, 2002, p. 20; Greeves & Wiggins 2003, pp. 49, 48 illus.; Nungesser, *Kunstforum International*, 2003, p. 265; Bastian (ed.) 2005, pp. 32–3, 58, 31 & 74 illus., 85 illus. (work in progress); Rosenblum 2005, pp. 111, 56–7 illus.; Raine, *Guardian*, 2006, p. 12; Greeves & Raine 2007, p. 73, 19, 61 illus.; Mueck et al. 2008, p. 68, 41 illus.

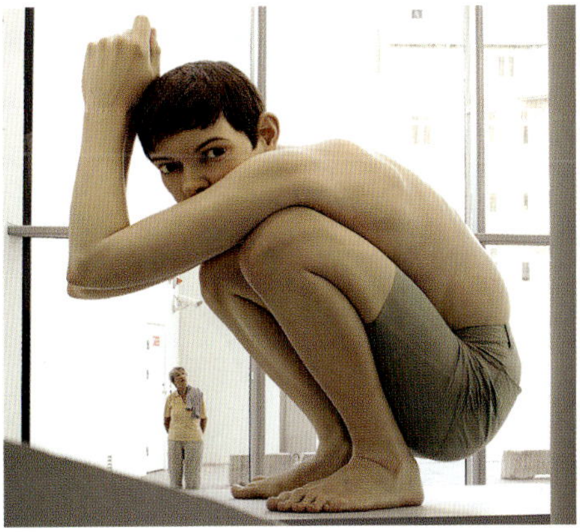

Boy **1999**
polyester resin, fibreglass, wood, steel cotton, ed. 1/1
490.0 × 490.0 × 240.0 cm
Aarhus Kunstmuseum, Denmark

EXHIBITIONS: *The Mind Zone*, Millennium Dome, London, 2000; *La Biennale di Venezia, 49: Esposizione Internazionale d'Arte: Platea dell'Umanità/Plateau of Humankind*, Corderie, Venice, 10 Jun. – 4 Nov. 2001.

LITERATURE: *Artforum International*, vol. 40, no. 1, 2001, cover illus.; Ingram, *Australian Financial Review*, 2001, p. 39; Leffingwell, *Art in America*, 2001, pp. 144; Mueck 2001, unpaginated illus. (work in progress); Naylor, *Art Monthly Australia*, 2001, p. 7 illus; Cocks et al., *Art Newspaper*, 2001, pp. 40, 41 illus.; Wilson in Szeemann & Liveriero Lavelli (eds) 2001, pp. 106, 107 illus.; Withers, *C: International Contemporary Art*, 2001, p. 22 illus. (detail); Acret, *ART AsiaPacific*, 2002, p. 20; Bruce, *Art & Australia*, 2002, p. 376; Herd, *Weekend Australian*, 2002, p. 12; Ingram, *Australian Financial Review*, 2002, p. 12 illus.; Lawrence 2002, unpaginated illus.; Morgan, Joyce, *Sydney Morning Herald*, 2002, p. 17; Pearlman, *Sydney Morning Herald*, 2002, p. 4; Sorensen, *Courier Mail*, 2002, p. 7; Usher, *Age*, 2002, p. 1; Baldissera 2003, p. 15; Greeves & Wiggins 2003, p. 49 illus.; Hill, *Sydney Morning Herald*, 2003, p. 23; Leydier, *Art Press*, 2003, p. 28; Nungesser, *Kunstforum International*, 2003, p. 263; Pietsch, *Art*, 2003, pp. 62–5 illus.; Théberge 2003, p. 56; Chapman, *Artlook*, 2004, p. 9; Kennedy, *Antiques and Art in New South Wales*, 2004, p. 11; Musa, *Canberra Times*, 2004, p. 3; Banks, *West Australian*, 2005, p. 14 illus.; Bastian (ed.) 2005, pp. 32, 8, 75 & 84 illus.; Clair, *Art Press*, 2005, pp. 13, 15; Clair 2005, p. 492; Rosenblum 2005, p. 111 illus.; Davies, Telegraph.co.uk, 2006; Farine, 'Ron Mueck: corps surhumains', *L'Oeil*, 2006, p. 62; Hill, *Art & Australia*, 2007, p. 245 illus.; Grosenick (ed.) 2008, p. 198; Heartney 2008, p. 201; Lindsay & Gott 2008, p. 2; Mueck et al. 2008, pp. 46–7 illus.

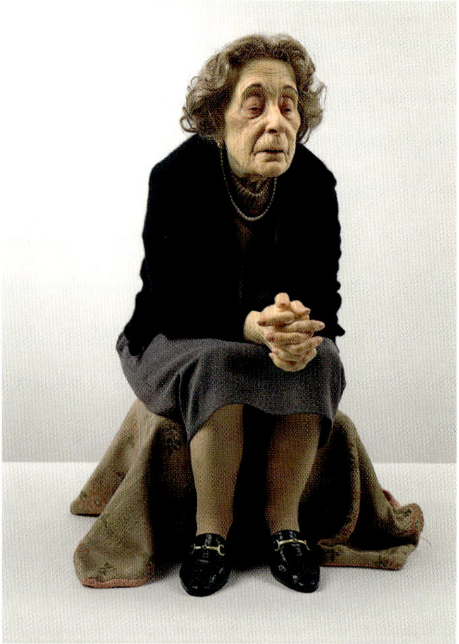

Seated woman 1999
polyester resin, fibreglass, silicone, polyurethane, aluminium wire, synthetic hair, fabric, leather, brass, costume jewellery, ed. 1/1
64.1 × 43.2 × 41.9 cm (overall)
Modern Art Museum of Fort Worth, Texas
Purchased, 2000

Seated woman 2000
polyester resin, fibreglass, silicone, polyurethane, aluminium wire, synthetic hair, fabric, leather, brass, costume jewellery, second edition, artist's proof
58.6 × 43.8 × 47.0 cm (overall)
The Broad Art Foundation, Santa Monica

EXHIBITIONS: *House of Sculpture*, Modern Art Museum of Fort Worth, Texas, 23 May – 8 Aug. 1999; touring: Museo de Arte Contemporáneo de Monterrey, Monterrey, Mexico, 19 Nov. 1999 – 20 Feb. 2000 (ed. 1/1); *Extra Ordinary*, James Cohan Gallery, New York, 18 May – 30 Jun. 2000 (ed. 1/1); *Ron Mueck: Hyperreal*, Nationalgalerie im Hamburger Bahnhof, Museum für Gegenwart, Berlin, 10 Sep. – 2 Nov. 2003 (A/P); *Ron Mueck*, Frans Hals Museum, De Hallen, Haarlem, 15 Nov. 2003 – 18 Jan. 2004 (A/P); *Ron Mueck*, Modern Art Museum of Fort Worth, Texas, 24 Jun. – 21 Oct. 2007 (ed. 1/1); *Real Life/La Vraie Vie: Ron Mueck and Guy Ben-Ner*, La Cité de l'Energie, Shawinigan, Quebec, 21 Jun. – 28 Sep. 2008 (ed. 1/1).

LITERATURE: National Museum of Modern Art, Tokyo 2002, p. 68 illus.; Greeves & Wiggins 2003, pp. 53, 59, 52 illus.; Leydier *Art Press*, 2003, p. 28; Nungesser, *Kunstforum International*, 2003, p. 264; Pietsch *Art*, 2003, p. 56 illus.; Bastian (ed.) 2005, pp. 33, 38–9, 35, 57, 75 illus.; Rosenblum 2005, p. 64, 69 & 111 illus.; Hartley 2006, p. 8; Shaughnessy 2008, p. 10 illus.

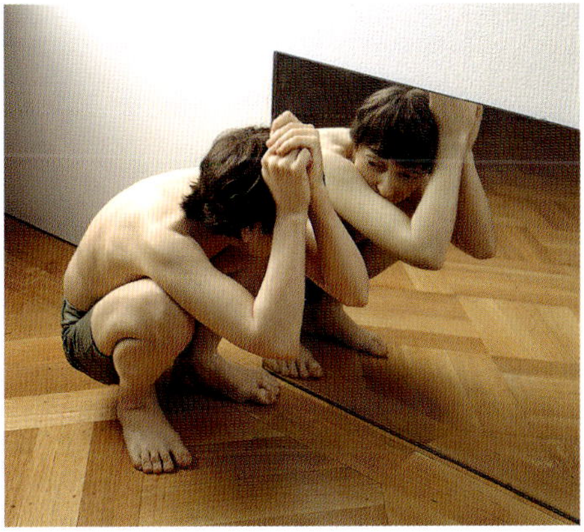

Crouching boy in mirror 1999–2002
polyester resin, fibreglass, synthetic hair, fabric, mirror, ed. 1/1
43.2 × 45.7 × 28 cm (figure);
45.7 × 55.9 × 0.6 cm (mirror)
The Broad Art Foundation, Santa Monica

EXHIBITIONS: *Ron Mueck: Sculpture*, Museum of Contemporary Art, Sydney, 19 Dec. 2002 – 2 Mar. 2003; *Ron Mueck: Hyperreal*, National-galerie im Hamburger Bahnhof, Museum für Gegenwart, Berlin, 10 Sep. – 2 Nov. 2003; *Ron Mueck*, Brooklyn Museum, New York, 3 Nov. 2006 – 4 Feb. 2007.

LITERATURE: James, *Sydney Morning Herald*, 1 January 2003, p. 18; Nungesser, *Kunstforum International*, 2003, pp. 263–4; Bastian (ed.) 2005, pp. 62, 63, 81, 85 cover illus.; Rosenblum 2005, pp. 58, 113, 48–9 illus.; Castro, *Sculpture*, 2007, p. 64.

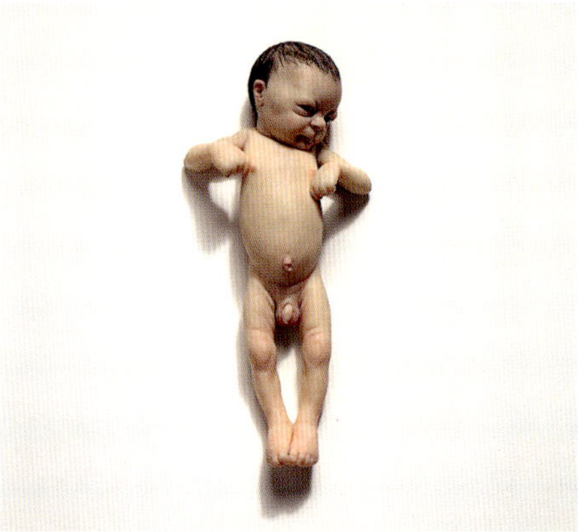

Baby 2000
polyester resin, fibreglass, synthetic hair, ed. 1/1
26.0 × 12.1 × 5.3 cm
Private collection, New York

Baby 2000
polyester resin, fibreglass, synthetic hair,
second edition, artist's proof
26.0 × 12.1 × 5.3 cm
Collection of Keith and Kathy Sachs, Philadelphia

Untitled (Baby) 2001
dental plaster, edition of 10
25.4 × 12.1 × 7 cm
Various collections

EXHIBITIONS: *Ron Mueck*, Anthony d'Offay, London, 15 Sep. – 9 Dec. 2000 (A/P); *La Biennale di Venezia, 49: Esposizione Internazionale d'Arte: Platea dell'Umanità/ Plateau of Humankind*, Corderie, Venice, 10 Jun. – 4 Nov. 2001 (A/P); *Directions: Ron Mueck*, Hirshhorn Museum and Sculpture Garden, Smithsonian Institution, Washington DC, 18 Jul. – 27 Oct. 2002 (ed. 1/1); *Face Off*, Robert Feldman Gallery, New York, 23 Oct. – 27 Nov. 2004 (A/P); *Ron Mueck*, Scottish National Gallery of Modern Art, Royal Scottish Academy Building, Edinburgh, 5 Aug. – 8 Oct. 2006 (A/P); touring: Modern Art Museum of Fort Worth, Texas, 24 Jun.–21 Oct. 2007 (A/P).

LITERATURE: Raine, *Areté*, 2000, pp. 117–18; Szeemann & Liveriero Lavelli (eds) 2001, p. 109 illus.; Acret, *ART AsiaPacific*, 2002, p. 20; Lawrence 2002, unpaginated illus.; National Museum of Modern Art, Tokyo 2002, p. 66 illus.; Greeves & Wiggins 2003, p. 41; Tanguay, *Sculpture*, 2003, p. 33 illus; Bastian (ed.) 2005, pp. 66, 77 illus.; Clair, *Art Press*, 2005, p. 15; Rosenblum 2005, pp. 58, 52 illus.; Greeves & Raine 2007, pp. 76, 28, 63 illus.; Mueck et al., 2008, p. 18 illus.

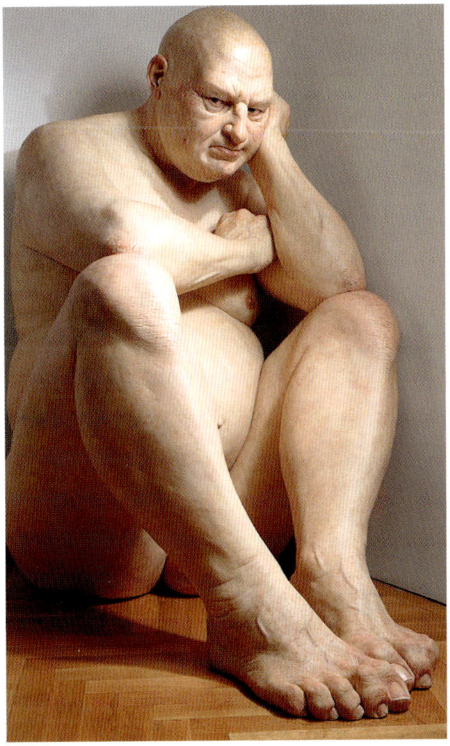

Big man 2000
polyester resin, fibreglass, ed. 1/1
205.7 × 117.4 × 209.0 cm
Hirshhorn Museum and Sculpture Garden, Smithsonian Institution, Washington DC
Museum purchase with funds provided by the Joseph H. Hirshhorn Bequest and in honor of Robert Lehrman, Chairman of the Board of Trustees, 1997–2004, for his extraordinary leadership and unstinting service to the Hirshhorn Museum and Sculpture Garden, 2001 (01.4)

EXHIBITIONS: *Ron Mueck*, Anthony d'Offay, London, 15 Sep. – 9 Dec. 2000; *Directions: Ron Mueck*, Hirshhorn Museum and Sculpture Garden, Smithsonian Institution, Washington DC, 18 Jul. – 27 Oct. 2002; *Ron Mueck*, Frans Hals Museum, De Hallen, Haarlem, 15 Nov. 2003 – 18 Jan. 2004; *Bodily Space: New Obsessions in Figurative Sculpture*, Albright-Knox Art Gallery, Buffalo, New York, 20 Apr. – 7 Sep. 2004; *Mélancolie: Genie et Folie en Occident*, Galeries Nationals du Grand Palais, Paris, 10 Oct. 2005 – 16 Jan. 2006; touring: Neue Nationalgalerie, Berlin, 17 Feb. – 7 May 2006; *Ron Mueck*, Brooklyn Museum, New York, 3 Nov. 2006 – 4 Feb. 2007; touring: National Gallery of Canada, Ottawa, 2 Mar. – 6 May 2007; Modern Art Museum of Fort Worth, Texas, 24 Jun. – 21 Oct. 2007.

LITERATURE: Raine, *Areté*, 2000, pp. 120–1; Wilson in Szeemann & Liveriero Lavelli (eds) 2001, p. 106; Lawrence 2002, unpaginated illus.; National Museum of Modern Art, Tokyo 2002, p. 69 illus.; Smith, *New York Times*, 2002, p. 27; Greeves & Wiggins 2003, pp. 41, 49, 51, 50 illus.; Leydier, *Art Press*, 2003, pp. 28, 25 illus.; Pietsch, *Art*, 2003, p. 60 illus; Tanguay, *Sculpture*, 2003, pp. 29–33, 30–1 illus. (work in progress); Bastian (ed.)

2005, pp. 32–3, 39, 19, 77 illus.; Clair 2005, pp. 492, 451 & 492 illus.; Clair, *Art Press*, 2005, p. 13; Clair & Leydier, *Art Press*, 2005, p. 25 illus.; Rosenblum 2005, pp. 63, 71–2, 73, 111 illus.; Frèrot, *Art Nexus*, 2006, p. 104 illus.; Hartley 2006, p. 8; Raine, *Guardian*, 2006, p. 12; Greeves & Raine 2007, pp. 73, 20 & 63 illus.; Hill, *Art & Australia*, 2007, p. 249 illus.; Johnson, *Art & Australia*, 2007, p. 612; Prieto, *Arte y Parte*, 2007, p. 95; Spaid, *ArtUS*, 2007, p. 59 illus.; Lindsay & Gott 2008, p. 5; Mueck et al. 2008, p. 25 illus.

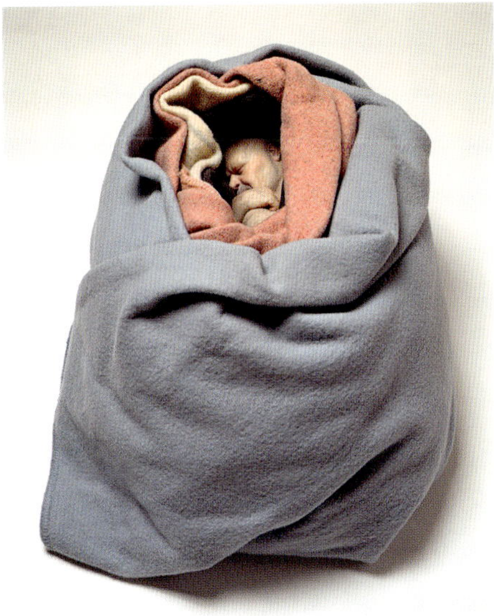

Man in blankets 2000
polyester resin, fibreglass, polyurethane, synthetic hair, wool, ed. 1/1
43.1 × 59.7 × 71.2 cm
Hoffman Collection, Dallas

Man in blankets 2001
polyester resin, fibreglass, polyurethane, synthetic hair, wool, second edition, artist's proof
43.1 x 59.7 x 71.2 cm
Kunstsammlung Nordrhein-Westfalen, Dusseldorf
Sammlung Ackermans, 2005

EXHIBITIONS: *Ron Mueck*, Anthony d'Offay, London, 5 Sep. – 9 Dec. 2000 (ed. 1/1); *Startkapital*, K21 Kunstsammlung Nordrhein-Westfalen, Dusseldorf, 18 Apr. 2002 – 27 Apr. 2003 (A/P); *Ron Mueck*, Frans Hals Museum, De Hallen, Haarlem, 15 Nov. 2003 – 18 Jan. 2004 (ed. 1/1); *Collection 2005*, K21 Kunstsammlung Nordrhein-Westfalen, Dusseldorf, 2 Jul. – 18 Sep. 2005 (A/P); *Ron Mueck*, Modern Art Museum of Fort Worth, Texas, 24 Jun. – 21 Oct. 2007 (ed. 1/1)

LITERATURE: Raine, *Areté*, 2000, pp. 119–20; Reust in Heynen (ed.) 2000, pp. 142, 31 & 119 illus.; Wilson in Szeemann & Liveriero Lavelli (eds) 2001, p. 106; National Museum of Modern Art, Tokyo 2002, p. 72 illus.; Greeves & Wiggins 2003, pp. 41, 56, 58, 57 illus.; Bastian (ed.) 2005, pp. 62, 47, 76, 78 illus.; Rosenblum 2005, pp. 63, 64 & 110 illus.; Spaid, *ArtUS*, 2007, p. 59; Mueck et al. 2008, p. 19 illus.

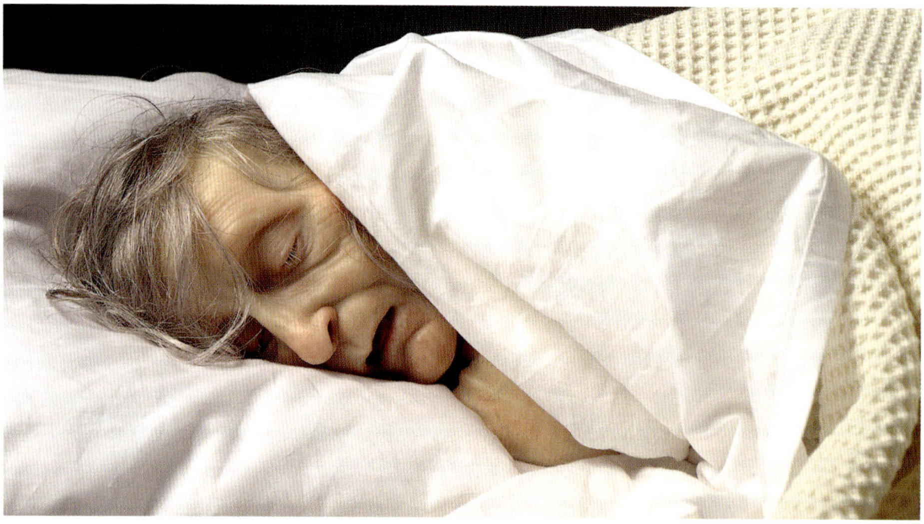

Old woman in bed 2000
polyester resin, fibreglass, silicone, polyurethane, synthetic hair, cotton, polyester, ed. 1/1
24.0 × 94.5 × 56.0 cm
National Gallery of Canada, Ottawa
Purchased, 2001 (40632)

Old woman in bed 2002
polyester resin, fibreglass, silicone, polyurethane, synthetic hair, cotton, polyester, second edition, artist's proof
25.4 × 94.0 × 53.9 cm
Art Gallery of New South Wales, Sydney
Purchased, 2003 (9.2003)

pp. 42, 44

EXHIBITIONS: *Ron Mueck*, Anthony d'Offay, London, 15 Sep. – 9 Dec. 2000 (ed. 1/1); *Directions: Ron Mueck*, Hirshhorn Museum and Sculpture Garden, Smithsonian Institution, Washington DC, 18 Jul. – 27 Oct. 2002 (ed. 1/1); *Ron Mueck, Sculpture,* Museum of Contemporary Art, Sydney, 19 Dec. 2002 – 2 Mar. 2003 (A/P); *Le Corps Transformé*, La Cité de l'Energie, Shawinigan, Quebec, 19 Jun. – 15 Oct. 2003 (ed. 1/1); *Ron Mueck: Hyperreal*, Nationalgalerie im Hamburger Bahnhof, Museum für Gegenwart, Berlin, 10 Sep. – 2 Nov. 2003 (A/P); *Ron Mueck*, Frans Hals Museum, De Hallen, Haarlem, 15 Nov. 2003 – 18 Jan. 2004 (A/P); *Silver:*

Dreams, Screens and Theories, Art Gallery of Greater Victoria, Canada, 28 Nov. 2003 – 8 Feb. 2004 (ed. 1/1); *In Bed: Images from a Vital Stage*, Toyota Municipal Museum of Art, Toyota City, Japan, 5 Oct. – 26 Dec. 2004 (ed. 1/1); *De Overkant/ Downunder: Den Haag Sculptuur 07*, Escher in het Paleis, The Hague, 1 Jun. – 9 Sep. 2007 (A/P); *Ron Mueck*, National Gallery of Canada, Ottawa, 2 Mar. – 6 May 2007 (ed. 1/1); touring: Modern Art Museum of Fort Worth, Texas, 24 Jun. – 21 Oct. 2007 (ed. 1/1); *Real Life/La Vraie Vie: Ron Mueck and Guy Ben-Ner*, La Cité de l'Energie, Shawinigan, Quebec, 21 Jun. – 28 Sep. 2008 (ed. 1/1); *Great Collections*, touring (Australia); Campbelltown Arts Centre, 12 Dec. 2008 – 18 Jan. 2009; Tweed River Art Gallery, 6 Feb. – 15 Mar. 2009; Western Plains Cultural Centre, 3 Apr. – 10 May 2009; Albury Library Museum and Albury Regional Gallery, 29 May – 6 Jul.; Ballarat Fine Art Gallery, 24 Jul. – 30 Aug. 2009 (A/P).

LITERATURE: Raine, *Areté*, 2000, p. 121; Lawrence 2002, unpaginated illus.; Clement, *Artlink*, 2003, pp. 57, 55 illus.; Greeves & Wiggins 2003, pp. 41, 58 illus.; Hill, *Sydney Morning Herald*, 2003, p. 23; Leydier, *Art Press*, 2003, p. 26 illus.; McDonald, *Australian Financial Review*, 2003, p. 48 illus.; Nungesser, *Kunstforum International*, 2003, p. 264; Théberge 2003, pp. 56, 57 illus.; Aoki et al. 2004, p. 104 illus.; Baldissera 2004, pp. 15, 36–7 illus.; Chapman, *Artlook*, 2004, p. 9; Banks, *West Australian*, 2005, p. 14 illus; Bastian (ed.) 2005, pp. 39, 62, 21, 36, 76, 79 illus.; Rosenblum 2005, p. 64, 111, 74–5 illus.; *Den Haag Sculptuur 2007*, 2007, pp. 151–3, 150 illus.; McPhee, 2008, p. 120 illus.; Mueck et al. 2008, p. 20 illus.; Shaughnessy 2008, pp. 18, 10–11 illus.

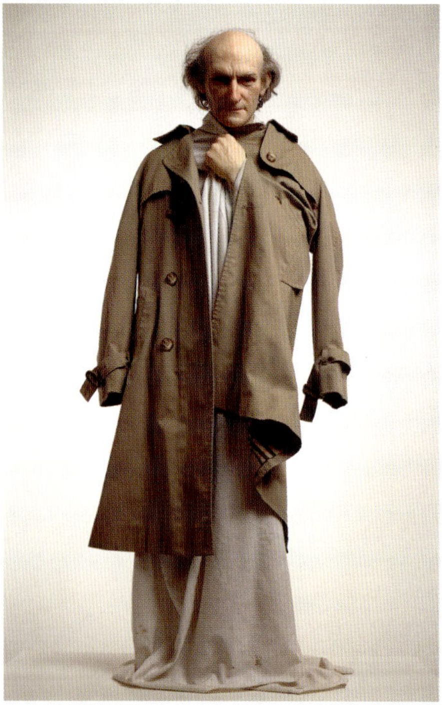

EXHIBITIONS: *Heavenly Creatures: Paula Rego and Ron Mueck*, British School at Rome, Rome, 10 Oct. – 15 Nov. 2002; *Eretica*, The Sant'Anna la Misericordia Complex, Palermo, 1 Aug. – 15 Sep. 2006.

LITERATURE: Leydier, *Art Press*, 2003, p. 3 illus.; Bastian (ed.) 2005, pp. 59, 76 illus.; Rosenblum 2005, pp. 47, 110 illus.; Mueck et al. 2008, p. 23 illus.

Standing man 2000
silicone, wood, aluminium, synthetic hair, wool, cotton, ed. 1/1
116.8 × 50.8 × 38.1 cm
Private collection, Milan

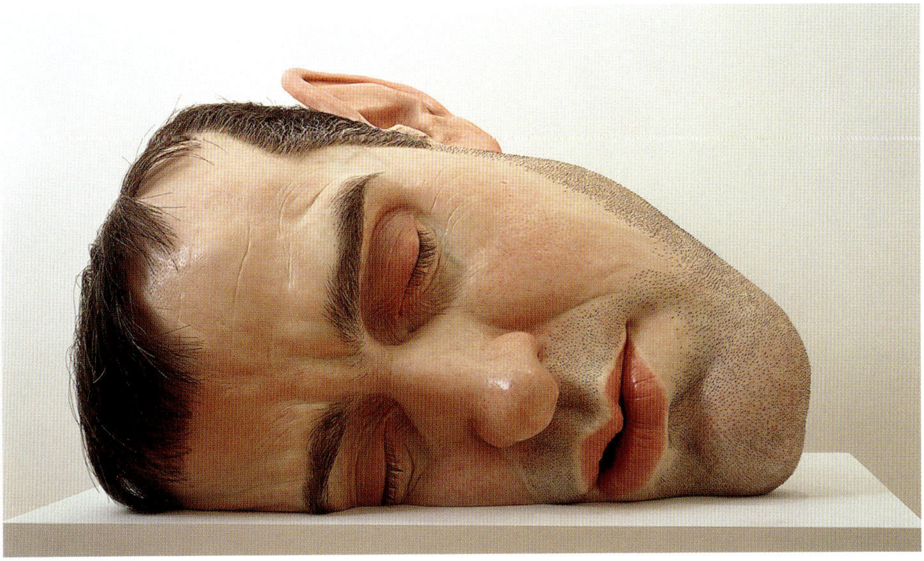

Mask II 2001
polyester resin, fibreglass, steel, plywood, synthetic hair, ed. 1/1
77.2 × 118.1 × 85.1 cm
San Francisco Museum of Modern Art, California
The Art Supporting Foundation to SFMOMA

Mask II 2002
polyester resin, fibreglass, steel, plywood, synthetic hair, second edition, artist's proof
77.0 × 118.0 × 85.0 cm
Private collection

pp. 48, 50, 52

EXHIBITIONS: *Ron Mueck*, James Cohan Gallery, New York, 12 May – 16 Jun. 2001 (ed. 1/1); *Directions: Ron Mueck*, Hirshhorn Museum and Sculpture Garden, Smithsonian Institution, Washington DC, 18 Jul. – 27 Oct. 2002 (A/P); *Ron Mueck: Sculpture*, Museum of Contemporary Art, Sydney, 19 Dec. 2002 – 2 Mar. 2003 (A/P); *Ron Mueck: Hyperreal*, Nationalgalerie im Hamburger Bahnhof, Museum für Gegenwart, Berlin, 10 Sep. – 2 Nov. 2003 (A/P); *Ron Mueck*, Frans Hals Museum, De Hallen, Haarlem, 15 Nov. 2003 – 18 Jan. 2004 (A/P); *In Bed: Images from a Vital*

Stage, Toyota Municipal Museum of Art, Toyota City, Japan, 5 Oct. –26 Dec. 2004 (A/P); *Ron Mueck*, Scottish National Gallery of Modern Art, Royal Scottish Academy Building, Edinburgh, 5 Aug. – 8 Oct. 2006 (A/P): touring: Brooklyn Museum, New York, 3 Nov. 2006 – 4 Feb. 2007 (ed. 1/1); National Gallery of Canada, Ottawa, 2 Mar. – 6 May 2007 (ed. 1/1); Modern Art Museum of Fort Worth, Texas, 24 Jun. – 21 Oct. 2007 (ed. 1/1); Andy Warhol Museum, Pittsburgh, 13 Dec. 2007 – 30 Mar. 2008 (A/P); 21st Century Museum of Contemporary Art, Kanazawa, 26 Apr. – 31 Aug. 2008 (A/P); *Statuephilia: Contemporary Sculptors at the British Museum*, British Museum, London, 4 Oct. 2008 – 25 Jan. 2009 (A/P); *ARTIST ROOMS: Ron Mueck*, Aberdeen Art Gallery and Museums, Aberdeen, 29 Aug. – 31 Oct. 2009 (A/P).

LITERATURE: Amy, *Sculpture*, 2001, pp. 73, 72 illus.; Leffingwell, *Art in America*, 2001, p. 144; Morgan, Robert, *Art Press*, 2001, p. 68; Saltz, *Village Voice*, 2001, p. 61 illus.; Herd, *Weekend Australian*, 2002, pp. 12, 13 illus.; Lawrence 2002, unpaginated illus.; Smith, *New York Times*, 2002, p. 27 illus.; Sorensen, *Courier Mail*, 2002, p. 7 illus.; James, *Sydney Morning Herald*, 1 January 2003, p. 18; Leydier, *Art Press*, 2003, p. 27 illus.; Nungesser, *Kunstforum International*, 2003, p. 264; Pietsch, *Art*, 2003, pp. 54–5 illus.; Adams 2004, p. 549 illus.; Bastian (ed.) 2005, pp. 41, 79, 80 (all illus.); Rosenblum 2005, pp. 112, 44–5 illus.; Hartley 2006, p. 11, pl. 4 illus.; Raine, *Guardian*, 2006, p. 12; Grosenick (ed.) 2008, pp. 198, 200 illus.; Massier, *Art Papers*, 2008, p. 71; Mueck et al. 2008, pp. 80–1, 11 illus.

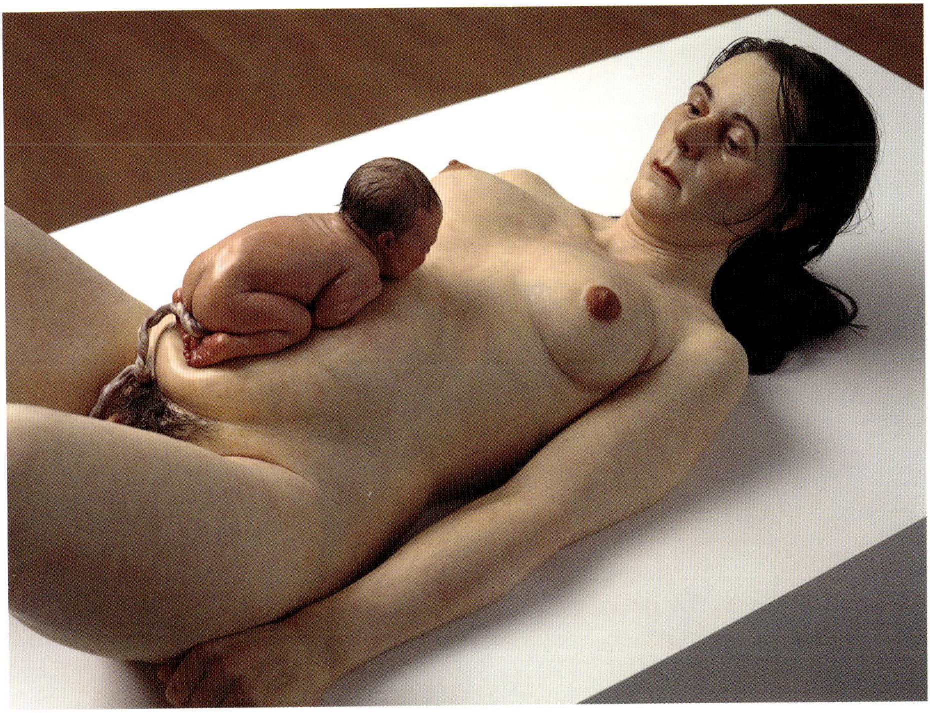

Mother and child 2001
polyester resin, fibreglass, silicone, synthetic hair, ed. 1/1
24.1 × 88.9 × 38.1 cm
Bayerische Staatsgemaeldesammlungen Munich, Museum Brandhorst, 2001 (UAB 293)

Mother and child 2004
polyester resin, silicone, synthetic hair, second edition, artist's proof
24.0 × 89.0 × 38.0 cm
Collection of Robert Lehrman

EXHIBITIONS: *Ron Mueck*, James Cohan Gallery, New York, 12 May – 16 Jun. 2001 (ed. 1/1); *Ron Mueck: Sculpture*, Museum of Contemporary Art, Sydney, 19 Dec. 2002 – 2 Mar. 2003 (ed. 1/1); *Ron Mueck: Making Sculpture at the National Gallery*, National Gallery, London, 19 Mar. – 22 Jun. 2003 (ed. 1/1); *Ron Mueck: Hyperreal*, Nationalgalerie im Hamburger Bahnhof, Museum für Gegenwart, Berlin,

10 Sep. – 2 Nov. 2003 (ed. 1/1); *Ron Mueck*, Frans Hals Museum, De Hallen, Haarlem, Netherlands, 15 Nov. 2003 – 18 Jan. 2004 (ed. 1/1); *Getting Emotional*, Institute of Contemporary Art, Boston, 18 May – 5 Sep. 2005 (A/P); *Real Life/La Vraie Vie: Ron Mueck and Guy Ben-Ner*, La Cité de l'Energie, Shawinigan, Quebec, 21 Jun. – 28 Sep. 2008 (A/P).

LITERATURE: Amy, *Sculpture*, 2001, pp. 72–3; Ingram, *Australian Financial Review*, 2001, p. 39 illus.; Kimmelman, *New York Times*, 2001, p. 34; Leffingwell, *Art in America*, 2001, pp. 144–5; Morgan, Robert, *Art Press*, 2001, p. 68; Saltz, *Village Voice*, 2001, p. 61 illus.; Herd, *Weekend Australian*, 2002, pp. 12, 13 illus.; Morgan, Joyce, *Sydney Morning Herald*, 2002, p. 17; Butler, *Courier Mail*, 2003, p. 1 illus. (detail); Chrisafis, *Guardian*, 2003, p. 13 illus.; Cumming, *Observer Review*, 2003, p. 10; Darwent, *Independent*, 2003, p. 8; Ebony et al. 2003, p. 150 illus.; Greeves & Wiggins 2003, pp. 23–7, 33–6, 24–7 illus. (work in progress), 64 illus.; Hill, *Sydney Morning Herald*, 2003, p. 23; James, *Sydney Morning Herald*, 1 January 2003, p. 18 illus.; Janusczack, *Sunday Times* 2003, pp. 6, 7 illus.; Leydier, *Art Press*, 2003, p. 28 illus.; Martin, *Art & Australia*, 2003, pp. 568–9, 569 illus.; McDonald, *Australian Financial Review*, 2003, p. 48; Pietsch, *Art*, 2003, pp. 64, 65 illus.; Russell Taylor, *Times*, 2003, p. 15; Tanguay, *Sculpture*, 2003, p. 33 illus.; Wiggins, *Art Review*, 2003, p. 92; Chapman, *Artlook*, June 2004, p. 9; Bastian (ed.) 2005, pp. 85, 28 & 78 illus.; Baume 2005, pp. 106-7 illus.; Rosenblum 2005, pp. 54, 58, 76, 111, 66–7 illus.; Hartley 2006, p. 10; Raine, *Guardian*, 2006, p. 12; Greeves & Raine 2007, pp. 74, 76–7, 30 & 63 illus.; Prieto, *Arte y Parte*, 2007, p. 95; Raine in Mueck et al. 2008, pp. 68, 29 illus.; Shaughnessy 2008, p. 4 illus.

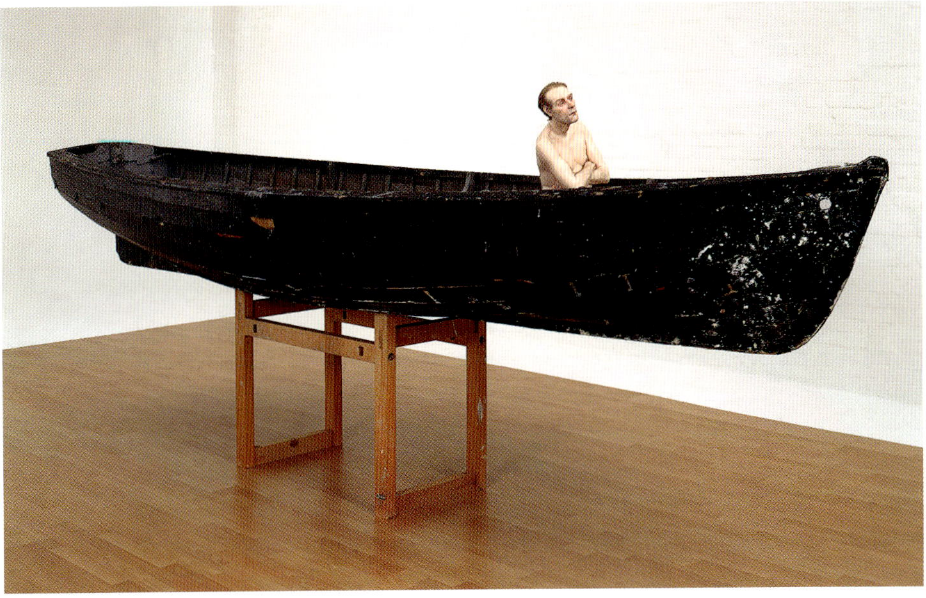

Man in a boat **2002**
silicone, polyurethane, synthetic hair, painted wood, metal, ed. 1/1
75.0 x 35.0 x 32.0 cm (man);
56.0 x 138.0 x 425.5 cm (boat);
76.5 x 53.4 x 100.0 cm (stand);
159.0 x 138.0 x 425.5 cm (overall)
Private collection

pp. 2, 60, 62

EXHIBITIONS: *Ron Mueck: Sculpture*, Museum of Contemporary Art, Sydney, 19 Dec. 2002 – 2 Mar. 2003; *Ron Mueck: Making Sculpture at the National Gallery*, National Gallery, London, 19 Mar. – 22 Jun. 2003; *Ron Mueck: Hyperreal*, Nationalgalerie im Hamburger Bahnhof, Museum für Gegenwart, Berlin, 10 Sep. – 2 Nov. 2003; *Ron Mueck*, Frans Hals Museum, De Hallen, Haarlem, 15 Nov. 2003 – 18 Jan. 2004; *Noah's Ark*, La Cité de l'Energie, Shawinigan, Quebec, 12 Jun. – 3 Oct. 2004; *Ron Mueck*, Scottish National Gallery of Modern Art, Royal

Scottish Academy Building, Edinburgh, 5 Aug. – 8 Oct. 2006; touring: Brooklyn Museum, New York, 3 Nov. 2006 – 4 Feb. 2007; National Gallery of Canada, Ottawa, 2 Mar. – 6 May 2007; Modern Art Museum of Fort Worth, Texas, 24 Jun. – 21 Oct. 2007; Andy Warhol Museum, Pittsburgh, 13 Dec. 2007 – 30 Mar. 2008; 21st Century Museum of Contemporary Art, Kanazawa, 26 Apr. – 31 Aug. 2008; *ARTIST ROOMS: Ron Mueck*, Aberdeen Art Gallery and Museums, Aberdeen, 29 Aug. – 31 Oct. 2009

LITERATURE: Saltz, *Village Voice*, 2001, p. 61 illus.; Herd, *Weekend Australian*, 2002, p. 12 illus. (detail); Clement, *Artlink*, 2003, p. 56 illus.; Cumming, *Observer Review*, 2003, p. 10; Darwent, *Independent*, 2003, p. 8 illus.; Greeves & Wiggins 2003, pp. 27–32, 40, 65, 29–32 illus. (work in progress), unpaginated illus.; James, *Sydney Morning Herald*, 1 January 2003, p. 18 illus.; Martin, *Art & Australia*, 2003, p. 569 illus.; Nungesser, *Kunstforum International*, 2003, pp. 265, 264 illus.; Pietsch, *Art*, 2003, pp. 64, 52–3 illus.; Théberge et al. 2004, pp. 10, 80, 81 & back cover illus.; Bastian (ed.) 2005, pp. 58, 60, 85, 52–3, 55, 79 illus. (detail); Clair, *Art Press*, 2005, pp. 14–5 illus.; Rosenblum 2005, pp. 76, 112, 60–2 illus.; Davies, Telegraph. co.uk, 2006; Farine, 'Ron Mueck: corps surhumains', *L'Oeil*, 2006, p. 63 illus. (detail); Hartley 2006, p. 9, pl. 3 illus.; Macmillan, *Scotsman*, 2006; Amy, *Art in America*, 2007, p. 132; Hill, *Art & Australia*, 2007, pp. 248, 247 illus. (detail); Johnson, *Art & Australia*, 2007, p. 612; Art & Australia 2008, p. 228; Grosenick (ed.) 2008, p. 199 illus.; Lindsay & Gott 2008, p. 2; Massier, *Art Papers*, 2008, p. 71; Mueck et al. 2008, pp. 80, 3–5 illus.

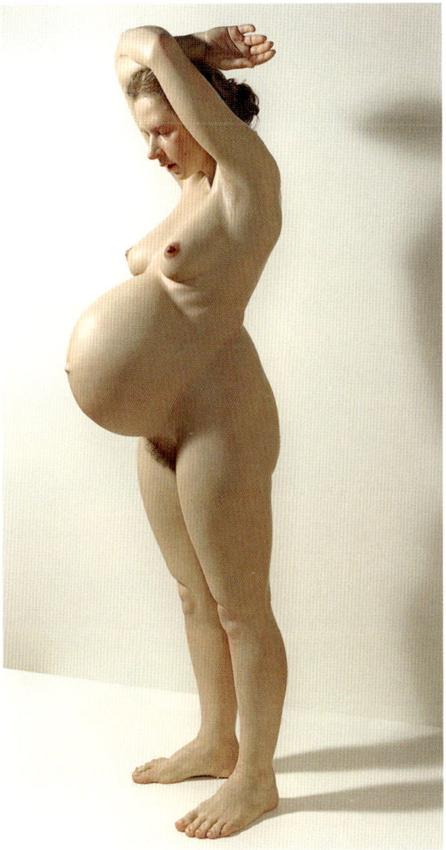

Pregnant woman 2002
polyester resin, fibreglass, silicone, aluminium, synthetic hair, ed. 1/1
252.0 × 73.0 × 68.9 cm
National Gallery of Australia, Canberra
Purchased with the assistance of Tony and Carol Berg, 2003 (NGA 2003.480)

pp. 54, 56, 58

EXHIBITIONS: *Ron Mueck: Sculpture*, Museum of Contemporary Art, Sydney, 19 Dec. 2002 – 2 Mar. 2003; *Ron Mueck: Making Sculpture at the National Gallery*, National Gallery, London, 19 Mar. – 22 Jun. 2003; *Ron Mueck: Hyperreal*, Nationalgalerie im Hamburger Bahnhof, Museum für Gegenwart, Berlin, 10 Sep. – 2 Nov. 2003; *Ron Mueck*, Frans Hals Museum, De Hallen, Haarlem, 15 Nov. 2003 – 18 Jan. 2004; *Ron Mueck: the making of* Pregnant woman *2002*, touring: National Gallery of Victoria, 29 Jan. – 27 Feb. 2005; Queensland Art Gallery, 12 Mar. – 5 Jun. 2005; *Ron Mueck @ McClelland*, McClelland Gallery + Sculpture Park, Langwarrin, 24 Aug. – 2 Nov. 2008.

LITERATURE: Albert, *Weekend Australian*, 2002, p. 9 illus.; Herd, *Weekend Australian*, 2002, p. 12; Moran, *Daily Telegraph*, 2002, p. 18; Joyce Morgan, *Sydney Morning Herald*, 2002, p. 17 illus.; Musa, *Canberra Times*, 2002, p. 1 illus.; Pearlman, *Sydney Morning Herald*, 2002, p. 4 illus. (work in progress); Sorensen, *Courier Mail*, 2002, p. 7 illus.; Usher, *Age*, 2002, p. 1 illus.; Chrisafis, *Guardian*, 2003, p. 13 illus.; Clement, *Artlink*, 2003, p. 54 illus.; Cumming, *Observer Review*, 2003, p. 10; Darwent, *Independent*, 2003, p. 8 illus.; Ebony et al. 2003, p. 151 illus.;

Greeves & Wiggins 2003, pp. 32–6, 34–7 illus. (work in progress), 66 illus.; Grishin, *Art & Australia*, 2003, p. 268; Hill, *Sydney Morning Herald*, 2003, p. 23 illus.; Hill, *Sydney Morning Herald*, 3 January 2003, p. 23 & illus.; James, *Sydney Morning Herald*, 1 January 2003, p. 18; Leydier, *Art Press*, 2003, p. 27 illus.; McDonald, *Australian Financial Review*, 2003, p. 48; Martin, *Art & Australia*, 2003, pp. 569, 568 illus.; Nungesser, *Kunstforum International*, 2003, p. 264; Pietsch, *Art*, 2003, pp. 64, 58–9 illus.; Russell Taylor, *Times*, 2003, p. 15; Tanguay, *Sculpture*, 2003, pp. 29, 32 illus.; Wiggins, *Art Review*, 2003, pp. 92, 93 illus., 94–5 illus. (work in progress); Chapman, *Artlook*, June 2004, pp. 9, 8 illus.; Kennedy, *Antiques and Art in New South Wales*, 2004, p. 11 illus.; Musa, *Canberra Times*, 2004, p. 3 illus.; Nadelman, *ARTnews*, 2004, p. 119 illus.; Banks, *West Australian*, 2005, p. 14 illus.; Bastian (ed.) 2005, pp. 80, 85, 27 illus., back cover illus. (detail); Clair, *Art Press*, 2005, p. 15; Makin, *Herald Sun*, 2005, p. 89 illus. (work in progress); Nelson, *Age*, 2005, p. 8 illus.; Rosenblum 2005, pp. 58, 76, 112 illus.; Raine, *Guardian*, 2006, p. 12; Greeves & Raine 2007, pp. 21, 73–4, 22 & 64 illus.; Prieto, *Arte y Parte*, 2007, p. 95; Art & Australia 2008, p. 228; Grosenick (ed.) 2008, p. 201 illus.; Heartney 2008, p. 201; Lindsay & Gott 2008, pp. 5, 3 illus.; Nelson, *Age*, 2008, p. 22; Raine in Mueck et al. 2008, pp. 68, 27 illus.

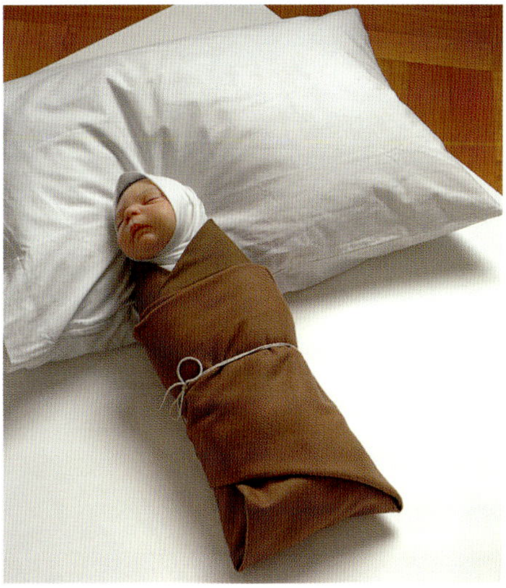

Swaddled baby **2002**
silicone, polyurethane, synthetic hair, wool, twine, ed. 1/1
18.4 × 21.6 × 49.5 cm (figure);
15.2 × 73.7 × 44.5 cm (pillow)
John and Amy Phelan Collection, New York

EXHIBITIONS: *Ron Mueck: Sculpture*, Museum of Contemporary Art, Sydney, 19 Dec. 2002 – 2 Mar. 2003; *Ron Mueck: Making Sculpture at the National Gallery*, National Gallery, London, 19 Mar. – 22 Jun. 2003; *Ron Mueck: Hyperreal*, Nationalgalerie im Hamburger Bahnhof, Museum für Gegenwart, Berlin, 10 Sep.–2 Nov. 2003.

LITERATURE: Herd, *Weekend Australian*, 2002, p. 12; Darwent, *Independent*, 2003, p. 8; Greeves & Wiggins 2003, pp. 37–41, 39–41 illus. (work in progress), 67 illus., unpaginated illus.; Janusczack, *Sunday Times*, 23 March 2003, pp. 6, 7 illus.; Nungesser, *Kunstforum International*, 2003, p. 264 illus.; Pietsch, *Art*, 2003, p. 61 illus.; Russell Taylor, *Times*, 2003, p. 15 illus.; Tanguay, *Sculpture*, 2003, p. 33 illus.; Bastian (ed.) 2005, pp. 62, 81, 49 illus.; Rosenblum 2005, pp. 58, 76, 113 illus.; Greeves & Raine 2007, pp. 77, 32 & 65 illus.

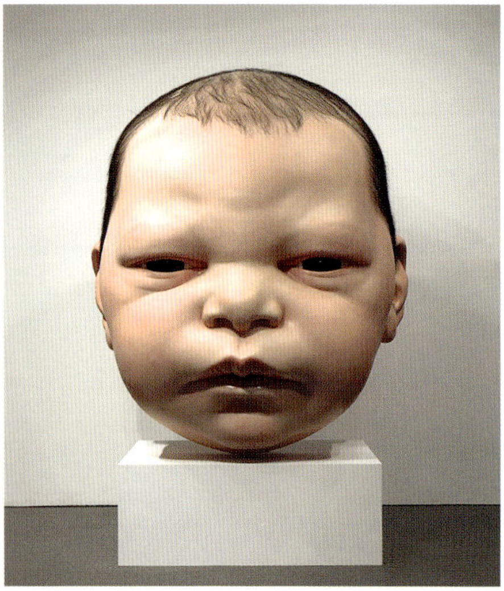

Head of a baby 2003
polyester resin, fibreglass, wood,
synthetic hair, wood, ed. 1/1
254.0 × 219.0 × 238.0 cm
National Gallery of Canada, Ottawa
Purchased, 2003 (41269)

EXHIBITIONS: *Le Corps Transformé*, La Cité de l'Energie, Shawinigan, Quebec, 19 Jun. – 15 Oct. 2003; *Real Life/La Vraie Vie: Ron Mueck and Guy Ben-Ner*, La Cité de l'Energie, Shawinigan, Quebec, 21 Jun. – 28 Sep. 2008.

LITERATURE: Théberge 2003, pp. 58–9 illus. (work in progress); Bastian (ed.) 2005, pp. 82, 68 illus.; Rosenblum 2005, pp. 113, 51 illus.; Greeves & Raine 2007, pp. 77, 65 illus.; Shaughnessy 2008, pp. 18, 13 illus.

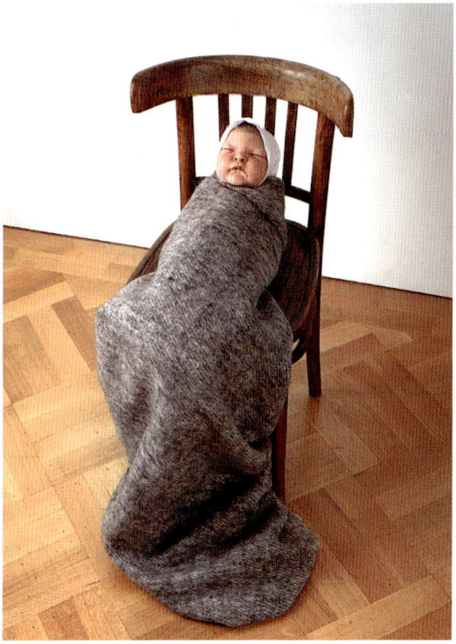

Baby on a chair 2004
silicone, polyurethane, synthetic hair, wood, fabric, cotton, ed. 1/1
18.4 × 21.6 × 49.5 cm (figure);
77.0 × 36.0 × 52.0 cm (overall)
Collection Glenn Fuhrman, New York

EXHIBITIONS: *Ron Mueck*, National Gallery of Canada, Ottawa, 2 Mar. – 6 May 2007.

LITERATURE: Bastian (ed.) 2005, pp. 82, 67 illus.; Rosenblum 2005, pp. 112, 70 illus.; Greeves & Raine 2007, pp. 77, 65 illus.; Mueck et al. 2008, p. 45 illus.

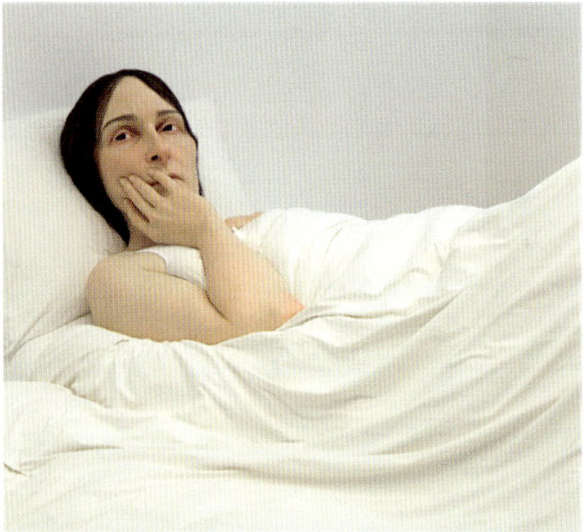

In bed 2005
polyester resin, fibreglass, polyurethane, horse hair, cotton, ed. 1/1
161.9 × 649.9 × 395.0 cm
Queensland Art Gallery, Brisbane
Purchased, Queensland Art Gallery Foundation, 2008 (2008.040)

pp. 26, 66, 68, 70

In bed 2005
polyester resin, fibreglass, polyurethane, horse hair, cotton, second edition, artist's proof
162.0 × 650.0 × 395.0 cm
Fondation Cartier, Paris
Purchased, 2006

EXHIBITIONS: *Ron Mueck*, Fondation Cartier pour l'Art Contemporain, Paris, 19 Nov. 2005 – 19 Feb. 2006 (A/P); touring: Scottish National Gallery of Modern Art, Royal Scottish Academy Building, Edinburgh, 5 Aug. – 8 Oct. 2006 (ed. 1/1); Brooklyn Museum, New York, 3 Nov. 2006 – 4 Feb. 2007 (ed. 1/1); National Gallery of Canada, Ottawa, 2 Mar. – 6 May 2007; Modern Art Museum of Fort Worth, Texas, 24 Jun. – 21 Oct. 2007 (ed. 1/1); Andy Warhol Museum, Pittsburgh, 13 Dec. 2007 – 30 Mar. 2008 (ed. 1/1); 21st Century Museum of Contemporary Art, Kanazawa, 26 Apr. – 31 Aug. 2008, (ed. 1/1); *Collection of the Fondation Cartier pour l'Art Contemporain at MOT Tokyo*, Tokyo Museum of Contemporary Art, Tokyo, 22 Apr. – 2 Jul. 2006 (A/P); *Real Life/La Vraie Vie: Ron Mueck and Guy Ben-Ner*, La Cité de l'Energie, Shawinigan, Quebec, 21 Jun. – 28 Sep. 2008 (A/P).

LITERATURE: Rosenblum 2005, pp. 89–90 illus. (work in progress), 23–30 & 113 illus., cover illus.; Davies, Telegraph.co.uk, 2006; Farine, 'Ron Mueck: corps surhumains', *L'Oeil*, 2006, p. 62 illus.; Hartley 2006, pp. 8–9, pl. 7 illus., p. 44 illus. (work in progress); Jones, *Guardian*, 2006, p. 22; Jones, *Guardian Weekly*, 2006, p. 21; Macmillan, *Scotsman*, 2006; Amy, *Art in America*, 2007, p. 132 illus.; Castro, *Sculpture*, 2007, p. 64; Hill, *Art & Australia*, 2007, pp. 247, 246 illus. (work in progress); Spaid, *ArtUS*, 2007, p. 59; Chambers, *Art Lines*, 2008, p. 23 illus.; Massier, *Art Papers*, 2008, p. 71 illus.; Mueck et al. 2008, pp. 79, 81, 6–7 illus.; Shaughnessy 2008, p. 9 & cover illus.

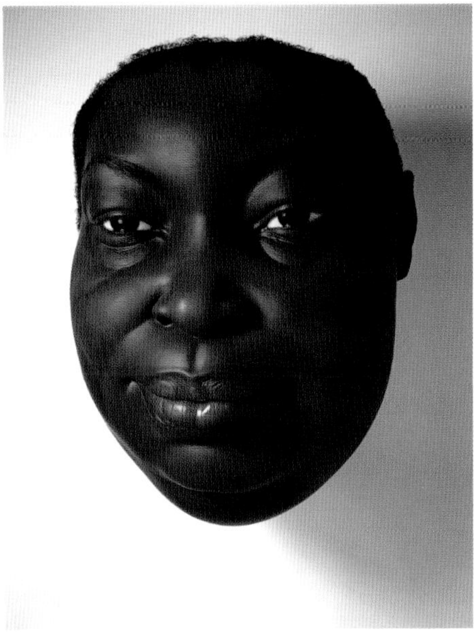

Mask III 2005
polyester resin, fibreglass, synthetic hair, synthetic polymer paint, ed. 1/1
155.0 × 132.0 × 113.0 cm
ARTIST ROOMS National Galleries of Scotland and Tate acquired jointly through The d'Offay Donation with assistance from the National Heritage Memorial Fund and The Art Fund, 2008 (AR00035)

EXHIBITIONS: *Ron Mueck*, Fondation Cartier pour l'Art Contemporain, Paris, 19 Nov. 2005 – 19 Feb. 2006; touring: Scottish National Gallery of Modern Art, Royal Scottish Academy Building, Edinburgh, 5 Aug. – 8 Oct. 2006; Brooklyn Museum, New York, 3 Nov. 2006 – 4 Feb. 2007; National Gallery of Canada, Ottawa, 2 Mar. – 6 May 2007; Modern Art Museum of Fort Worth, Texas, 24 Jun. – 21 Oct. 2007; Andy Warhol Museum, Pittsburgh, 13 Dec. 2007 – 30 Mar. 2008; 21st Century Museum of Contemporary Art, Kanazawa, 26 Apr. – 31 Aug. 2008; *ARTIST ROOMS: Ron Mueck*, Aberdeen Art Gallery and Museums, Aberdeen, 29 Aug. – 31 Oct. 2009.

LITERATURE: Rosenblum 2005, pp. 86–8, 14–16 illus., 92–3 illus. (work in progress), 113 illus.; Hartley 2006, p. 11 illus. (work in progress) & pl. 8 illus.; Raine, *Guardian*, 2006, p. 12; Amy, *Art in America*, 2007, p. 132; Castro, *Sculpture*, 2007, p. 64; Hill, *Art & Australia*, 2007, p. 250 illus.; Massier, *Art Papers*, 2008, p. 71; Mueck et al. 2008, p. 13 illus.

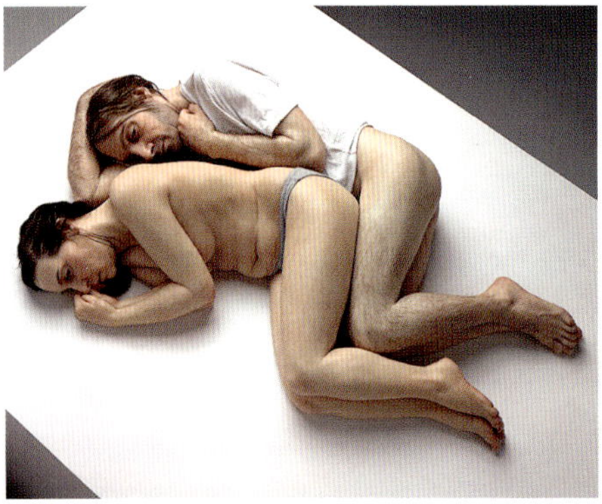

Spooning couple 2005
polyester resin, fibreglass, silicone, synthetic hair, cotton fabric, ed. 1/1
14.0 × 65.0 × 35.0 cm
Collection Glenn Fuhrman, New York

Spooning couple 2005
polyester resin, fibreglass, silicone, synthetic hair, cotton fabric, second edition, artist's proof
14.0 × 65.0 × 35.0 cm
ARTIST ROOMS National Galleries of Scotland and Tate acquired jointly through The d'Offay Donation with assistance from the National Heritage Memorial Fund and The Art Fund, 2008 (AR00033)

EXHIBITIONS: *Ron Mueck*, Fondation Cartier pour l'Art Contemporain, Paris, 19 Nov. 2005 – 19 Feb. 2006 (A/P); touring: Scottish National Gallery of Modern Art, Royal Scottish Academy Building, Edinburgh, 5 Aug. – 8 Oct. 2006 (A/P); Brooklyn Museum, New York, 3 Nov. 2006 – 4 Feb. 2007 (A/P); National Gallery of Canada, Ottawa, 2 Mar. – 6 May 2007 (A/P); Modern Art Museum of Fort Worth, Texas, 24 Jun. – 21 Oct. 2007 (A/P); Andy Warhol Museum, Pittsburgh, 13 Dec. 2007 – 30 Mar. 2008 (A/P); 21st Century Museum of Contemporary Art, Kanazawa, 26 Apr. – 31 Aug. 2008 (A/P); *Attention to Detail*, Flag Art Foundation, New York, 27 Jan. – 30 Apr. 2008 (ed. 1/1); *ARTIST ROOMS: Ron Mueck*, Aberdeen Art Gallery and Museums, Aberdeen, 29 Aug. – 31 Oct. 2009 (A/P).

LITERATURE: Clair, *Art Press*, 2005, p. 15 illus. (work in progress); Rosenblum 2005, pp. 58, 63; 83, 94–6 illus. (work in progress); 33–8, 112 illus.; Davies, Telegraph.co.uk, 2006; Farine, 'Les grandes personnes de Ron Mueck', *L'Oeil*, 2006, p. 64 illus. (work in progress); Hartley 2006, p. 10, pl. 6 illus.; Raine, *Guardian*, 2006, p. 12 illus; Amy, *Art in America*, 2007, p. 132; Greeves & Raine 2007, pp. 16, 71–2, 66 illus.; Johnson, *Art & Australia*, 2007, p. 612 illus.; Spaid, *ArtUS*, 2007, p. 59; Massier, *Art Papers*, 2008, p. 71; Mueck et al. 2008, pp. 66–7, 79, 81, 52 illus. (work in progress), 16–17 illus.

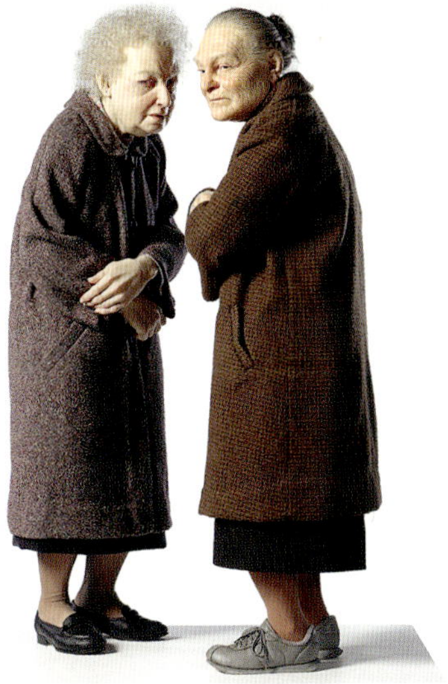

Two women 2005
polyester resin, fibreglass, silicone, polyurethane, aluminium wire, steel, wool, cotton, nylon, synthetic hair, plastic, metal, ed. 1/1
82.6 × 48.7 × 41.5 cm (variable)
National Gallery of Victoria, Melbourne
Purchased, Victorian Foundation for Living Australian Artists, 2007 (2007.120)

pp. 15, 72, 74, 76

Two women 2005
polyester resin, fibreglass, silicone, polyurethane, aluminium wire, steel, wool, cotton, nylon, synthetic hair, plastic, metal, second edition, artist's proof
82.6 × 48.7 × 41.5 cm (variable)
Collection Glenn Fuhrman, New York

EXHIBITIONS: *Ron Mueck*, Fondation Cartier pour l'Art Contemporain, Paris, 19 Nov. 2005 – 19 Feb. 2006 (A/P); touring: Scottish National Gallery of Modern Art, Royal Scottish Academy Building, Edinburgh, 5 Aug. – 8 Oct. 2006 (A/P); Brooklyn Museum, New York, 3 Nov. 2006 – 4 Feb. 2007 (A/P); National Gallery of Canada, Ottawa, 2 March – 6 May 2007 (A/P); Modern Art Museum of Fort Worth, Texas, 24 Jun. – 21 Oct. 2007 (A/P); *Ron Mueck @ McClelland*, McClelland Gallery + Sculpture Park, Langwarrin, 24 Aug. – 2 Nov. 2008 (ed. 1/1); *Bizarre Perfection*, The Israel Museum, Jerusalem, 19 Dec. 2008 – 13 Jun. 2009 (A/P).

LITERATURE: Rosenblum 2005, pp. 84–5, 95, 97 illus. (work in progress); 113, 19–23 illus.; Davies, Telegraph.co.uk, 2006; Hartley 2006, p. 10, 44 illus. (work in progress) & pl. 9 illus.; Macmillan, *Scotsman*, 2006; Amy, *Art in America*, 2007, p. 132; Castro, *Sculpture*, 2007, p. 64; Hill, *Art & Australia*, 2007, p. 246 illus. (work in progress); Prieto, *Arte y Parte*, 2007, p. 95 illus.; Holzwarth 2008, pp. 324, 327 illus.; Lindsay & Gott 2008, pp. 5, 3 illus.; Nelson, *Age*, 2008, p. 22.

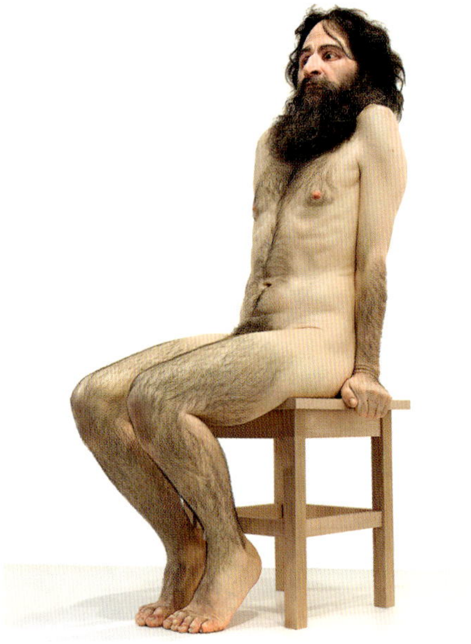

Wild man 2005
polyester resin, fibreglass, silicone, aluminium, wood, horse hair, synthetic hair, ed. 1/1
285.0 × 162.0 × 108.0 cm
McClelland Gallery + Sculpture Park, Langwarrin
Purchased by the Elisabeth Murdoch Sculpture Foundation and The Balnaves Foundation, 2008 (2007.25)

pp. 78, 80, 82

Wild man 2005
polyester resin, fibreglass, silicone, aluminium, wood, horse hair, synthetic hair, second edition, artist's proof
285.0 × 162.0 × 108.0 cm
ARTIST ROOMS National Galleries of Scotland and Tate acquired jointly through The d'Offay Donation with assistance from the National Heritage Memorial Fund and The Art Fund, 2008 (AR00034)

EXHIBITIONS: *Ron Mueck*, Fondation Cartier pour l'Art Contemporain, Paris, 19 Nov. 2005 – 19 Feb. 2006 (A/P); touring: Scottish National Gallery of Modern Art, Royal Scottish Academy Building, Edinburgh, 5 Aug. – 8 Oct. 2006 (A/P); Brooklyn Museum, New York, 3 Nov. 2006 – 4 Feb. 2007 (A/P); National Gallery of Canada, Ottawa, 2 March – 6 May 2007 (A/P); Modern Art Museum of Fort Worth, Texas, 24 June – 21 Oct. 2007 (A/P); Andy Warhol Museum, Pittsburgh, 13 Dec. 2007 – 30 March 2008 (A/P); 21st Century Museum of Contemporary Art, Kanazawa, 26 Apr. – 31 Aug. 2008 (A/P); *Ron Mueck @ McClelland*, McClelland Gallery + Sculpture Park, Langwarrin, 24 Aug. – 2 Nov. 2008 (ed. 1/1); *ARTIST ROOMS: Ron Mueck*, Aberdeen Art Gallery and Museums, Aberdeen, 29 Aug. – 31 Oct. 2009 (A/P).

LITERATURE: Clair, *Art Press*, 2005, p. 14 illus. (work in progress); Rosenblum 2005, pp. 63; 82, 91–3, 98 illus. (work in progress); 9–13, 112 illus.; Davies, Telegraph.co.uk, 2006; Farine, 'Les grandes personnes de Ron Mueck', *L'Oeil*, 2006, p. 65; Farine, 'Ron Mueck: corps surhumains', *L'Oeil*, 2006, p. 62 illus. (work in progress); Hartley 2006, p. 10–11, 44 illus. (work in progress) & pl. 5 illus.; Jones, *Guardian*, 2006, p. 22; Jones,

Guardian Weekly, 2006, p. 21 illus.; Hill, *Art & Australia*, 2007, pp. 251, 246 illus. (work in progress), 247 illus.; Johnson, *Art & Australia*, 2007, p. 612; Spaid, *ArtUS*, 2007, p. 59; Art & Australia, 2008, p. 228; Holzwarth 2008, p. 324, p. 325 illus.; Kitazawa, *Art iT*, 2008, p. 21; Lindsay & Gott 2008, pp. 1, 5, 8; 4, 6, 9 illus. (work in progress); 7 illus.; cover illus. (detail); Massier, *Art Papers*, 2008, p. 71; Money & Carbone, *Age*, 2008, p. 20; Mueck et al. 2008, pp. 81, 53 illus. (work in progress), 15 illus.; Nelson, *Age*, 2008, p. 22 illus; *ARTIST ROOMS: Ron Mueck*, Aberdeen Art Gallery and Museums, Aberdeen, 29 Aug. – 31 Oct. 2009.

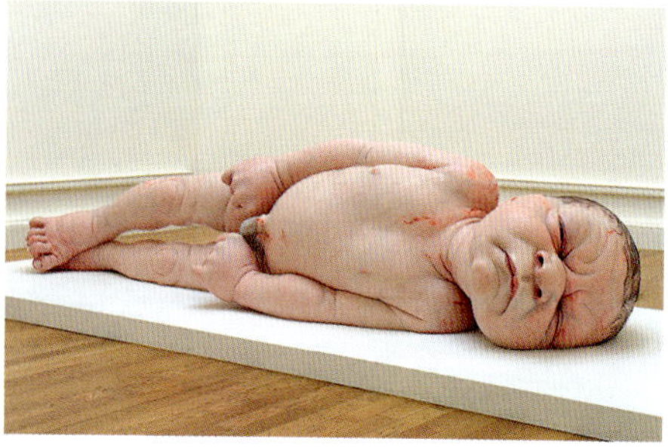

A girl **2006**
polyester resin, fibreglass, silicone, synthetic hair, synthetic polymer paint, ed. 1/1
110.5 × 501.0 × 134.5 cm
National Gallery of Canada, Ottawa
Purchased with the generous support of F. Harvey Benoit and Dr Lynne Freiburger-Benoit, 2007 (42161)

A girl **2006**
polyester resin, fibreglass, silicone, synthetic hair, synthetic polymer paint, second edition, artist's proof
110.0 × 501.0 × 134.5 cm
Scottish National Gallery of Modern Art, Edinburgh
Purchased with assistance from The Art Fund, 2007 (GMA 4821)

pp. 84, 86, 88

EXHIBITIONS: *Ron Mueck*, Scottish National Gallery of Modern Art, Royal Scottish Academy Building, Edinburgh, 5 Aug. – 8 Oct. 2006 (ed. 1/1); touring: Brooklyn Museum, New York, 3 Nov. 2006 – 4 Feb. 2007 (ed. 1/1); National Gallery of Canada, Ottawa, 2 Mar. – 6 May 2007 (ed. 1/1); *Ron Mueck: a Girl*, Contemporary Art Centre, Málaga, 30 Mar. – 17 Jun. 2007 (A/P); Modern Art Museum of Fort Worth, Texas, 24 Jun. – 21 Oct. 2007 (ed. 1/1); Andy Warhol Museum, Pittsburgh, 13 Dec. 2007 – 30 Mar. 2008 (A/P); 21st Century Museum of Contemporary Art, Kanazawa, 26 Apr. – 31 Aug. 2008 (A/P); *Real Life/La Vraie Vie: Ron Mueck and Guy Ben-Ner*, La Cité de l'Energie, Shawinigan, Quebec, 21 Jun. – 28 Sep. 2008 (ed. 1/1); *ARTIST ROOMS: Ron Mueck*, Aberdeen Art Gallery and Museums, Aberdeen, 29 Aug. - 31 Oct. 2009.

LITERATURE: Davies, Telegraph.co.uk, 2006; Hartley 2006, p.11, pl. 10 illus.; 44–6 illus. (work in progress); Jones, *Guardian*, 2006, p. 22 illus.; Jones, *Guardian Weekly*, 2006, p. 21 illus.; Miller, *Herald*, 2006, illus.; Amy, *Art in America*, 2007, p. 132; Castro, *Sculpture*, 2007, p. 64 illus; Greeves & Raine 2007, pp. 69, 74–6, 78, 35–49 illus. (work in progress), 50–4, 67 illus.; Johnson, *Art & Australia*, 2007, p. 612; Prieto, *Arte y Parte*, 2007, p. 95 illus.; Spaid, *ArtUS*, 2007, p. 59; Kitazawa, *Art iT*, 2008, p. 21 illus.; Holzwarth 2008, pp. 324, 326 illus.; Massier, *Art Papers*, 2008, p. 71; Mueck et al. 2008, pp. 60, 69, 80, 48–51 illus. (work in progress), 8–9 illus.; Shaughnessy 2008, pp. 13, 18, 15 illus. (work in progress), 6–7 illus.

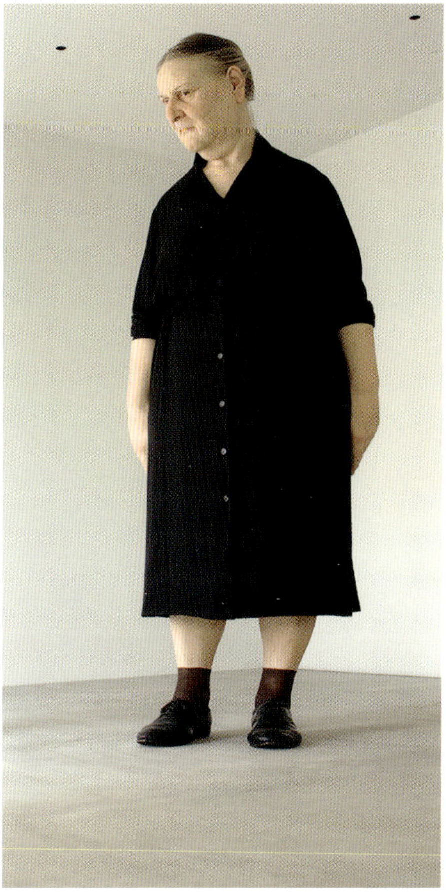

Standing woman 2007
silicone, polyurethane, aluminium wire, horse hair, synthetic hair, fabric, leather, ed. 1/1
405.0 × 155.0 × 110.0 cm
Towada Arts Center, Towada City, Japan

LITERATURE: Mueck et al. 2008, p. 43 illus.

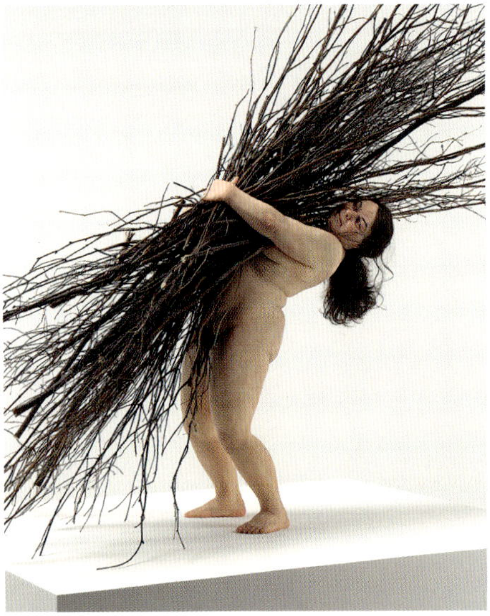

Woman with sticks 2008
silicone, polyurethane, steel, wood,
synthetic hair, ed. 1/1
170.0 × 183.0 × 120.0 cm
Anthony d'Offay, London

pp. cover, 7, 90

Woman with sticks 2010
silicone, polyurethane, steel, wood,
synthetic hair, artist's proof
170.0 × 183.0 × 120.0 cm
John and Amy Phelan Collection, New York

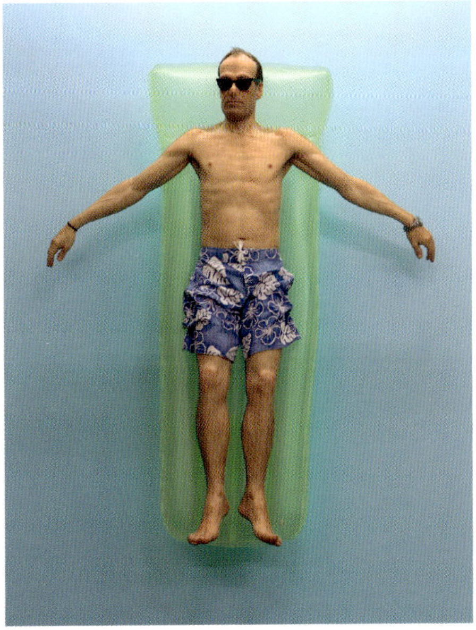

Drift 2009
silicone, synthetic hair, polyester resin, fibreglass, polyurethane, aluminium, plastic, fabric, ed. 1/1
118.0 × 96.0 × 21.0 cm
John and Amy Phelan Collection, New York

pp. 100, 102, 104

Drift 2010
silicone, synthetic hair, polyester resin, fibreglass, polyurethane, aluminium, plastic, fabric, artist's proof
118.0 × 96.0 × 21.0 cm
Anthony d'Offay, London

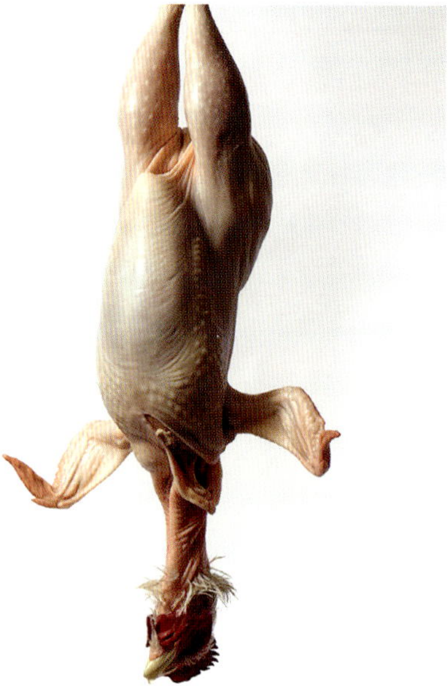

Still life 2009
silicone, polyurethane, aluminium, feathers,
stainless steel, nylon rope, ed. 1/1
215.0 × 89.0 × 50.0 cm
Anthony d'Offay, London

pp. 106, 108, 110

Still life 2010
silicone, polyurethane, aluminium, feathers,
stainless steel, nylon rope, artist's proof
215.0 × 89.0 × 50.0 cm
Private collection, Switzerland

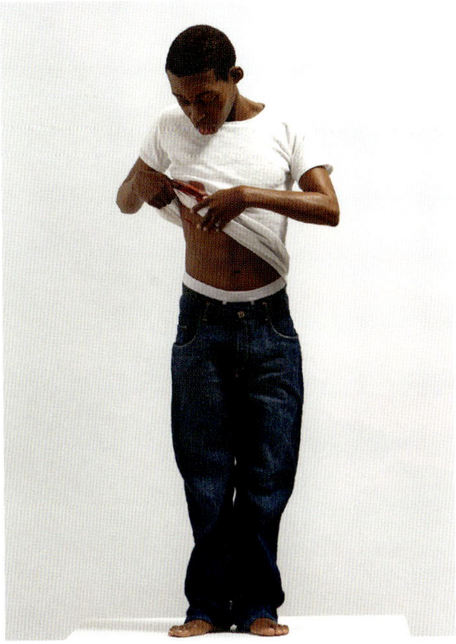

Youth 2009
silicone, polyurethane, steel,
synthetic hair, fabric, ed. 1/4
65.0 × 28.0 × 16.0 cm
Anthony d'Offay, London

pp. 94, 96, 98

Youth 2010
silicone, polyurethane, steel, synthetic
hair, fabric, artist's proof
65.0 × 28.0 × 16.0 cm
Anthony d'Offay, London

Youth 2010
silicone, polyurethane, steel,
synthetic hair, fabric, ed. 2/4
65.0 × 28.0 × 16.0 cm
Anthony d'Offay, London

SELECTED BIBLIOGRAPHY

BOOKS

Adams, Brook, Lisa Jardine, Martin Maloney, Norman Rosenthal & Richard Shone. *Sensation: Young British Artists from the Saatchi Collection* (exh. cat.). Thames and Hudson in association with the Royal Academy of Arts, London, 1997.

Adams, Laurie Schneider. *A History of Western Art*. 4th edn, rev. McGraw-Hill, Boston, 2004.

Amman, Jean-Christophe & de Ligt, Natalie. *Ich Will, dass Du mir glaubst! 9. Triennale Klienplastik Fellbach* (exh. cat.). Stadt Fellbach, Fellbach, 2004.

Aoki, Masahiro, Stephan Kohler, and Masatoshi Tsuzuku. *In Bed: Images from a Vital Stage*. Toyota Municipal Museum, Toyota, 2004.

Art & Australia (ed.). *Current: Contemporary Art from Australia and New Zealand*. Dott Publishing, Paddington, Sydney, 2008.

Baldissera, Lisa. *Silver: Dreams, Screens and Theories* (exh. cat.). Art Gallery of Greater Victoria, Victoria, Canada, 2004.

Bastian, Heiner (ed.). *Ron Mueck* (exh. cat.). 2nd edn, rev. Hatje Cantz Publishers, Ostfildren-Ruit, 2005.

Baume, Nicholas (ed.). *Getting Emotional* (exh. cat.). Institute of Contemporary Art, Boston, 2005.

Bowron, Edgar Peters, Carolyn Rose Rebbert, Robert Rosenblum & William Secord. *Best in Show: the Dog in Art from the Renaissance to Today* (exh. cat.). Yale University Press, New Haven, 2006.

Chanzit, Gwen F. *In Limbo* (exh. cat.). School of Art and Art History, University of Denver, Denver, 2005.

Clair, Jean. *Mélancolie: Génie et Folie en Occident* (exh. cat.). Réunion des Musées Nationaux: Gallimard, Paris, 2005.

Close, Chuck. *Attention to Detail: Curated by Chuck Close* (exh. cat.). FLAG Art Foundation, New York, 2008.

Collins, Judith. *Sculpture Today*. Phaidon, London, 2007.

De Cruz, Gemma. *Ant Noises at the Saatchi Gallery* (exh. cat.). Saatchi Gallery, London, 2000.

De Hallen Haarlem & Frans Hals Museum. *Ron Mueck* (exh. cat.). De Hallen, Haarlem, 2003.

Den Haag Sculptuur 2007. *De Overkant = Down Under: Den Haag Sculptuur 07* (exh. cat.). Veenman, Rotterdam, 2007.

Deuchar, Stephen & Anne Goodchild. *Tate Sculpture: the Human Figure in British Art from Moore to Gormley* (exh. cat.). Millennium Galleries, Sheffield, 2005.

Dodd, Philip & Ian Christie. *Spellbound: Art and Film* (exh. cat.). British Film Institute Hayward Gallery, London, 1996.

Ebony, David, Jane Harris, Frances Richard, Martha Schwendener, Sarah Valdez & Linda Yablonsky. *Curve: the Female Nude Now* (exh. cat.). 1st edn. New York University, New York, 2003.

Ellis, Patricia. *100: the Work that Changed British Art*. Jonathan Cape in association with the Saatchi Gallery, London, 2003.

Falkenberg, Merrill & Eric Fischl. *All the More Real* (exh. cat.). Parrish Art Museum, Southampton, New York, 2007.

Fayet, Roger, Cornelia Meyer & Marina Warner. *Haare: Obsession und Kunst*. Museum Bellerive, Zurich, 2000.

Gerchow, Jan & Hans Belting. *Ebenbilder: Kopien von Körpern – Modelle des Menschen* (exh. cat.). Hatje Cantz Publishers, Ostfildern-Ruit, 2002

Greeves, Susanna & Craig Raine. *Ron Mueck: a Girl* (exh. cat.). Gestión Cultural y Comunicacón, Santander, 2007.

Greeves, Susanna & Colin Wiggins. *Ron Mueck* (exh. cat.). National Gallery Company, London, 2003.

Grosenick, Uta (ed.). *Art Now. Vol. 2: the New Directory to 81 International Contemporary Artists*. Taschen, Los Angeles, 2008.

Grynsztejn, Madeleine. *Supernova: Art of the 1990s from the Logan Collection*. San Francisco Museum of Modern Art, San Francisco, 2003

Guldemond, Jaap (ed.). *Imagine, You Are Standing Here in Front of Me: Caldic Collectie*. Museum Boijmans van Beuningen: Caldic Collectie: NAi Publishers, Rotterdam, 2002.

Hartley, Keith. *Ron Mueck*. National Galleries of Scotland, Edinburgh, 2006.

Hayward, Vicky, Robert Timms & Alexandra Bradley (eds). *Young British Art: the Saatchi Decade*. Booth-Clibborn Editions Abrams, New York, London, 1999.

Heartney, Eleanor. *Art & Today*. Phaidon, London, 2008.

Heynen, Julian (ed.). *Sammlung Ackermans: Christian Boltanski ... [Et Al.]*. Hatje Cantz Publishers, Ostfildern-Ruit, 2002.

———. (ed.). *Startkapital: K21, Kunstsammlung Nordrhein-Westfalen*, English edn. Hatje Cantz Publishers, Ostfildern-Ruit, 2002.

Holzwarth, Hans Werner. *Art Now. Vol. 3: a Cutting Edge Selection of Today's Most Exciting Artists*. Taschen, London, 2008.

Kelley, Mike, John C. Wekhman & Christoph Grunenberg. *The Uncanny: by Mike Kelley, Artist* (exh. cat). Konig, Koln, 2004.

Lai, Hsiang-ling & Goang-Ming Yuan. *Slowtech*. Contemporary Art Foundation, Museum of Contemporary Art, Taipei, 2006.

Lawrence, Sidney. *Directions: Ron Mueck* (exh. cat.). Smithsonian Institution Press, Washington DC, 2002.

LeVitte-Harten, Doreet. *Heaven*. Hatje Cantz Publishers, Ostfildern-Ruit, 1999.

Lindsay, Robert & Ted Gott. *Ron Mueck @ McClelland*. McClelland Gallery + Sculpture Park, Langwarrin, 2008.

McPhee, John. *Great Collections: Treasures from the Art Gallery of New South Wales, Australian Museum, Botanic Gardens Trust, Historic Houses Trust of New South Wales, Museum of Contemporary Art,*

Powerhouse Museum, State Library of New South Wales, State Records New South Wales (exh. cat.). Museums & Galleries New South Wales, Woolloomooloo, 2008.

Mueck, Ron. *Boy: by Ron Mueck; Photographs by Gautier Deblonde* (exh. cat.). Anthony d'Offay Gallery, London, 2001.

Mueck, Ron, Craig Raine, Katsura Funakoshi & Daisuke Murata. *Ron Mueck* (exh. cat.). Foil, Tokyo, 2008.

National Museum of Modern Art Tokyo. *A Perspective on Contemporary Art: Continuity/Transgression* (exh. cat.). National Museum of Modern Art, Tokyo, 2002.

Price, Dick. *The New Neurotic Realism* (exh. cat.). Saatchi Gallery, London, 1998.

Rinder, Lawrence & Nancy Crowley. *Spaced Out: Late 1990s Works from the Vicki and Kent Logan Collection*. California College of Arts and Crafts, San Francisco, 1999.

Rosenblum, Robert. *Ron Mueck* (exh. cat.). Fondation Cartier pour l'Art Contemporain, Paris, 2005.

Schmidt, Hans-Werner & Beate Ermacora. *Unsichere Grenzen: Daniele Buetti, Bea Emsbach, Martin Honert, Dieter Huber, John Isaacs, Ron Mueck, Tony Oursler, Diego Schindler-Castro* (exh. cat.). Kerber, Bielefeld, 1999.

Schoppmann, Wolfgang, Eva Schmidt & Peter Friese (eds). *Ohne Zogern: die Sammlung Olbricht Teil 2 = Without Hesitation: the Olbricht Collection, Part 2* (exh. cat.). Edition Braus, Heidelberg, 2001.

Shaughnessy, Jonathan. *Real Life = La Vraie Vie: Guy Ben-Ner, Ron Mueck* (exh. cat). National Gallery of Canada, Ottawa, 2008.

Szeemann, Harald, Cecelia Liveriero Lavelli & Lara Facco (eds.). La Biennale di Venezia: 49. *Esposizione Internazionale d'Arte: Platea dell'Umanitá/Plateau of humankind* (exh. cat.). 2 vols. Electa, Milan, 2001.

Théberge, Pierre. *The Body Transformed* (exh. cat.). National Gallery of Canada, Ottawa, 2003.

Théberge, Pierre, Mayo Graham & Kitty Scott. *Noah's Ark* (exh. cat.). National Gallery of Canada, Ottawa, 2004.

Windsor, Alan (ed.). *British Sculptors of the Twentieth Century.* Ashgate, Aldershot, England, 2003.

NEWSPAPERS, PERIODICALS AND DVDS

'Mueck's baby delivered to capital', *BBC News*, 13 March 2007, reproduced at <news.bbc.co.uk/2/hi/uk_news/scotland/edinburgh_and_east/6446619.stm>.

'Naked ambition', *Age*, 5 August 2008, p. 20.

'Ron Mueck: a model artist', *Australian Magazine*, 29–30 July 2000, p. 43.

'Sculptor Ron Mueck to open first Canadian show', *CBC News*, 1 March 2007, reproduced at <www.cbc.ca/arts/artdesign/story/2007/02/28/mueck-show.html>.

Acret, Susan. '49th Venice Biennale: Northern Hemisphere blues', *ART AsiaPacific*, no. 33, 2002, pp. 20–2.

Albert, Jane. 'Sculptor's work bares fruit', *Weekend Australian*, 21 December 2002, p. 9.

Amy, Michael. 'New York: Ron Mueck: James Cohan Gallery', *Sculpture*, vol. 20, no. 10, 2001, pp. 72–3.

——. 'Ron Mueck at the Brooklyn Museum', *Art in America*, vol. 95, no. 4, 2007, p. 132.

Artforum International, vol. 40, no. 1, 2001.

Banks, Ron. 'The modelling of a marvellous career', *West Australian*, 12 February 2005, p. 14.

Barrett, David. '"Sensation": Royal Academy of Arts, London, 18 September –28 December, 1997', *Artext*, no. 60, 1998, pp. 93–4.

Bevan, Roger. 'Saatchi Britart sell-off continues', *Art Newspaper*, vol. 14, no. 156, 2005, p. 41.

Bishop, Louise. 'Model family', *Creative Review*, vol. 17, no. 4, 1997, pp. 36–8.

Black, Catriona. 'Mortal contact', *Glasgow Sunday Herald*, 13 August 2006, reproduced at <i1.exhibit-e.com/jamescohan/eff272ca.pdf>.

Bruce, Candice. '49th Biennale of Venice 2001: spectacle, wizardry and disrupted narratives', *Art & Australia*, vol. 39, no. 3, 2002, pp. 373–6.

Butler, Rex. 'Shock art: forget trying to work out what it means. Sensational art is getting back to basics', *Courier Mail*, 22 February 2003, p. 1.

Castro, Jan Garden. 'Ron Mueck: Brooklyn Museum', *Sculpture*, vol. 26, no. 6, 2007, p. 64.

Centro de Arte Contemporáneo de Málaga. *Ron Mueck [a Girl]: Cacmálaga, Centro De Arte Contemporáneo De Málaga*. cedeCOM, videorecording, Spain, 2007.

Chambers, Nicholas. 'Ron Mueck: *In Bed*, 2005', *Art Lines*, no. 3, 2008, p. 23.

Chapman, Chris. 'Naked ambition', *Artlook*, June 2004, p. 9.

Chrisafis, Angelique. 'Pregnant pause', *Guardian*, 18 March 2003, p. 13.

Clair, Jean & Richard Leydier. 'Immortal melancholy', *Art Press*, no. 316, 2005, pp. 24–30.

Clair, Jean & T.S. Torgoff 'Ron Mueck', *Art Press*, no. 317, 2005, pp. 12–15.

Clement, Tracey. 'Warped reflections: [hyperrealism]', *Artlink*, vol. 23, no. 3, 2003, pp. 52–7.

Cocks, Anna Somers, Louisa Buck & Cristina Ruiz. 'The Venice Biennale: very moving', *Art Newspaper*, vol. 12, no. 116, 2001, pp. 38–41.

Cooper, Emmanuel. 'Merely craft', *Crafts*, no. 203, 2006, p. 10.

Crone, Bridget. 'Saatchi Gallery, London: YBAs take over County Hall', *Art & Australia*, vol. 41, no. 2, 2003, pp. 218–19.

Cumming, Laura. 'Natal attraction', *Observer*, 23 March 2003, p. 10, reproduced at ‹www.guardian.co.uk/theobserver/2003/mar/23/1›.

Cumming, Laura. 'Where there's Mueck, there's class', *Guardian*, p. 13, August 2006, reproduced at ‹www.guardian.co.uk/artanddesign/2006/aug/13/art.edinburgh2006›.

Darwent, Charles. 'It looks real: so why is it so spooky?', *Independent*, 23 March 2003, p. 8.

Davies, Serena. 'Ron Mueck: bigger than Monet?', Telegraph.co.uk, 15 August 2006, reproduced at ‹www.telegraph.co.uk/culture/art/3654545/Ron-Mueck-bigger-than-Monet.html›.

de Wavrin, Isabelle. 'Collection Saatchi: La publicité a l'oeuvre', *Beaux Arts Magazine*, no. 177, February 1999, pp. 108–9.

Etherington-Smith, Meredith. 'Saatchi's new sensation', *Art Review*, vol. 54, 2003, pp. 60–5.

Farine, Manou. 'Les grandes personnes de Ron Mueck', *L'Oeil*, no. 576, 2006, pp. 64–5.

——. 'Ron Mueck: corps surhumains', *L'Oeil*, no. 576, 2006, pp. 62–3.

Fenner, Felicity. 'Venice Biennale: dreams and conflicts', *Art & Australia*, vol. 41, no. 2, 2003, pp. 214–17.

Frèrot, Christine. 'La melancolie: genius and insanity in the West', *Art Nexus*, vol. 5, no. 60, 2006, pp.102–4.

Gayford, Martin. 'Umbillically symbolic', *Sunday Telegraph*, 23 March 2003, p. 7.

Glueck, Grace. 'Giant Baby, Dead Dad and others, realer than real', *New York Times*, 10 November 2006, p. 35, reproduced at ‹www.nytimes.com/2006/11/10/arts/design/10muec.html?_r=1&scp=1&sq=giant%20baby%20glueck&st=cse›.

Grishin, Sasha. 'The rise and rise of the National Gallery of Australia', *Art & Australia*, vol. 41, no. 2, 2003, pp. 256–71.

Haase, Amine. 'Melancholie – genie und wahnsinn', *Kunstforum International*, no. 179, 2006, pp. 352–6.

Hatton, Rita. 'Letter from London: what has Charles Saatchi got in his satchel?', *Art Monthly Australia*, no. 162, 2003, pp. 10–11.

Hatton, Rita & John A. Walker. 'The new neurotic capitalism', *Art Monthly Australia*, no. 119, 1999, pp. 16–19.

Herd, Juliet. 'In like skin', *Weekend Australian*, 21–22 December 2002, pp. 12–13.

Hill, Peter. 'New model army', *Sydney Morning Herald – Metro*, 3–9 January 2003, p. 23.

——. 'Ron Mueck: the un-special effects man', *Art & Australia*, vol. 45, no. 2, 2007, pp. 242–51.

Ingram, Terry. 'Australian artists soar on fresh appeal', *Australian Financial Review*, 3 January 2002, p. 12.

——. 'The birth of a famous Australian', *Australian Financial Review*, 12 July 2001, p. 39.

James, Bruce. 'Stand and deliver', *Sydney Morning Herald*, 1 January 2003, p. 18.

Januszczak, Waldemar. '... Ron Mueck sails into history ...', *Sunday Times*, 23 March 2003, pp. 6–7.

Jocks, Heinz-Norbert. 'Heaven', *Kunstforum International*, no. 147, 1999, pp. 386–9.

Johnson, Paddy. 'Ron Mueck', *Art & Australia*, vol. 44, no. 4, 2007, p. 612.

Jones, Jonathan. 'If you like this, you need to get out more', *Guardian*, 9 August 2006, reproduced at <www.guardian.co.uk/stage/2006/aug/09/comedy.edinburgh20063>.

——. 'A parody of people', *Guardian Weekly*, 25–31 August 2006, p. 21.

Kennedy, Brian. 'Ron Mueck's *Pregnant Woman*', *Antiques and Art in New South Wales*, 2004, p. 11.

Kimmelman, Michael. 'Veering from the end of life to the beginning, with lucidity and awe', *New York Times*, 1 June 2001, p. 34.

Kitazawa, Hiromi. 'Ron Mueck: pursuing a universal series', *ART iT*, vol. 6, no. 3, 2008, pp. 20–1.

Leffingwell, Edward. 'Ron Mueck at James Cohan', *Art in America*, vol. 89, no. 11, 2001, pp. 144–5.

Leydier, Richard. 'Le realisme de Ron Mueck/Ron Mueck's psychological realism', *Art Press*, no. 288, 2003, pp. 24–8.

McDonald, John. 'It's all in the detail: Ron Mueck: the lure of the hyperreal', *Australian Financial Review*, 30 January 2003, p. 48.

McEwen, John. 'Something disturbing in silicon', *Sunday Telegraph*, 18 February 1996.

Macmillan, Duncan. 'Contemporary visions aren't dead in the water', *Scotsman*, 19 December 2006, reproduced at <news.scotsman.com/duncanmacmillan/Contemporary-visions-arent-dead-in.2836231.jp>.

MacRitchie, Lynn. 'Rude Britannia', *Art in America*, vol. 86, no. 4, 1998, pp. 36–9.

Majendie, Paul. 'Saatchi art show for the filthy rich', *Age*, 16 April 2003, p. 12.

Makin, Jeff. 'Bursting to be noticed', *Herald Sun*, 7 February 2005, p. 89.

Martin, Colin. 'Ron Mueck: technical mastery and the human condition, *Art & Australia*, vol. 40, no. 4, 2003, pp. 568–9.

Massier, John. 'Ron Mueck: Pittsburgh', *Art Papers*, vol. 32, no. 4, 2008, p. 71.

Miller, Phil. 'Art show sees larger than life sculptures', *The Herald*, 1 August 2006, reproduced <www.heraldscotland.com/sport/spl/aberdeen/art-show-sees-larger-than-life-sculptures-1.13261>.

Money, Lawrence & Suzanne Carbone. '*Age* diary', *Age*, 5 August 2008, p. 20.

Moran, Jason. 'Gallery hopes *Pregnant Woman* will woo art lovers', *Daily Telegraph*, 21 December 2002, p. 18.

Morgan, Joyce. 'Destination piece will be back to stay', *Sydney Morning Herald*, 20 December 2002, p. 17.

Morgan, Robert C. 'Ron Mueck: James Cohan Gallery', *Art Press*, no. 271, 2001, p. 68.

Musa, Helen. 'NGA buys nude for $800,000', *Canberra Times*, 20 December 2002, p. 1.

———. 'Ultra-realism in gallery's latest unveiling', *Canberra Times*, 6 March 2004, p. 3.

Myers, Terry R. 'Ron Mueck: Anthony d'Offay Gallery, London', *Artext*, no. 63, 1998, pp. 84–5.

Nadelman, Cynthia. 'Middle-aged gods and giant babies', *ARTnews*, vol. 103, no. 11, 2004, pp. 116–21.

National Gallery, London. *Ron Mueck*, National Gallery, London, DVD, 2008.

Naylor, Stephen. 'The Australian Pavilion dances to Lyndal Jones' vaporetto vista', *Art Monthly Australia*, no. 141, 2001, pp. 5–9.

Nelson, Robert. 'High, wild and handsome: Mueck's outsider is a force of nature', *Age*, 10 September 2008, p. 22.

———. 'A monumental work pregnant with heroic proportions', *Age*, 16 February 2005, p. 8.

Nungesser, Michael. 'Ron Mueck', *Kunstforum International*, no. 167, 2003, pp. 263–5.

O'Connell, Alex. 'It's big and it's very, very clever', *Times*, 2 August 2006, reproduced at <entertainment.timesonline.co.uk/tol/arts_and_entertainment/article696390.ece>.

O'Hagan, Sean. 'Ron Mueck: from Muppets to motherhood', *Observer*, 6 August 2006, reproduced at <www.guardian.co.uk/artanddesign/2006/aug/06/art2>.

Pearlman, Jonathan. '*Boy* too fragile, but *Dead Dad* may make journey', *Sydney Morning Herald*, 24 July 2002, p. 4.

Pietsch, Hans. 'Allein mit sich selbst', *Art*, no. 5, May 2003, pp. 52–65.

Prieto, Julia. 'Ron Mueck', *Arte y Parte*, no. 68, 2007, p. 95.

Prince, Mark. 'On sculpture', *Art Monthly*, no. 282, 2004–05, pp. 7–10.

Raine, Craig. 'The body beautiful', *Guardian*, p. 12, 12 August 2006, reproduced at <www.guardian.co.uk/artanddesign/2006/aug/12/art.edinburgh2006>.

——.'Ron Mueck', *Areté*, no. 4., Winter, 2000, pp. 117–18.

——. 'To the life', *Modern Painters*, vol. 11, no. 3, 1998, pp. 20–3.

Restany, Pierre. 'La Biennale del Banale 2001', *D'Ars*, vol. 41, no. 166, 2001, pp. 4–14.

Restorff, Jörg. 'Flügelwesen und Bruchpiloten: von guten und bösen Engeln', *Kunstzeitung*, no. 52, December 2000, p. 1

Russell Taylor, John. 'All Mueck and magic', *Times – T2*, 19 March 2003, p.15.

Saltz, Jerry. 'Like life', *Village Voice*, 5 June 2001, reproduced at <www.villagevoice.com/2001-06-05/art/likelife>.

Smith, Roberta. 'Art review: every which way to paint', *New York Times*, 30 August 2002, p. 27.

Sorenson, Rosemary. 'Mother of all sculptures stretches the imagination', *Courier Mail*, 21 December 2002, p. 7.

Spaid, Sue. 'Ron Mueck', *ArtUS*, 2007, no. 20, winter 2007, p. 59.

Tanguay, Sarah. 'The progress of big man: a conversation with Ron Mueck', *Sculpture*, vol. 22, no. 6, 2003, pp. 28–3.

Thompson, Mitra. 'Saatchi art up the river', *Herald Sun*, 18 April 2003,p. 29.

Turner, Grady T. 'Sensation–"sick stuff"!', *Flash Art*, vol.32, no.209,1999, p. 57.

Usher, Robin. 'I am strong, I am invincible, I am woman (all 2.5 metres of me)', *Age*, 21 December 2002, p. 1.

Wiggins, Colin. 'Pregnant pauses', *Art Review*, vol. 54, 2003, pp. 92–5.

Wilson, Michael. 'Shop front', *Art Monthly*, no. 237, 2000, pp. 7–10.

Withers, Rachel. 'Venice Biennale: hunting the sphinx', *C: International Contemporary Art*, fall 2001, p. 21–3.

Page numbers in italics indicate illustrations.

Published in association with
Yale University Press
P.O. Box 209040
New Haven, CT 06520-9040
yalebooks.com

© 2011 National Gallery of Victoria
All rights reserved.
This book may not be reproduced, in whole or in part, including illustrations, in any form (beyond that copying permitted by Sections 107 and 108 of the U.S. Copyright Law and except by reviewers for the public press), without written permission from the publishers.

Library of Congress Control Number: 2011927133

Published for the exhibition *Ron Mueck*, NGV International, 180 St Kilda Road, 22 January 2010 – 18 April 2010, then touring to Queensland Art Gallery, Brisbane, 8 May – 8 August 2010; Christchurch Art Gallery Te Puna o Waiwhetu, New Zealand 30 September 2010 – 23 January 2011.

'Wild men of the woods' was first published in *Ron Mueck @ McClelland*, courtesy of McClelland Gallery + Sculpture Park, Langwarrin.

All works © Ron Mueck courtesy Anthony d'Offay, London; p. 15 © Emily Floyd courtesy Anna Schwartz Gallery, Melbourne; p. 58 © Francis Bacon. Licensed by ARS & VISCOPY, Australia; p. 40 © Jasper Johns. Licensed by VAGA & VISCOPY, Australia

Photography credits: Mark Ashkanasy: pp. 78, 80, 166; Brooklyn Museum Archives: pp. 18, 23; Mike Bruce: pp. 7, 90, 170; Jenni Carter: pp. 42, 44, 148; Anthony d'Offay, London: pp. 2, 21, 24, 48, 88, 128–30, 133–40, 142–6, 150–5, 159–61, 163–4, 192; Gautier Deblonde: pp. 26, 28, 60, 82, 134; Ray Fulton: p. 66, 68, 162; Natasha Harth: p. 70; Poul Ib Henriksen: p. 141; David Hurlston: p. 31; Samir Hussein / Getty Images p. 50; Katarzyna Krzywania: p. 62; Peter Macdiarmid / Getty Images p. 52; Daniel Mahon: pp. 15, 76; Christian Markel: p. 33; National Gallery of Australia: pp. 54, 56, 58, 157; National Gallery of Victoria: p.72, 102, 104; Antonia Reeve: pp. 84, 86, 168; John Spiller: pp. 94, 6, 98, 100, 106, 108, 110, 171–3; Towada Art Center: p. 169; Michael Tropea: pp. 36, 38, 40, 131; Narelle Wilson: p.74, 165.

Editors: Paige Amor, Margaret Trudgeon and Catherine Cradwick
Design: Jessica Gommers
Permissions and copyright: Megan Patty
Publications Officer: Judy Shelverton
Publications Manager: Jasmin Chua
Pre-press: Philip White
Indexer: Fay Donlevy
CTP and printing: 1010 Printing International Pty Ltd, China
Cover stock: 296gsm IP High Yield Board
Endpapers: 120gsm Rives Design Bright White
Text stock: 170gsm Hanno Satin
Exhibition ID & publication font: National

The views expressed in this publication are those of the authors and do not necessarily reflect those of the publisher.

10 9 8 7 6 5 4 3 2 1